American Institute of Graphic Arts

AIGA

Professional Practices in Graphic Design

Edited by Tad Crawford

ALLWORTH PRESS
NEW YORK

CO-PUBLISHED WITH THE AMERICAN INSTITUTE OF GRAPHIC ARTS

07 06 05 04 03   8 7 6 5 4
Published by Allworth Press
An imprint of Allworth Communications
10 East 23rd Street, New York NY 10010

Co-published with the American Institute of Graphic Arts

Designed by Paul Montie, Fahrenheit, Boston, MA

Page composition/typography by Sharp Des!gns, Lansing, MI

ISBN: 1-880559-89-7

Library of Congress Catalog Card Number: 97-072223

Printed in Canada

Contents

Part II. Management

Part III. Marketing

Part IV. Rights

Preface

The American Institute of Graphic Arts (AIGA) is dedicated to advancing excellence in graphic design as a discipline, profession, and cultural force. It is committed to leadership in the exchange of ideas and information, the encouragement of critical analysis and research, and the advancement of education and ethical practice.

This book is the AIGA's first comprehensive guide on professional practices for designers at all stages of their careers. The contents were developed in response to questions raised regularly by our members—working professionals. The authors have each worked regularly with practicing designers. The AIGA seeks to bring designers to solutions for the challenges they face.

In a broader sense, we also hope this book helps designers to establish an accepted set of norms for professional practices, which—through wide adoption within the profession—will develop respect for the consistent, responsive, and businesslike tenor of relations between designers and their clients. As designers assume greater responsibility for the critical role of intermediary between information and understanding, they deserve respect and trust in the business environment. This respect should always be a response to the quality of their work, but it will be more easily gained if potential clients also appreciate the integrity of the profession's business practices.

Richard Grefé, executive director
American Institute of Graphic Arts

Part I.

Relationships

CHAPTER 1

Worst of Times,
Best of Times

by Ellen Shapiro

For nearly ten years, I have been trying to identify and isolate the secret ingredients in successful designer-client relationships. What is it that makes the difference between doing just another job and one that advances not only the client's enterprise but also the annals of design? What, exactly, do those rare clients and designers do together that engenders work that looks wonderful and possesses that elusive something that makes people respond: take notice, support a cause, change their behavior, laugh, cheer?

This is a year—a decade—that has produced some of the most extraordinary graphic design, ever. This spring's new crop of design books celebrates work that is breathtaking in its complexity, sophistication, wit, and technical wizardry. To find out how it came about, especially in relation to the client's role, I recently called some of the nation's top designers and opened the conversation by asking, "What do you do to cultivate successful, long-term client relationships?" Many of the answers stunned me:

"You've gotta be kidding."

"You're asking me?"

"Even long-time clients are looking for cheaper vendors."

"How would I know?"

"We're in the process of losing our biggest client right now."

Words and phrases were used that sounded like they belonged in a different kind of book:

"One-night stand."

"Ships passing in the night."

"Flash in the pan."

"Hit and run."

"Date rape."

Date rape! Even Michael Mabry, identified in a recent national survey as "having the most influence and name recognition among graphic designers in nine key U.S. cities," told me that he and his wife Sarah, who manages their San Francisco studio, talk every couple of weeks about what they'll do when they can't make a living as graphic designers any more. "We seem to be existing day in and day out on one-night stands—one package, one identity, one brochure," he says. "And we do twice as much work for the same money as five years ago. We wonder if there's a future in this profession." When asked if he really wants readers of this book to see those thoughts in print, Mabry had no hesitation. "It's sad. But it's what all designers talk about when we get together. The root of the problem is that we want to find interesting work, and clients want to buy a commodity. Companies are buying a style based on what a new vice president or product manager thinks will work. Nothing's long-term; there's no strategy. At the end, you hand over the logo or identity to people who want to do it in-house or use a lower-cost vendor, and they don't understand it, and then you watch it go south."

This pessimism was echoed in the response of Tom Carnase, who calls himself "one of the few survivors." Carnase, who's created exquisite letterform design for more than thirty-five years, including twelve as Herb Lubalin's partner, said, "Marketing people don't have the same savvy any more. Some things they ask me to do don't make any sense. I ignore them in disgust." He mused about a Kabuki dancer honored as a national treasure in Japan. "Did you ever hear of that here? So many talented people can't make it. With all the money in this country! All you find is cheating and (doing) what you can get away with, from the top down."

When veterans like Carnase reminisce about "the good old days," they're recall-ing those thoughtful clients, top New York corporate communications directors, educated in the arts and concerned with quality, who got washed away in the tidal wave of downsizings and mergers that followed the October 1987 stock market crash. And who have been re-placed in part by the callow youths, glorified administrative assistants, and cunningly ag-gressive arm-twisters many of us have to deal with these days. Carnase is not alone. Most people I talked to commented that business ethics have changed, and the standards are emanating from the top down. After all, it was pointed out, if the president of the United States deflects charges of obstruction of justice and uses expediency as his guide, why should we expect a mere vice president of marketing to be any more noble. "Trust me," a client

implored recently, claiming she was too busy to read and sign a design firm's client agreement. The designer was nearly finished with the project by the time a twenty-page "agreement" arrived from a mega law firm; the designer would have to assign all the firm's intellectual property rights, not take credit for the work except with the client's prior approval "in every instance in which designer wishes to use work for the design firm's promotional purposes, designer shall submit a copy of same, which shall be reviewed by client, who shall suggest any changes to be made, which designer shall make within ten days," and agree to many other onerous conditions. Upon signing, the firm would get paid for the work. Some people might call that blackmail.

If things are tough for you, you are not alone. This is a harsh business world for everyone. And a difficult one to figure out. New and mind-boggling things happen every day. Maybe date rape is not such a far-fetched analogy. You, the alleged victim, knew the person. You entered into some kind of relationship. Was the bad thing that happened to you consensual or not? Let the jury decide. It's tempting to fantasize that while designers are sipping wine with cheese at AIGA events and drooling over the latest visiting superstar, the clients are attending seminars run by former marine commandos on techniques for squeezing the most work out of vendors for the least money, and for getting out of people what they don't really want to give. After all, part of every client's job description is mastering the arts of manipulation, control, and exploitation. Only it's called being a good manager, getting the organization what it needs.

But when it comes to matters of aesthetics and effective communication, we graphic designers think we know better. And increasingly, it seems, those disrespectful clients aren't listening. In 1991, I wrote a "Clients and Designers" piece for *Communication Arts* magazine on the relationship of Pentagram partner Kit Hinrichs and The Nature Company. This was one designer-client partnership that seemed to have it all. And it may have come the closest to unlocking that elusive secret: I learned that Kit Hinrichs and The Nature Company founder Tom Wrubel drove around the Bay Area together and talked about life! If you could be like Kit, then you wouldn't be a vendor! Not even a service provider or a creative. You would be a consultant, a valued advisor, a confidant! Hinrichs's identity, packaging, and catalogs for The Nature Company not only won a zillion design awards, they used the power of design to help build a single Berkeley store that sold walking sticks and field glasses into a $90 million, international empire. Kathy Tierney, the company's executive vice president, claimed that The Nature Company's commitment to being a leader meant finding "the best

designer" who could "conjure up the experience of being in the natural world" with "a mix-ture of fun and serious . . . that creates a feeling people love . . . so they want to buy a piece of the feeling." Today, alas, The Nature Company catalogs look like every other, the Hinrichs magic apparently traded in for the conventional square-inch analysis that the client, bought by a conglomerate, formerly eschewed.

The question remains—begs us to grapple with it—how can we deal with the way things are now? Neither Paul Rand nor his near-mythical client I.B.M. chairman Thomas Watson, Jr. are with us any more. But they did establish a paradigm based on the principle that if you do something that's truly distinctive and gets results, it will be sought after. Maybe not forever, but long enough to create excellent work, to make a difference. It might be as simple—and difficult—as that.

To not be treated like a commodity, you can't be a commodity. Almost everyone I interviewed asked me to be sure to include that in the story.

Ironically, many designers spend more time copying each other's successful work—at least as measured by the standards of design annuals—than developing their own signa-ture strengths. A book proposal I submitted recently was rejected on the grounds that there are only two kinds of books graphic designers will buy: "how-to books and annuals and com-pendiums with a lot of stuff they can copy."

That's depressing. In the arts, there's only a limited amount of room at the top. And none for copycats. If you're Kiri Te Kanawa, your calendar is booked years in advance with singing and recording engagements around the world. You get lucrative endorsement con-tracts to advertise that your time is so precious it can only be measured by an eighteen-karat, diamond-studded Rolex. If you're one of the thousands of wanna-be opera singers—even if you're very talented by average standards—you're waiting tables around Lincoln Center and counting the hours between singing lessons on your Timex. If you're Los Angeles de-signer April Greiman, you're not studying design annuals and figuring out whom and what to copy. Instead, your clients, like Southern California Institute of Architecture director Michael Rotundi, are finding you indispensable and saying such things about you as: "She's an evolved spirit. She's energy. You go near her and it's like you plug yourself into a wall socket. You look at her work and know it is the way it should be. It feels good and you just want to keep doing it." Rotundi advises his own students that it's easier to get a job when you're inventive and you've found your own voice. "Your work is identifiable. The passion comes through."

Unfortunately, much graphic designer passion goes into imitation. And clients know

it. If Michael Vanderbyl wins an award for a logo with a cute drawing of a little dog, for the next two years the annuals are filled with little dog logos, not quite so cute. The next year it's noble workers. Then it's ecologically correct C. S. Anderson look-alikes in green on recycled, brown-bag paper. Sure, awards are one indication of success. But they're ephemeral. They're not about the long-lasting quality and brain power that will keep you from being viewed as a commodity-style purveyor. In Michael Mabry's words, "Everybody (including the judges, apparently) wants to do the same thing." The style of the minute. It's easy to get lulled into thinking that if you don't have your own ideas, you can always use someone else's. As an instructor at Parsons School of Design in New York, I realized that design school is a place where more than a few young people with little artistic talent—and no aptitude in the verbal skills that are essential to mass communication—can end up. And some of the students are not smart enough to copy the best work that's being done. I actually found myself asking some of them to copy. They could have learned a lot by doing a good Vignelli imitation.

With all this going on, should we be surprised that books and annuals are so full of gorgeous, innovative posters, brochures, announcements, and packages? No, and the reason, says Mabry, is obvious. "There are so many more designers. There is so much more work for the judges—and clients—to choose from." Everybody has access to the same technical bag of tricks.

If you labor long and hard at it, you can succeed—at least at the razzle-dazzle aspects of it. Godzilla is to *The Lost World: Jurassic Park* as the graphic design of the seventies through late eighties is to the work being done today. No one wants to go back to the days when an award-winning brochure consisted of a full-bleed photograph juxtaposed with three columns of Helvetica set flush left, rag right. Boring, boring, boring. But because kids like my fifteen-year-old son have surpassed most of us over forty at technical wizardry, in order to be of value to the client, we have to be able to deliver more. Therein lies the other secret that practically every successful designer and design firm principal was willing to share: You have to "become a partner" with the client to "really get to know the client's business."

There are usually two ways to do that. The small way and the big way. I tried the small way. I decided to try to understand and emulate the Paul Rand model. Consultant to captains of industry who paid him $100,000 for a single logo (at least insofar as the legend goes), Rand worked solo, out of his house, and answered his own phone. That I know for sure. I interviewed him a few times and he answered the phone, "Hello." Not "Rand

Associates" or anything like that. "What happens when you're sick?" I asked him once, naively. "They have to wait," he said. Talent—unique and inimitable talent—counts for a lot. But most clients can't live with the 100 percent solo practitioner unless you're another Rand—and who is?—or maybe Leonardo da Vinci. And they'd probably expect even Leonardo to have assistants who can complete and FedEx or messenger (or e-mail; it has to be done faster and faster all the time) the packages full of the work they want, when they want it. I'll never get $100,000 for a logo, but the small way works for me because, when clients want a designer/writer, they know good writing comes from individuals, not from large organizations.

Effective marketing communications, however, usually emanates from large organizations. I have found that many of the successful designers these days, those who can't or don't want to become April Greimans or Paul Rands or Ernest Hemingways, have built relatively large companies. Not as big as the clients', but big enough to marshal talent, resources, and power.

A case in point is Stan Richards. Fresh out of Pratt Institute on a trip across the country, Richards discovered that Dallas was "a cow town, a retarded advertising community." He decided to set up shop there instead of Los Angeles, where the competition was strong, and built an entity that at last count had more than 300 employees, $300 million in annual billings, and a private jet to whisk him to meetings with clients around the country and back in time to be home for dinner. "I saw that Dallas was going to grow and flourish," says Richards. "Good work was going to be really difficult to sell. But if I could stick to it, I could become the predominant designer. It took a lot of years, but we did it." Richards attributes his success to hiring the best people and getting the best out of them—and to offering clients more than graphic design, a lot more, namely advertising and all kinds of related and high-billing marketing services. "Some clients who see me as an advertising guy don't even know I'm a graphic designer. And don't care," he claims. "The difference is the business relationship. Being a designer is a project-based relationship; you're purely focused on one aspect of the work, the design of it. In advertising, it's a long-term, overarching business relationship, which can take place over many, many years. You do anything and all things to enhance the client's business. It could be TV, print, radio."

Frankfurt Balkind Partners is another powerhouse that grew out of a boutique design studio. With more than 150 people in offices in New York, Los Angeles, and San Francisco, the firm has cultivated clients for which it can be the agency of record. "They might

not last forever," says principal Aubrey Balkind of his firm's client relationships, "but we want them to be broad and deep. It's not good enough any more to say, 'We can do this for you.' You have to be able to tell them what they should do, and have thought it through enough so they believe you because what you're saying makes a lot of sense." Frankfurt Balkind Partners executive creative director Ken Hunter adds, "Design sells itself too short. Suddenly you're out of favor. To be involved in big projects, big relationships, you have to structure the account side and invest a lot of effort in research to consistently be of value on a strategic level."

In the Chicago suburb of Dundee, Illinois, Samata/Mason principal Pat Samata says her firm is getting into areas they swore ten years ago they'd never touch. "We did annual reports. Now everybody wants advertising, identity, Web sites." But, like her new partner Dave Mason, who moved from Vancouver, B.C., to merge his annual report firm with the Samatas', clients want to do business with them. With the Samatas, you may not feel like you're plugged into a wall socket. It's more like a special, warm, family. "The way we've approached everyone in life is that if there's anything meaningful we will nurture it and it will grow into a friendship," says Pat Samata. "I can't tell you how many times I've said, 'This friend of mine, she's a client, she's also a friend.'" Like many designers, the Samatas aren't interested in traditional client entertainment based on wining and dining and tickets to sports events. Instead, their clients—executives of Fortune 100 industrial companies— might be invited to supper at the Samata home. They'll share a bottle of wine husband/partner Greg uncorks while the two-year-old twins are running around the table legs and Parker, the four-year-old, is coloring. The friendship might start by swapping kid stories in the downtime at the printer's while waiting for the next sheet. "Press checks are times when everyone is equal," Samata states, adding that she and Greg won't work with anybody they wouldn't want to have as a friend. A few years ago, the firm took the initiative to break off with a long-standing client, its biggest biller. "The client felt they had control over us and were chewing up and spitting out our staff. People were afraid to pick up the phone. Life is too short for that." Greg took the client to lunch and said, "This is not good for either of us."

Judy Kirpich, who heads the twenty-five-person Grafik Communications firm in Alexandria, Virginia, maintains that she, too, won't do business with someone she senses at the outset might want to mistreat her or her employees, or who seems to want something for nothing. Adding another twist to the date rape analogy, Kirpich says, "You have to know who you're going to be sleeping with for the next six months." She says she's worked the

hardest at being perceived as a really smart strategic player. To be selected for projects such as identities for the PBS Business Channel, "projects that small freelancers can't touch," she reads every marketing study she can get her hands on, talks to researchers, and goes to every training seminar. "I try to build up the client's intellectual trust. That's the only way they won't look at you as someone who does whacked-out type."

This is not to say there's no hope for the small firm—five to ten people—that has been the mainstay of our business. But you might have to be the kind of person, like Drew Hodges, who thrives on spontaneity. Hodges, who runs entertainment-industry-oriented Spot Design out of a small loft in New York's flower-import-export district, says, "We're like designated hitters who work for people who have wonderful art departments, like Nickelodeon. At any given moment we could be working on ten things, or just one project. I've trained myself not to look for stability."

Perseverance is also a virtue. Toni Schowalter, who's headed a five-person New York design office for ten years, said she finds these times frustrating and also recalled a recent moment of triumph: a logo she'd designed for a culinary organization was adapted by the client three-and-a-half years—and two management changes—after she'd first presented it. She took it to a James Beard event and buttonholed the organization's new director. "The quality shone through and they finally recognized it."

Craig Bernhardt, of New York's Bernhardt/Fudyma design group, reports that his firm is still hanging in there—actually doing very well—but they've had to change the way they operate. "It used to be that clients would call and say, 'We have a project, can you take a look at it and give us a price?' Today, we're one of seventeen firms; they get it down to six proposals. Who are we bidding against? It might be Pentagram at one end and someone working out of his apartment at the other." Bernhardt said he and partner/wife Janice Fudyma started paying careful attention to the ways clients like to work, even if it's not the way they prefer. Clients were recently sent a survey that asked them to rate from one (lowest) to ten (highest) how well they thought Bernhardt/Fudyma understood their message, how creative the execution was, how well the firm followed up on details, and whether things like notifications of costs of changes were made in a timely manner. "We got lots of eights and nines," Bernhardt says. "But also some fives and sixes, which let us know where they thought we were falling short so we could modify our way of working."

"Really flexible" is a phrase also used by Michael Mabry. "You learn to roll with the flow. We change and they change." Although Mabry claims he is pessimistic about the

future of graphic design, he acknowledges that marketing people still believe that identity and packaging have an important direct effect on sales. And that will mean continuing work for him and his firm.

So is this the flash-in-the-pan era of ships passing in the night? Or is it the cusp of the millennium when strong firms are being built to do powerful, enduring work that reshapes national and international organizations? And when great solo-practitioner starships also rule the skies?

Like Dickens's "best of times, worst of times," it is a little of both. There are opportunities for those with the talent and the will, and who can put up with the frustrations.

CHAPTER 2

Negotiating: Lessons
from a Caveman

By Ed Gold

A few weeks ago I saw a production of Rob Becker's show *Defending the Caveman*. It's another of those one-actor shows that producers turn to when Andrew Lloyd Webber stops returning their calls, and it's a pretty good example of this particular genre.

In the show, Becker draws parallels between the behavior of modern men and women and that of cave men and cave women. I have to say that he's very good at doing this, although I myself am well past the age of "guyhood" and had a hard time identifying with most of the "guy" attitudes and behaviors he was describing.

As I sat there watching Becker, however, I began to realize that much of what he was saying on stage could easily apply to designers and how they try to get what they want.

For example, Becker describes a scene in which four men are sitting around a coffee table watching a football game when they realize that the chip bowl needs to be refilled. They begin the process of trying to identify which of them will have to get off his butt, go into the kitchen, and refill the bowl.

"I bought the chips," says the first.

"I put the bowl on the table," says the second.

"I filled the bowl," says the third.

The fourth man kind of sheepishly says, "I did all I could do. I *ate* the chips."

The others all look at him accusingly until he finally gets up and trudges off to the kitchen, chip bowl in hand.

According to Becker, what they've been doing has been searching for the one with the weakest excuse, who is then tagged as the loser in the game and sent off to their personal Siberia, the kitchen, to refill the bowl.

In other words, they are "negotiating."

According to Becker, modern men negotiate almost all the time, over practically everything, because negotiating allows them metaphorically to focus on a specific target, hunt it down, kill it, and drag its carcass back to their cave to be presented as proof of their skill as a hunter, just as their cavemen ancestors did.

I agree with Becker. Negotiating is about winning and losing.

It would be nice to think that the secret handshake admitting a designer to the exclusive club of successful designers is the ability to orchestrate mutual cooperation and satisfaction between designer and client. After all, it seems obvious that, in any relationship, both parties have to feel satisfied with whatever they are getting from each other or the relationship can't last.

The problem is, when it comes to conflicts between designers and their clients, seldom are both sides really seeking cooperation; they are seeking a win. They are not looking for mutual satisfaction; they are trying to get whatever it is they want, and whatever it is they want, they want it all. They are willing to settle for less, if necessary, but not without a fight. We call this battle "negotiating," and like all battles, if one wants to come away with all of one's body parts intact, there are certain rules to follow and tactics to employ.

Most designers I've met are already convinced that they are great negotiators. After all, that's practically all they've been doing ever since they began to design. But, if designers are so good at negotiating, why do they complain so often that their clients don't respect them, don't listen to them, don't understand design, and almost always screw up their jobs?

The sad fact is that most designers are actually pretty bad at getting what they want from a client. Here are what I believe to be the most common reasons why they don't:

They don't know what they want: Sharpening the spear.

The most important part of the process of negotiating takes place long before the negotiating begins. It begins when the parties figure out what they are really trying to come away with. For most designers the answer to the question, "What are you trying to get from your client?" is easy. "What am I asking for?" Sometimes it's a job, sometimes it's a price, sometimes it's the freedom to do things their way.

But, most of the time, it's not that simple. If all the designer wanted was just to be given the job, then all he or she would have to do would be to find out what the client was looking for and provide it. But we know that "Tell me what you want and how much you're

willing to pay for it" seldom works, and when it does, both parties feel cheated and suspicious of the other. The relationship is shaky at best.

When closely examined, the answer to the question "What does 'getting what you want from a client' really mean to you?" can be complex. It could mean achieving a short-term goal, such as making a sale or getting a particular design approved or getting paid the price you asked. But it could also mean establishing a long-term relationship or getting the client to trust your advice.

Each of these goals requires a different strategy, and, since no two clients are exactly alike, each client requires that a different strategy be employed to accomplish the same goal. Furthermore, each designer is different, with a different set of values and limits. While one designer couldn't care less if a client wanted to use a snapshot of his five-year-old grandchild holding a bowling ball on the cover of the client's annual report, as I once was asked to do, another might have picked up the nearest sharp instrument and thrown it at the client, as I once also did. Luckily, my aim is so bad that I didn't come close to hitting the client.

The fact is, we all have individual goals and limits. Before a designer can complete a negotiation successfully, he or she must have a clear idea of what these goals and limits are. A designer needs to identify precisely the least that he or she would be willing to accept, as well as know when to walk away from the table. If the client won't give a designer the least that designer will take, the designer hasn't lost anything by walking.

They don't know what the other guy wants: Tracking the raptor.

Human nature dictates that, when it comes to conflicts, we tend to think more about what *we* want than about what the *other* party wants. This may explain why everyone who argues with us seems to be so damn hardheaded, stubborn, or just plain stupid. The fact of the matter is that it doesn't make any difference how dumb other people's ideas may be or why they believe their ideas will work. These ideas happen to be their beliefs, like it or not, and these beliefs will drive them forward relentlessly, regardless of whether or not you agree with them. In fact, the more you attack these beliefs, the more they will dig their heels in and defend them.

But people are not made of cardboard. They are multidimensional and have many beliefs and needs, some stronger than others, some in great conflict with each other. If the purpose of any negotiation is to get the other person to give you what you want, then the fastest way to do this, other than pulling out an Uzi, is not to try to change the other person's

mind about one strongly held belief, but to search for another that allows the other person to cooperate more willingly.

Several years ago I was asked to design an annual report for a new client. The report was one I really wanted to work on, since the budget was good and the quality of the report had consistently been high over the years. But the CEO of the company had a reputation for mistrusting the advice of everyone, when it came to running his business. This was especially true of designers, whom he placed, in terms of pecking order and behavior, on the same level as his chiropodist . . . someone he knows he needs once in a while, but who is quite below him and has to be watched carefully.

The person I was working with was convinced that the CEO always wanted his people to present him with a completed design that they had all agreed upon, which he then proceeded to reject because it didn't express exactly what he wanted to say. Of course, he didn't know what he wanted to say until he had some ideas to react to. Based on the CEO's new directions, everyone went back to the drawing board and started over. Eventually, after several false starts, deadlines began to dictate that one of the designs already created be approved. The report was finally printed, having gone over budget and bringing everyone involved to the point of panic and frustration.

I was certain that the CEO would not let me proceed with the job until he had satisfied his need to show me how much more he knew about his business than I or anyone else did. Until he got this out of his system, it would make no difference what I said, how good the work I showed was, or how many different designs I did.

I knew that a preplanning session was probably going to be useless because the CEO's normal way of working was to wait until he was presented with various options, which would then bring other possibilities to his mind. But I also knew that the CEO was proud of his company's reputation for promoting teamwork and cooperation. I decided that I might be able to use these two beliefs to help me avoid the hassle of doing endless different designs.

Rather than just producing many alternative designs, I asked my contact to set up two formal brainstorming sessions to which the CEO would be invited. I would serve as the facilitator at the sessions. The first would explore several possible design options; the second would choose one of these options to proceed with. I thought this might give the CEO lots of concepts to choose from, let us all hear input, and, at the same time, satisfy his sense that this was a true team effort.

It worked. By the end of the second session we had made a choice. The work proceeded smoothly and effortlessly. The job was finished on time, well under budget, and was a design I was satisfied to put in my portfolio. Furthermore, from then on, the CEO's perceptions of the value of a designer changed completely. I was no longer just another in a string of prima donnas, but a member of his corporate team.

How? It depends not only on what kind of negotiation the parties are involved in, but also on the differences between clients. In any case, it can't happen at all if the designer doesn't put the client's needs and wants before his or her own. Unless the client believes that he or she is getting something desired, the differences between the two parties are sure to cause frustration and a possible deadlock.

In any negotiating exchange, the person with the most knowledge of the other is usually the one who wins. If you hope to be successful in a negotiation, you must shift your focus from you to your clients. You must know who they are, what they expect to get out of the negotiations, where their bottom line is, and what ingrained attitudes and beliefs they hold. This information can only come from asking questions of them and of those who know them, and from listening carefully to the answers.

A few weeks ago I was having lunch with a designer. He was telling me how difficult it is to find good clients. I asked him what his definition of a good client was. He said that a good client is one who allows him to do great work and pays him a lot of money to do it.

I agreed that this sounds like a pretty good client to have. I then asked him how many clients he had had that fit this description. He replied, "Not enough to live on."

The fact is that most clients have the potential to fit this description. While all of us will encounter a few unscrupulous people in the course of our professional careers, most of the clients that hire us are honest and fair. They do not enter into a relationship with a designer with the intention of destroying the relationship and coming out of it with a bad job and an unpleasant experience. The problem is that both parties in the relationship see things only from their own perspectives and are interested only in achieving their own objectives.

It would be wise for the designer to recognize that the client usually doesn't understand the process of design very well, often views the relationship as if contracting to have a house painted, couldn't care less about what the designer will be getting out of the relationship, and really has only one interest, "What can you do for me?"

They think too much about themselves and not enough about the other guy: When attacking the beast, it's not a good idea to look at your own feet.

In the midst of a heated negotiating session, most designers' minds are focused on what their next move will be. This gets in the way of where their minds should be, on the ultimate result they want. The ultimate result will be determined more by what their clients are willing to give them at the moment than it is by what the designers want or what the clients might give them in the long run. As a matter of fact, the clients probably have no idea at that point how much they really are willing to give. They might be persuaded to move a little from their established position, but probably not much.

In order for designers to get what they want, they will have to stop trying to change their clients' minds and focus on trying to figure out what other strategy to adopt that will get their clients to cooperate. Sometimes it means doing some research in order to validate claims and opinions. At other times it means trying to win a small concession from the client based on something the designer knows the client would be willing to agree to, and, in a series of small steps, gradually move the client closer and closer to your position.

They think compromising is a dirty word: Sometimes retreat is the best attack.

No one likes to compromise. There's something wimpy about compromising. Our nation was built on a tradition of going for it. We celebrate examples of our refusal to compromise or surrender. Remember the Alamo! Remember McAuliffe's "Nuts!" at Bastogne? We seem to think that anything less than unconditional surrender somehow translates into a loss. Which is why we fight so hard to hold our positions at all costs, even if it may be absolutely the wrong thing to do.

The truth is that compromise is just one of many tactics used in the process of negotiating. Use it when appropriate to do so, in order to arrive at the position, after the difference has been split, where you were willing to be before the negotiations began.

They use the same negotiating technique again and again: No two dinos are alike.

It goes without saying that every client is different, just as every person is different. This may seem obvious, but it affects every aspect of the negotiating process. Unless a designer has done some homework on how a client has responded in similar situations, has really studied the client's personality, is listening for conversational cues that can tip a designer off to a client's attitudes and perceptions, and is consciously planning and adjusting a

strategy that fits the characteristics of the client, negotiation might not work with that particular client at that particular time.

They try to solve the wrong problem: A knife is no match for a raptor.

Let's say a designer is hired to produce a capabilities brochure. The designer designs the best damn capabilities brochure in history. When the design is presented to the client it is obvious that the client has had second thoughts. "Maybe we don't really need a capabilities brochure. Maybe what we really need is a whole new look. Maybe what we really need is an identity program!" Warning bells start going off in the mind of the designer. He or she knows that, sooner or later, this will become a problem, and it usually does, in the form of disputed bills, finger-pointing, and blaming.

Clients are notorious for coming to designers with requests to help solve the wrong problems. If designers aren't on their toes, they can find themselves the messenger who has to be killed.

The best way to avoid a sticky negotiation is to be alert to situations that cause the need for a negotiation in the first place. If, right at the outset, the designer had dug deep enough to uncover the real problem the client faced, not only would there be no need to negotiate the extra time and costs, but the designer would have been transformed from a mere puppet who moves when a string is pulled by the client to someone who stands beside the client helping to pull the strings.

They don't recognize the hidden agendas: There's more of them in the bushes.

Sometimes a designer will be negotiating with one person, sometimes more than one. The designer should always be aware that the people sitting across from him or her, whether one person or many, have their own agendas. These agendas aren't always easy to recognize.

Sometimes a client's agenda has to do with getting brownie points from the big kahuna. Sometimes it has to do with undermining someone else in the company. Sometimes there's an internal struggle for power that has absolutely nothing to do with the on going negotiations. Any of these hidden agendas can end up affecting those negotiations dramatically.

It pays for designers to try to find out as much as possible about who they will be dealing with and to be alert to the agendas that may be driving the arguments of their negotiating counterparts. These may have a greater impact on negotiations than the stated issues themselves.

They let their emotions get in the way of their goals: A T-Rex can smell fear.

Many designers approach the negotiating process prepared for a calm, logical exchange of positions, leading to a friendly resolution sealed with a handshake and a glass of wine. In your dreams.

The negotiating process, by its very nature, means giving and taking. Expect the client to try to move you from your stated position. Sometimes you will be pushed by tough and experienced negotiators who will be searching desperately to find just the buttons that will set you off and make you lose it.

Don't cooperate. They want you to lose your cool and force a deadlock. When you do this, they achieve their goals. The status remains unchanged. They don't have to give an inch. The result: you lose, they win.

No matter what your adversaries are doing or saying, never forget that your ultimate purpose in negotiating is to get them to do something that is to *your* benefit, not theirs. At the same time, you should recognize that you won't get anything if they don't think they have benefited as well. Although this often means getting less than you want, it should always mean getting at least as much as you think is fair.

They don't recognize an opportunity for closure when they're given it: When a raptor shows you its belly, you better not miss.

Don't forget that the whole purpose of beginning the negotiating process at all is to close it as fast as possible. Be alert. When the opportunity for closure presents itself, grab it. Otherwise, you may lose it forever.

They don't spend enough time reviewing results: It's okay to look back—they're gone.

It wouldn't make much sense for a designer to go through hours of negotiating without having learned anything from it, and we know that the only way to learn anything is to consciously study the subject. After each negotiating session designers should take time to reflect on what went right and what went wrong. They should try to figure out why things worked or didn't and make plans to use the information the next time they run into a similar situation.

We should consider ourselves lucky. Unlike the cave man, if we lose a battle, we can always hunt again tomorrow.

CHAPTER 3

The Process of Setting Fees

by Eva Doman Bruck

There are three fundamental conditions to consider during the process of setting fees. One is the cost of staying in business (overhead), second is a best estimate of the nature and complexity of the proposed project (variable costs), and third is knowing the intrinsic value of the final product (market conditions).

No matter the size of the organization, it is most likely to enjoy long-term success when there is detailed, up-to-date information available on its consumption of resources translated into financial terms. Resources may be staff and freelance personnel, supplies and materials, and outside services. Therefore, it is imperative to set up a record keeping system that tracks time, payables, and income. Record keeping can be approached in a variety of ways. An experienced accountant should be retained in helping to determine whether the business requires a customized bookkeeping system or whether off-the-shelf software may be suitable.

Overhead and Setting the Hourly Rate

Start the fee setting process by examining in detail the constant costs of the business, or in bookkeeping parlance what is called the overhead. Included in the overhead category are rent, utilities, equipment leases, office supplies, business insurance, salaries, taxes and benefits, accounting and legal services, and the cost of nonbillable time devoted to self-promotion and administrative chores. Don't forget to include profit in this equation; a healthy business should aim to generate about 20 percent of annual profit after all expenses have been paid. For the purpose of determining your hourly rate, these costs are calculated on an annual basis. The total dollar amount is divided by the total number of hours you have estimated are available for billing to clients for the year. The best way to learn how much of

your time is available to devote to paying projects is to gain some experience in tracking actual time spent on billable versus nonbillable work. You should be able to bill out at least 50 to 80 percent of your time. If you find you have less time than this for project work, take a hard look at your daily activities and see how you can gain some efficiencies and free up more time for billable activities.

To calculate the hourly rate:

Annual Overhead (including salary + profit) ÷ Annual Billable Hours = Hourly Rate Time

Unless you are being hired on an hourly basis, your hourly rate should be relevant only to you; for most pricing situations the hourly rate should be transparent in the fee structure. Studio members also need to understand how to control and keep track of time, not only to meet project deadlines, but also to allow for administrative, marketing, and maintenance chores. It helps to inform everyone from the beginning why this information is needed (cost control, client billing, and staffing information), and that disciplined time management allows for significantly more time for creative work.

Studio members should transfer pertinent aspects of this information to standardized time sheets. They should track time spent on active assignments regardless of whether such time is directly billable. In flat fee situations, the information is used periodically to calculate how much budget is left to work with and finally, how profitable the job was or wasn't.

How detailed should a time sheet be? It depends on management's need to know and client requirements. Some design companies want to know how much time is spent on every aspect of an assignment from briefing meetings to print/fabrication supervision. This information is useful in tracing the relative levels of job costs phase by phase and can also be used to help price similar assignments in the future. Unfortunately, it's also a large inputting headache for this level of detail and many smaller companies avoid excessive subcoding. Although, there are intranet programs that make it possible for each employee to enter information on an electronic time sheet that is then transferred to a database for tracking and report generation. Agencies and design companies also track time spent preparing presentation materials used to pitch accounts; they may also want to see how long administrative and studio maintenance takes. This information is used to monitor studio staff's productiv-

ity, that is, how much of a person's time is billable, how much is used to bring in future income, and how much is simply downtime.

Materials

Supplies that are routinely a part of the studio's activities are part of the overhead, while materials that are billable back to projects must be accounted for in such a way that you can show evidence of the purchase. Code these invoices with the project number and keep a set of copies to back up bills to clients. It is best for one person to be in charge of ordering general supplies and shared equipment, while individuals requisition what they need only for their own projects. Naturally, there has to be a purchase order system for items over some specified amount, and a trusted staff person should be authorized to approve these orders.

Services

All outside services need to be documented. Whether it's for retouching, illustration and photography, model making, outputting, slide production, or independent contractors and freelance personnel, there has to be a written record of what is being requested, by whom, at what price, and for illustration, photography, and copywriting, and under what kind of terms (copyright, usage rights, credit lines, etc.). The purchase order system for materials is just as useful for outside services. However, remember that a purchase order is a legal commitment to pay, so don't issue any purchase orders if you are only intending to evaluate a product or service. It is also useful to include standardized terms and conditions that are part of each purchase order regarding such issues as ownership, copyright, payment terms, confidentiality, and any other items you consider important to the protection of your interests. Included in payment terms can be the payment schedule which is generally one-third in advance to begin work, one-third upon approval of design drawings, and one-third upon completion.

Project Estimating

The difference between a good estimate and a bad estimate is the difference between profit and loss. The key to an accurate estimate is a thorough understanding of the project specifications as well as the production process. Make sure you have an opportunity to see firsthand what the project looks like, either from prior examples, or competitive ones.

If you know what is being requested and also know how to produce it, and build in a certain amount of safety, you have an excellent chance of setting an accurate fee.

Most professionals break down a project into phases: preproduction for initial client briefings, competitive research, and concept development; design development begins with refinements to the concept sketches based on client input, and then application of the approved concept to the project's main components; production of finished art and design follows after approval; and finally, printing and/or fabrication of all the project elements. Phases are further classified into tasks, which then can be analyzed in terms of duration. An important element of successful estimating is knowing approximately how long it takes to do specific tasks and adding on just enough to allow for hitches and breakdowns in the process. Certain contingencies, such as delayed client approvals can be covered in the project agreement, but delayed delivery of outside elements, such as photography or copy, is the designer's headache and requires an allowance to be built into the production process.

Once you have outlined all of the elements and their production requirements, attach to each step the number of different personnel, their hourly rates, and how long it will take each of them to carry out the necessary steps. Some firms calculate rates per each individual, other firms have a tiered system of rates. A tiered system is preferred, especially in instances where it is necessary to reveal to clients what the firm's hourly rates are. In this way, different levels of personnel are grouped by levels of rates. Generally, the categories are: principals, senior designers, junior designers, and production personnel. In this way, you also avoid revealing salary information to anyone within your organization, as well as to your clients. Add up the personnel hours/days, making sure to account for time to prepare for presentations and client approvals, as well as the delivery of those elements they are supposed to provide. Count in responsibilities for art direction, print supervision, and fabrication of three-dimensional elements. Multiply the final total by approximately 15 percent for contingencies. For well-defined projects of a simple nature, the contingency allowance can be smaller; for large, complicated, vaguely defined projects, the contingency allowance should be greater. You now have your design fee.

Out-of-Pocket Expenses

Estimate all of the out-of-pocket expenses which are reimbursable. These items are usually standard, but with some clients they may have to be negotiated. Generally, the following items are included in this category: outside services, such as illustration, photogra-

phy, copywriting, prototyping, and outputting, delivery services; and items such as models, props, and unique references. Most often, these are expenses that the designer may mark up in order to cover the administrative expenses of researching, bidding, and supervising, as well as for laying out and carrying their costs. Some designers mark up printing and fabrication. Others prefer to have clients pay for them directly. This is a negotiable matter. In the event the client is going to pay directly, but the designer is still responsible for supervision, the fee for supervision needs to be built into the estimate.

Changes and Additions

The tiered system of staff rates is especially useful when clients request changes and additions to their original project specifications. Changes and additions should be considered separately in the project agreement. A brief statement which describes what is considered outside of the project's scope of work, followed by the tiered rates will take care of this thorny, but frequent contingency. It is especially useful to document such additions and changes in advance of doing them and have the client sign off, in writing if possible.

Market Conditions

Aside from the actual time and expense it takes to create something, there is another critical factor to consider: the inherent worth of that particular item. Inherent worth isn't the same as actual cost. Inherent worth has to do with how much someone is willing to pay to have something or it's market value. An annual report for a Fortune 500 corporation is going to have a much greater inherent worth than an in-house newsletter for a small regional trade association. This is not because the large corporation is necessarily better, but because it has a more urgent need to communicate effectively with a greater number of people, and because it has far more money to pay for what it wants. There is no social or moral value involved. A bottle that holds $100 per ounce perfume may have the same market value as a bottle that holds $1.29 dishwashing soap. A two-page, full-color spread that appears in a minor, local newspaper may pay the same as a quarter-page, black and white insert in a national consumer magazine. Value has to do with distribution, exposure, and the kind of industry being served. Advertising and corporate clients tend to pay the higher rates, but they are also the most sought after and, usually, the most demanding to service.

Usage Rights

Always remember to consider future uses of your work. The prospect of building future "passive" income is not only attractive financially, but important in terms of professional prestige. If you designed a two-color poster for an off-Broadway play that then became a huge Broadway hit, but did not reserve the right to your artwork for collateral uses, it could happen that your artwork could be used on book covers, posters, movie ads, and billboards, and possibly even for promotional items, and none of these would carry your credit line.

Do designers have the same rights issues as photographers, illustrators, and artists? Yes and no. Corporate identity is a nonissue. Annual reports and time or event-based materials have limited life spans. On the other hand, cover designs for books, posters, product literature, advertisements, and other items which may be expanded in terms of media, print-run, and time, should be considered as more open-ended opportunities for future use and future income. Therefore, a general rule of thumb is to limit usage rights and pricing to only those media and applications that the client is requesting, and reserve all other rights. And, always do so in writing. A complete buy out requires a significantly higher fee. Consider what the compensation might be for future uses of the design. In the event that you are sharing copyrights with other artists for the same item, try to coordinate your efforts. Either make sure you own all rights to the various design elements, or carry separate agreements that specify future compensation for them. Avoid making the client have to think about negotiating with a group of different artists for one design.

Negotiations

While checking with colleagues and other sources, such as pricing guidelines, can be useful, it is usually best to find out directly from the client how much they have budgeted for the project. This information is helpful for the designer to gage the client's expectations. There may be an opportunity to expand a project, or if necessary, to walk away from it in the event the designer believes it is not possible to do justice to it for the level of renumeration.

In most instances of business life, negotiation is a key activity. In the course of normal operations, you will be negotiating with clients, employers, partners, suppliers, landlords, among many others. Negotiation is an important skill, and one that can be learned and improved continually. Fundamentally, it is necessary to understand the goal of productive negotiations—that both parties must feel that they have gotten a fair value and can proceed in

good faith. Good relations rarely follow horrible negotiations. There must be the transmission of a certain level of trust and good will on both sides. Neither side should be made to feel like a loser. Neither side should feel that they have been unfairly coerced.

Once you have identified what you are seeking—whether it is a higher fee, a more prominent credit line, or free portfolio samples—identify those areas upon which you are willing to trade a smaller markup on out-of-pocket expenses, additional sketches, changes at no cost, or print supervision at a lower rate; the choices may be quite extensive. Also, always ask for a little more and know the point below which you will not proceed. Negotiation is an ancient human activity (hobby to some people) and the nature of it is such that one always expects to get a little more for a little less. As long as you know your upper and lower ranges, finding the comfortable medium is a matter of building your case to support your demands. Be prepared, know what you are talking about, and never feel obliged to commit to a number on the spot if you are not sure it is the right number. It is always possible to stall in order to give yourself a chance to make new calculations or just simply weigh the advantages and disadvantages of the proposition. Naturally, in instances where fees are fixed, or in a competitive situation where the lowest bidder wins automatically, there is little opportunity for discussion. The opportunity afforded by the work, whether monetary or otherwise, is the only basis on which to make a final decision. In such cases, you may decide a lower fee is worth the widespread exposure a project offers; or the prospect of a longer-term commitment for additional work outweighs the limitations of an uninspiring project. Many designers take on bread and butter assignments to cover their overhead and let high fee projects support those in which they have a personal interest, but may pay little or nothing.

There are many opportunities and many trade-offs. The trick is to balance them well enough to have an overall sense of satisfaction and progress. Which, ultimately, is further promoted when you have mastered the technique of setting fees accurately.

The AIGA Standard Form
of Agreement

by Roger Whitehouse

I came to the United States from England in 1967 as an architect to teach at Columbia University. As part of my move from East to West, I eventually defected into the ranks of graphic design. However, my initial years practicing as an architect both in London and New York had gotten me into certain habits. In those days, whenever you started work for a client you simply reached for an RIBA or AIA standard form of agreement, scribbled in a few numbers, and away you went. Other than the fact that you inevitably had to slash your fees, the contract was never really an issue because it had gained such widespread acceptance.

Graphic design was different, however. Agreements generally seemed to revolve around a one-page letter or some numbers casually mentioned during a meeting or phone call. After that, 50 percent of your time was spent on the design process and the rest on diplomatically making sure you got paid.

After a few such episodes, I reluctantly decided it was time to sit down and write my own version of a proper contract. This mainly consisted of having heated arguments with myself about contractual issues, much to the alarm of my family and staff who happened upon me on these occasions. Obviously, I needed to seek professional help. I called AIGA and after a few brief sessions, I agreed to grab the bull by the horns and work with Marjorie Katz, who was then heading AIGA's Professional Practice Committee, on a standard form of agreement between designer and client.

To start with, we sent about one hundred requests to designers for copies of their contractual materials. About fifty replied. Of these, twenty had simple terms and conditions and five had fairly sophisticated documents, a couple of which could even be described as vicious. The rest returned a collection of strange forms, beautifully printed with rules and rows of little dots, but we couldn't decipher what they were for. There is a limit to how much

6-point Bodoni, printed gray on gray, one can read without wanting to take up kelp farming or some other more fundamental pursuit.

I did a cull, cut, and paste of all the various clauses that comprised these contracts, and put together the basic structure of a standard document. Interestingly, there is a fair degree of similarity between many of the clauses. Whether this is evidence of the fact that we share all these concerns and issues regardless of the type of practice or location, or whether the staff get into the file cabinets and hand the stuff around to other offices, I'm not sure.

There were, of course, some clauses in everyone's contracts that attested to some recent bitter experience such as, "The client agrees that under no circumstances shall the design or designs be submitted to any third parties for review or comment including the client's spouse, children, or in-laws, particularly with regard to details of the color treatment." These we omitted in the belief that the final printed document should be terse and not require more than the signatures of two parties.

At last, we put out a first draft and sent it to a test group of designers for comment and review. Of these, most have never spoken to me again and the rest told me they would pass it on to their attorneys for comment.

I tried again, this time trapping people at social events or in elevators. I even got some to read the draft and sit down with me to discuss some of the details. They harangued me with the belief that the document was much too long and complicated. Then, they read through it again and insisted, however, that nothing could be taken out.

Finally, after a well-attended, working session on the projected contract that was organized by the AIGA/NY chapter, we came to the realization that it was as finished as it was ever going to be, and sent it to Marcus Strock for legal comment and, if possible, to translate it back into English.

Inevitably, no contract can ever cover all eventualities, although this one has been conceived to cover as wide a range of projects as possible. The following notes describe in detail the reasons for most of the clauses and give suggestions regarding a variety of opportunities to customize it.

Almost a decade has passed since we labored together over the AIGA contract. In evaluating whether our efforts were a success, I think that I can fairly say that the contract has been used and looked to for what is fair and ethical in designer-client relationships. It has helped both as a form for use and as a checklist for consideration when in the midst of negotiations. I believe the contract is a living document, one that may well be improved to

keep pace with changes in technology and changes within the design profession. Until that time, however, the AIGA Standard Form of Agreement for Graphic Design Services can serve as a uniform basis for designers' contractual arrangements with their clients.

Some of the material included will be familiar to designers, some will not be. The clauses have all been developed in response to specific issues, and the purpose of these notes is to explain what these issues are and how they affect the designer. The notes follow the numbering sequence of the contract itself which is reproduced at the end of the chapter.

Provision is made here for the client's and designer's names and addresses to be entered, together with the name by which the project will be known. A job number or purchase order number may also be included here if required.

1.1. Description of Project

In order for the contract to be clear, it is important to describe the project carefully. With simple projects, the description could be a single sentence. For example:

> A four-page, one or two color, 8½-by-11-inch brochure, consisting of text only, describing your company's services.

However, with more complex projects, the description could cover several pages, describing areas of research and consultation and including many potential printed or fabricated pieces, including what services will be provided for each, how work will be phased, and when and what each presentation will entail. In this event, it may be advisable to refer to an appendix or other document, such as a proposal, in which this information is contained.

The most important consideration is that both the designer and client should be clear as to the scope of the project. This is essential in the frequent event that the scope changes as the work proceeds, and revisions to the fees become necessary.

2.1. Basic Services

The starting point for these documents was to define clearly what services we offer our clients. As designers we provide professional services. That means we have studied and amassed a body of knowledge and expertise in our area of practice, graphic design, and make that knowledge and expertise available to our clients in the form of advice and the formulation of solutions to their needs. These basic consultation services, which are common to all

designers, include research, conceptualization, design, documentation of our ideas to enable them to be implemented, coordination of all other individuals involved in the project, and quality control of the implementation of the finished design.

2.2. Supplementary Services

There are many other services that specific designers include beyond that of basic consultation. Many of these, such as copy development, illustration, etc., are referred to in this clause. What is important is that the contract makes clear what services you are and are not including. Space has been included on the form for you to list any supplementary services you intend to provide.

2.3. Implementation

In attempting to construct a standard form of agreement for designers, the most difficult issue has been that of including any implementation services such as printing, fabrication, and installation.

Some designers do not wish to include any implementation services in their contract. The reasons for this are twofold: firstly, they feel it is contrary to their status as a consultant; and, secondly, for the important reason that if they did, they would probably be considered a vendor rather than a consultant by most sales tax authorities and would have to charge sales tax on their billings, including consultations.

3.1. Fees

Clearly state fees, either the total sum or other basis for compensation. For example:

For the fixed sum of $0,000.00

or:

Hourly, at the rates stated in this contract, not to exceed $0,000.00

or, by referring to another document:

See Appendix A, "Schedule of Fees," attached.

3.2. Hourly Rates

The hourly rates for the calculation of any additional services should be inserted here. These are most commonly stated as dollar amounts for various levels of staff (i.e., principals, senior staff, junior staff). Another alternative is to express the rates as a multiplier of an employee's salary. This multiplier is normally between 2.5 and 3.5 to allow for benefits, overhead, and profit.

3.3. Initial Payment

There are several functions the initiating fee performs. It confirms the client's good faith prior to the work commencing. Because the fee is not refundable, it serves to compensate the designer for nonreimbursable overhead costs and arranging for staff to be engaged in the event that the contract is abandoned at an early stage. It also assists the designer in financing the project. This is particularly important where there can be considerable sums expended in wages and reimbursable expenses. The initiating fee helps to cover this cost during the time it takes to invoice and collect. It also insures that the client does not become unduly in debt to the designer, thus giving the client excessive leverage in the relationship.

The amount asked for in an initiating fee can vary considerably from 10 percent on a long-term project without excessive expenses to 50 percent on a short-term, staff-intensive contract with potentially high reimbursable costs. Most commonly used figures are 20 percent, 25 percent, and 33.3 percent. In calculating this figure, a good rule of thumb is that it cover the amount of an average invoice for both fees and reimbursables for one month.

3.4. Payment Schedule

State the way in which fees and expenses are to be disbursed. For example:

In three equal payments: one-third upon signing the contract, one-third upon approval of the completed design, one-third upon completion of the project

or:

Monthly, based upon time expended, within the agreed totals

or:

Initiating Fee	$0,000.00
Completion of Preliminary Design Phase	$0,000.00
Completion of Design Development Phase	$0,000.00
Completion of Drawings and Mechanicals	$0,000.00
Completion of Project	$0,000.00

3.5. Revisions and Additions

A designer's services are essentially paid for on a time basis even in a fixed sum contract. Consequently, it is important that a designer not end up with a far greater time commitment than that quoted for, and this clause fulfills an important function in preventing that. It is only enforceable, however, if the original description of the project is clear and accurate, and the designer carefully monitors and documents hours spent.

3.6. Rush Work

A designer should be properly compensated for having to work unusual hours in exactly the same way that the printer and other individuals involved in the project will expect to be. The surcharge rates most commonly charged are 50 or 100 percent. Each individual designer will need to determine what is appropriate in his or her case.

3.7. Reimbursable Expenses

It is normal to add a reasonable handling charge to all reimbursable expenses. The most commonly used markups are 15, 17.5, or 20 percent. In determining the amount, it should be remembered that the purpose of this charge is to cover the administrative costs of handling the payment of bills and invoicing rather than considering it as an extra fee. Consequently, the percentage charged should be appropriate for the service provided. It may also be appropriate for larger items of expenditure to be billed directly to the client. In these instances, the large sums involved make it convenient for the client to establish their own account with the supplier.

3.8. Reimbursables and Implementation Budgets

While it is a designer's responsibility to use his or her best efforts to keep within stated budgets, it is also important that clients understand that expenses are their responsibility and are not always under the control of the designer.

It is important to resist any attempt to link the designer's fee and implementation costs under an upset figure. It is the client's responsibility to decide, based on the designer's advice, what ultimately to spend on their project. A single upset total implies that if the implementation costs exceed a certain amount, the excess should be paid for out of the designer's fee. This clause provides for a separate upset to be set for both fees and implementation costs and application made to the client to extend either budget if necessary.

3.10. Late Payment

Invoices are most commonly payable within thirty days. A service charge for collection of overdue accounts can be added. Most commonly used is 1.5 percent per month (18 percent per annum). There are legal limits to this amount. For example, in most states any figure over 1.5 percent is considered usury and is illegal. It is common practice to include such a clause in a contract, but not to attempt to collect on it unless litigation becomes necessary. The cumulative interest stated in the contract is then added to the collectible total.

4.1. Client Representative

This clause is important to prevent conflicting instructions being given to a designer by more than one member of a client organization. Even if it is impossible for one person to give all information and approvals directly, it is important to have a liaison on a client's staff who is responsible for obtaining and providing such information and arranging for approvals to be made.

4.2. Materials to be Provided by the Client

An important issue in making the extent of the designer's work clear is to clearly define what materials and services the client will be providing for use on the project. Space has been provided on the form to list such items as existing photography, drawings, or illustrations and such services as copy development, editing, proofreading, etc.

4.3. Liability of Designer

If a client insists on the designer taking some liability for items to be provided by the client, such as photographs or illustrations, the amount of the liability should be limited. Also, the designer should determine whether it would be wise to obtain insurance coverage for valuable items such as original transparencies.

5.1. Rights

Designers should retain as many rights as possible to their designs. It is implicit in the concept of being a professional consultant. It is a foundation concept of the copyright law. It is the basis upon which a designer is considered a provider of services rather than vendor of property in the eyes of the sales tax authorities in many states. It preserves the rights of designers to prevent unauthorized modification of their work. It provides a basis for the designer to receive further remuneration if the design is used beyond the purposes for which it was originally intended. In our digital era, it is ever more important to grant only limited rights. The value of electronic usages are particularly difficult to estimate at this time. By negotiating for limited rights and reserving all other rights, the designer ensures fair compensation at the time a use is to made. Presumably at that time, the value of the use will be easier to ascertain.

The effectiveness of this clause is, of course, dependent on the accuracy of the descriptions of the rights to be transferred. It is not the intention of the contract to prevent the use of the design for any of the purposes for which it was commissioned. Any listing of uses to which the design can be put can therefore be lengthy, but should still be finite. After the grant of rights, the designer would be wise to add, "All other rights, including but not limited to electronic rights, are reserved to the Designer." If electronic rights, such as for a Web site design, are in fact being transferred, the phrase might read, "All other rights, including but not limited to nonelectronic rights, are reserved to the Designer." If a mixture of electronic and nonelectronic rights are being transferred, the recitation might be, "All other rights are reserved to the Designer."

5.3. Third Party Contracts

Third party contracts is an important area of consideration. We are often asked to act on behalf of our clients to obtain the services of other creative people. Photographers, illustrators, writers, and others, all have their own professional organizations and contrac-

tual requirements, and it is often our responsibility to resolve them with our client's interests. Most important of these is rights. To simplify the process, this document proposes, unless specified otherwise in the write-in space provided, the granting of the same rights that have been negotiated for the designer's work. This is valuable to insure that our work is not put to a use for which rights have not been obtained from other members of the creative team. It is important, therefore, during any negotiation of fees with third parties to explain precisely what rights are to be transferred.

6.1. Code of Ethics

Adherence to the AIGA Code of Ethics and Professional Conduct is voluntary. This clause may be deleted if you do not wish to bind yourself to its conditions.

6.5. Sales Tax

This clause has been included to assist the designer in collecting any sales taxes that are retroactively assessed in an audit of the designer's invoices.

6.8. Termination

The most commonly specified notice for termination is ten business days. It can also be stated as zero where it is preferred that immediate cancellation can take effect.

6.9. Arbitration

The amount entered here, for arbitration, should be the maximum allowed for small claims court, which varies from jurisdiction to jurisdiction.

The Joint Ethics Committee (JEC), of which the AIGA is a sponsor, is a mediating and arbitrating organization which specializes in cases dealing with the creative professions. Only cases involving infringement of the JEC Code of Fair Practice are considered. Copies of the Code of Fair Practice are available from: The Joint Ethics Committee, Post Office Box 179, Grand Central Station, New York, NY 10017.

8. Continuations and Other Conditions

This section of the document, Continuations and Other Conditions, is provided for the designer to add any special clauses which are necessary to cover particular circumstances of the project.

10. Signatures

At the end of the contract, space has been provided for both parties to sign. Each signature should be followed by a description of the legal business entity and the title held by the party signing. It is important to be sure that the person signing the contract on the client's behalf has the authority to do so.

AIGA

The American Institute of Graphic Arts

Standard Form of Agreement for Graphic Design Services

General Edition

This document is intended to be used as a basis of agreement between designers and their clients. It has important legal consequences. Consultation with an attorney is encouraged with regard to its completion or modification.

The Client and Designer agree as follows:

Agreement made as of date

Between the Client

And the Designer

For the Project referred to as

Document Number
1988-01
October 1988 Edition

© 1988
The American Institute
of Graphic Arts

1059 Third Avenue
New York, New York 10021
Telephone 212.752.0813

Page Number 1

WHITEHOUSE · 39

**Standard Form of
Agreement for
Graphic Design Services**

General Edition

1.   THE PROJECT

Description of the Project   1.1.   The Project that is the subject of this agreement shall consist of:

Document Number   *© 1988*   *1059 Third Avenue*   *Page Number 2*
1988-01   *The American Institute*   *New York, New York 10021*
October 1988 Edition   *of Graphic Arts*   *Telephone 212.752.0813*

**Standard Form of
Agreement for
Graphic Design Services**

General Edition

---

2. SERVICES

The Designer shall provide the Basic and Supplementary Services specified below.

Basic Services

2.1. The Designer shall provide Basic Services for the Project consisting of consultation, research, design, checking quality of Implementation, and coordination of the Project and its Execution. In connection with performing Basic Services, the Designer shall prepare and present materials to the Client that demonstrate or describe the Designer's intentions and shall prepare various materials, such as artwork, drawings, and specifications, to enable the design to be printed, fabricated, installed, or otherwise implemented.

Supplementary Services

2.2. In addition to the Basic Services described above, the Designer's fee may also include the provision of certain specialized Supplementary Services, but only to the extent described below. Such Supplementary Services might include: Creative services including copy development, writing, editing, photography, and illustration. Preparation of special artwork including drawing of logotypes, nonstandard typefaces, maps, diagrams, and charts, and preparation of existing materials for reproduction such as partial or complete redrawing, line conversion, retouching, captioning within an illustration, diagram, or map, and making camera-ready color separation overlays. Production services including typesetting and proofreading. Preparation of special presentation materials including detailed renderings, models, mockups, and slide presentations. If any of these other services are required, but are not to be provided by the Designer as Supplementary Services, they will be coordinated by the Designer, provided by others, and billed to the Client as reimbursable expenses.

The Supplementary Services to be provided by the Designer with respect to the Project shall consist of:

Implementation

2.3. The Designer's services under this Agreement do not include Implementation such as printing, fabrication, and installation of the Project design. The Client and Designer agree that any such Implementation is to be provided by others, and the Designer's services with respect to such Implementation shall be restricted to providing specifications, coordination, and quality-checking. Unless otherwise specified in this Agreement, the Designer shall have no responsibility to the providers of such Implementation, and charges therefor shall be billed directly to the Client. While not responsible for Implementation, in a supervisory capacity the Designer may assume responsibility for paying such charges, and the Designer shall be entitled to reimbursement from the Client for Implementation costs plus such handling charge as is specified in Section 3.7.

Document Number
1988-01
October 1988 Edition

© 1988
The American Institute
of Graphic Arts

1059 Third Avenue
New York, New York 10021
Telephone 212.752.0813

Page Number 3

---

3. COMPENSATION

Fees

3.1. The Client shall pay the Designer for the services described in this Contract as follows:

Hourly Rates

3.2. Where specified in this contract, the Client shall pay the Designer at the Designer's standard rates as in effect at this time.

The Designer's standard rates currently in effect are as follows:

No change shall be made in the Designer's standard rates prior to

Initial Payment

3.3. Upon signing this Agreement, the Client shall make a payment of

This initial payment shall be credited against the amounts due hereunder as follows:

Payment Schedule

3.4. After receipt of an invoice, the Client shall make payments within

The Designer may render invoices according to the following schedule:

Document Number
1988-01
October 1988 Edition

© 1988
The American Institute
of Graphic Arts

1059 Third Avenue
New York, New York 10021
Telephone 212.752.0813

Page Number 4

| *Revisions and Additions* | 3.5. | A fixed fee or fee estimated not to exceed a specified amount is based upon the time estimated to complete the services specified in this Agreement during normal working hours. Any revisions or additions to the services described in this Agreement shall be billed as additional services not included in any fixed fee or estimated fee specified above. |

Such additional services shall include, but shall not be limited to, changes in the extent of work, changes in the complexity of any elements of the Project, and any changes made after approval has been given for a specific stage of design, documentation, or preparation of artwork.

The Designer shall keep the Client informed of additional services that are required and shall request the Client's approval for any additional services which cause the total fees, exclusive of any surcharge for rush work, to exceed the fixed or estimated fees set forth in section 3.1. by more than the following amount:

Rush Work   3.6.   The Client shall pay a surcharge for any services requiring work to be performed outside of normal working hours by reason of unusual deadlines or as a consequence of the Client not meeting scheduled times for delivery of information, materials, or approvals.

The surcharge for rush work shall be at the standard rates plus

Normal working hours for this Project are as follows:

Reimbursable Expenses   3.7.   The Client shall reimburse the Designer for all out-of-pocket expenses incurred by the Designer with respect to the Project including, but not limited to, expenditures for: Implementation, typesetting, photostats, photoprints, photography, film and processing, acetate color overlays, transfer proofs, presentation and artwork materials, electrostatic (xerographic) copies, Fax and long-distance telephone charges, postage, and local deliveries, including messengers, out-of-town travel, and shipping.

Automobile travel will be charged at a standard rate per mile of

Reimbursable Expenses will be billed at cost plus a surcharge of

Reimbursable and   3.8.   Any budget figures or estimates for Reimbursable Expenses or Implementation charges such
Implementation Budgets   as printing, fabrication, or installation are for planning purposes only. The Designer shall use his or her best efforts to work within stated budgets but shall not be liable if such expenses exceed budgets.

Records   3.9.   The Designer shall maintain records of hours and reimbursable expenses and shall make such records available to the Client for inspection on request.

Late Payment   3.10.   The Client shall pay a service charge for all overdue amounts of

Document Number
1988-01
October 1988 Edition

© 1988
The American Institute
of Graphic Arts

1059 Third Avenue
New York, New York 10021
Telephone 212.752.0813

Page Number 5

4.   CLIENT'S OBLIGATIONS

Client's Representative   4.1.   The Client shall appoint a sole Representative with full authority to provide or obtain any necessary information and approvals that may be required by the Designer. The Client's Representative shall be responsible for coordination of briefing, review, and the decision-making process with respect to persons and parties other than the Designer and its sub-contractors. If, after the Client's Representative has approved a design, the Client or any other authorized person requires changes that require additional services from the Designer, the Client shall pay all fees and expenses arising from such changes as additional services.

Materials to be Provided by the Client   4.2.   The Client shall provide accurate and complete information and materials to the Designer and shall be responsible for the accuracy and completeness of all information and materials so provided. The Client guarantees that all materials supplied to the Designer are owned by the Client or that the Client has all necessary rights in such materials to permit the Designer to use them for the Project.

The Client shall indemnify, defend, and hold the Designer harmless from and against any claim, suit, damages and expense, including attorney's fees, arising from or out of any claim by any party that its rights have been or are being violated or infringed upon with respect to any materials provided by the Client.

All copy provided by the Client shall be in a form suitable for typesetting. Where photographs, illustrations, or other visual materials are provided by the Client, they shall be of professional quality and in a form suitable for reproduction without further preparation or alteration. The Client shall pay all fees and expenses arising from its provision of materials that do not meet such standards. The Designer shall return all materials provided by the Client within 30 days after completion of the project and payment of amounts due. The Client shall provide the following materials and services for the Project:

Liability of Designer   4.3.   The Designer shall take reasonable precautions to safeguard original or other materials provided by the Client. The Designer shall, however, not be liable for any damage to, or loss of any material provided by the Client, including artwork, photographs, or manuscripts, other than or on account of willful neglect or gross negligence of the Designer.

Approval of Typesetting and Final Artwork   4.4.   The Client shall proofread and approve all final type before the production of artwork. The signature of the Client's Representative shall be conclusive as to the approval of all artwork drawings and other items prior to their release for printing, fabrication, or installation.

Instructions to Third Parties   4.5.   The Client specifically grants to the Designer the right to act on the Client's behalf to give instructions on behalf of the Client to any person or entity involved in the Project, such as photographers, illustrators, writers, printers, and fabricators. Any such instructions or approvals by the Client may only be made through the Designer. The Client shall be bound by all such instructions given by the Designer within the scope of this Agreement.

Document Number
1988-01
October 1988 Edition

© 1988
The American Institute
of Graphic Arts

1059 Third Avenue
New York, New York 10021
Telephone 212.752.0813

Page Number 6

5.   RIGHTS AND OWNERSHIP

Rights

5.1.   All services provided by the Designer under this Agreement shall be for the exclusive use of the Client other than for the promotional use of the Designer. Upon payment of all fees and expenses, the following reproduction rights for all approved final designs created by the Designer for this project shall be granted:

Ownership

5.2.   All drawings, artwork, specifications, and other visual presentation materials remain the property of the Designer. The Client shall be entitled to temporary possession of such materials only for the purpose of reproduction after which all materials shall be returned, unaltered, to the Designer.

All preliminary concepts and visual presentations produced by the Designer remain the property of the Designer and may not be used by the Client without the written permission of the Designer.

The Designer shall retain all artwork, drawings, and specifications, for which reproduction rights have been granted for a specified period from the date of the signing of this Agreement. Upon expiration of this period, all such materials may be destroyed unless the Client has requested, in writing, that they be retained and agrees to pay reasonable storage charges. The Client shall have reasonable access to all such materials for the purpose of review.

The specified time for the Designer to retain such materials shall be

Third Party Contracts

5.3.   The Designer may contract with others to provide creative services such as writing, photography, and illustration. The Client agrees to be bound by any terms and conditions, including required credits, with respect to reproduction of such material as may be imposed on the Designer by such third parties.

The Designer will endeavor to obtain for the Client the same reproduction rights with respect to materials resulting from such services as the Designer is providing the Client under this Agreement except as specified below:

*Document Number
1988-01
October 1988 Edition*

*© 1988
The American Institute
of Graphic Arts*

*1059 Third Avenue
New York, New York 10021
Telebone 212.752.0813*

Page Number 7

6.   MISCELLANEOUS

Code of Ethics

6.1.   The Designer's services shall be performed in accordance with the AIGA Code of Ethics and Professional Conduct for Graphic Designers.

Credit

6.2.   The Designer shall have the right to include a credit line on the completed designs or any visual representations such as drawings, models, or photographs and this same credit shall be included in any publication of the design by the Client. The Client shall not, without written approval, use the Designer's name for promotional or any other purposes with respect to these designs. The Designer's credit line shall read as follows:

Samples and Photographs

6.3.   The Client shall provide the Designer with samples of each printed or manufactured design. Such samples shall be representative of the highest quality of work produced. The Designer may use such copies and samples for publication, exhibition, or other promotional purposes.

The number of samples to be provided to the Designer shall be

The Designer shall have the right to photograph all completed designs or installations and shall have the right to use such photographs for publication, exhibition, or other promotional purposes.

Confidentiality

6.4.   The Client shall inform the Designer in writing if any portion of any material or information provided by the Client or if any portion of the Project is confidential.

Sales Tax

6.5.   The Client shall pay any sales, use, or other transfer taxes that may be applicable to the services provided under this Agreement, including any tax that may be assessed on audit of the Designer's tax returns.

Applicable Law

6.6.   This Agreement shall be governed by the Law of the principal place of business of the Designer.

Assignment

6.7.   Neither the Client or the Designer may assign or transfer their interest in this Agreement without the written consent of the other.

Termination

6.8.   Either party may terminate this Agreement upon giving written notice to the other as specified below. Upon termination of this Agreement by the Client or by the Designer for cause, the Designer may retain any initial payment and the Client shall pay the Designer for all hours expended on the Project, up to the date of termination, at the Designer's standard rates together with all other amounts due hereunder. Any initial payment that has been received shall be credited against any such amounts due. All indemnities shall continue even after any such termination.

The amount of written notice to be given by either party shall be

Document Number
1988-01
October 1988 Edition

© 1988
The American Institute
of Graphic Arts

1059 Third Avenue
New York, New York 10021
Telephone 212.752.0813

Page Number 8

| *Arbitration* | 6.9. | Either party may request that any dispute arising out of this Agreement shall be submitted to binding arbitration before a mutually agreed upon arbitrator pursuant to the rules of the American Arbitration Association. The arbitrator's award shall be final and judgment may be entered upon it in any court having jurisdiction thereof. |

| *Entire Agreement* | 6.10. | This Agreement represents the entire agreement between the Client and the Designer and may be changed or modified only in writing. |

| *Representations* | 6.11. | The Client represents that it has full power and authority to enter into this Agreement and that it is binding upon the Client and enforceable in accordance with its terms. |

The Designer represents that it has full power and authority to enter into this Agreement and that it is binding upon the Designer and enforceable in accordance with its terms.

7. TIME SCHEDULE

The Designer and Client agree that the work shall be completed according to the following schedule:

The Designer reserves the right to adjust the schedule in the event that the Client fails to meet agreed deadlines for submission of materials or granting approvals and to allow for changes in the scope or complexity of services from those contemplated by this Agreement.

Document Number
1988-01
October 1988 Edition

© 1988
The American Institute
of Graphic Arts

1059 Third Avenue
New York, New York 10021
Telephone 212.752.0813

Page Number 9

8.   CONTINUATIONS AND OTHER CONDITIONS

*Document Number
1988-01
October 1988 Edition*

*© 1988
The American Institute
of Graphic Arts*

*1059 Third Avenue
New York, New York 10021
Telehone 212.752.0813*

Page Number 10

DEFINED TERMS

9. Basic Services   As described in Section 2.1.
    Client   As defined on page 1.
    Designer   As defined on page 1.
    Implementation   As described in Section 2.3.
    Project   As described in Section 1.
    Reimbursable Expenses   As described in Section 3.7.
    Supplementary Services   As described in Section 2.2.

SIGNATURES

10. This Agreement was entered into between the Designer and the Client as of the day and date set forth on page 1.

    Designer

    Client

Document Number
1988-01
October 1988 Edition

© 1988
The American Institute
of Graphic Arts

1059 Third Avenue
New York, New York 10021
Telebone 212.752.0813

Page Number 11

AIGA

Standard Form of Agreement for Graphic Design Services

General Edition

The AIGA Standard Form of Agreement for Graphic Design Services, General Edition, is intended to be used by graphic designers and their clients as the basis of agreement for a broad range of graphic design projects. It should be thoroughly studied for its appropriateness in the context of the intended project, carefully edited, and any neccesary extra clauses added to ensure that it is precisely tailored to the needs of the project.

To assist in the tailoring process, write-in space has been provided for including much of the project-specific information required. As an alternative to write-in information, or where there is insufficient room, exhibits may be attached to the back of the document. Any exhibits, which may be in the form of correspondence between designer and client, should be clearly identified as "Exhibit A" etc. and reference made to them in the write-in space provided, such as "See Exhibit A Attached."

For more information regarding this document and its use, refer to AIGA Publication 1988-02 "Notes on the Standard Form of Agreement for Graphic Design Services, General Edition."

Document Number
1988-01
October 1988 Edition

© 1988
The American Institute
of Graphic Arts

1059 Third Avenue
New York, New York 10021
Telephone 212.752.0813

Page Number 12

The AIGA Standard Terms and Conditions
for Designer/Client Relationships

by Emily Ruth Cohen

To satisfy the need for a friendlier and condensed alternative to the AIGA's existing Standard Form of Agreement for Graphic Design Services, the AIGA is pleased to launch a new, shorter document entitled The AIGA Standard Terms and Conditions for Designer/Client Relationships. This project evolved in response to the continued interest and support shown by the chapters and has been researched, organized, and written with extensive experience writing estimates and agreements for a wide variety of projects and clients in the graphic design profession.

This short agreement, when attached to a designer's project estimate and/or proposal, can be used as a written confirmation of terms and conditions between the designer and client. In order for the agreement to work effectively, the estimate/proposal needs to include certain important criteria and information. This information is described in an accompanying outline of instructions for appropriate usage of the standard terms and conditions. The "short agreement" was written to be friendly and understandable, while at the same time protecting the rights of both the designer and client.

The input of our members and AIGA's staff, combined with their commitment to creating a shorter form, helped this two-year project come to fruition. I'd also like to express my thanks to Alina Wheeler and Robert Meyer, whose earlier efforts and research helped launch this project. Additional thanks are due to lawyers James Silverberg and Tad Crawford, who reviewed the final versions and offered their professional advice and critique.

Instructions for Usage of AIGA Standard Terms and Conditions for Designer/Client Relationships

In order for this agreement to work effectively, we have assumed that the designer will include the following information in his or her estimate/proposal. (Note: the following list includes examples of possible project criteria. However, each project will have unique requirements that should be outlined clearly in the estimate/proposal.)

Client's Name and Address

- Name of Client Representative
- Date
- Designer's Name and Address
- Name of Project

Project Description and Specifications, such as:

- Project goals
- Number of components
- Size
- Page count
- Colors
- Artwork requirements (including commissioned or stock artwork, photography, hand lettering, etc.)

Third-Party Relationships (such as Editorial Services)

Client Responsibilities

A list or description of the materials/services client will be providing (such as copy on disk, proofreading, images, etc.)

Project Stages, Responsibilities, and Presentations

This is the most important part of the estimate/proposal and is crucial to future negotiations of additional services and costs not anticipated or described (see information

listed under "Services"). Following are suggestions for the kinds of information you may want to include (some information may not apply to your particular project):

- Project stages
- Number of sample pages, layouts, design solutions, etc. included in each design phase (and the outlined fee structure).
- Type of presentations included (rough thumbnails, black and white layouts, tight color comps, etc.)
- Number and complexity of revisions included within fee structure (such as quantity of pass pages, quantity and complexity of design revisions, type changes, etc.)
- Electronic versus camera-ready mechanicals, low- or high-resolution scans, etc.
- Production responsibilities (obtaining printing estimates, review of press proofs, on-press supervision, etc.)

Usage Rights

The estimate/proposal should indicate any limitations on usage that the outlined fees are based on (i.e., limiting the allowable time of usage, the type of medium, the way the design/concept can be used, the geographical area to be exposed to the project, etc.)

Project Schedule

The schedule should include delivery dates for each project stage as well as client approval dates for each stage. If a complete schedule cannot be determined when the estimate/proposal is written, then include any known scheduling information. For example, "The following estimate is based on a nonrush schedule of four weeks. A written schedule will be issued for the client's approval before the project is begun."

Project Fees (see "Out-of-Pocket Expenses")

Include all costs for the project stages, responsibilities, and presentations listed in the estimate/proposal. You may also include separate rates for undefined responsibilities, such as day rates for on-press or photo supervision, client meetings, and any applicable sales tax. For information on sales tax, speak with your accountant and local AIGA chapter. It may also be helpful, especially for longer or more complex projects, to list fees for each project

stage or responsibility. Pricing details will help determine any cancellation fees that may need to be assessed (see "Cancellation").

Out-of-Pocket Expenses

List out-of-pocket expenses that are not included in your fees, such as overnight couriers, messengers, travel costs, computer output (Iris prints, color lasers, linotronic output, film), supplies, etc. Provide an estimate of these costs or state that all such costs will be billed additionally. Indicate the percentage of your markup on these expenses (and which expenses are not marked up).

Payment Schedule

A payment schedule should include all amounts due and the date payment is expected. We suggest that you include a payment schedule after the initial estimate/proposal has been approved. Typically, payments are either made in thirds or adjusted to reflect the project schedule (i.e., for smaller projects, one-half payments may be more appropriate; for larger projects, several monthly payments extended over the length of the project). Also, for client revisions, author alterations (AAs), and out-of-pocket expenses, include the payment terms (i.e., net thirty days). Payments are often due on a particular date or upon delivery (or approval) of certain project phases. The first payment should be due before any work begins on the project.

Additional Recommendations

We suggest that you submit and negotiate the project estimate/proposal prior to attaching the terms and conditions and payment schedule for written confirmation. This allows the client to concentrate on and approve all the necessary project criteria before reviewing the additional terms and conditions.

We do not recommend that you use the form Standard Terms and Conditions for Designer/Client Relationships for complicated or long-term projects, which may require a lengthier contract. Such projects may include, but are not limited to, multimedia projects, signage programs, retainer-based relationships, etc.

Although we have researched the information extensively, we still recommend that you have the terms and conditions reviewed by your lawyer.

Ultimately, the designer is fully liable to the client for all the conditions outlined in

the short agreement, including providing the client with a summary of additional costs and services incurred, as the project progresses, that are above and beyond the agreed-upon criteria and fee structure.

AIGA Standard Terms and Conditions for Designer/Client Relationships

Services

The Designer agrees to provide all the services outlined in the attached estimate/proposal within the criteria specified. If, however, the client changes any of the criteria during the project requiring additional services, a revision/AA fee will be charged.

Additional services will include, but are not limited to, changes in the extent of work, changes in schedule, changes in the complexity of any elements of the project, and any changes made after client approval has been given for a specific stage of the project according to the agreed-upon schedule, including concept, design, composition, and production of mechanicals.

The Designer will keep the Client informed of additional services that are required and obtain the Client's approval for any services that cause the total fees to exceed those outlined in the attached estimate/proposal.

Schedules/Overtime/Rush Work

The Designer reserves the right to adjust the schedule and/or charge additionally in the event that the Client fails to meet the agreed-upon deadlines for delivery of information, materials, approvals, payments, and for changes and additions to the services outlined in the estimate/proposal.

Client Approval

The Client will approve and proofread all final designs and type before the production of mechanicals. The Client's approval of all tangible materials and artwork will be assumed after the work has been submitted to the client for review, unless the client indicates otherwise in writing.

Rights/Ownership

All tangible materials in all circumstances remain the property of the Designer. All rights and ownership apply to preliminary concepts, works in progress, and finished material, whether the project is completed or canceled. The Client will be entitled to limited and

specific usage rights of such materials only for the purpose of reproduction, after which all materials will be returned, unaltered, to the Designer within thirty days of use.

Upon payment of all fees and expenses, the Designer will grant all reproduction and/or usage rights, as outlined in the attached estimate/proposal, for all approved final materials created by the Designer for this project.

If the Client wishes to make any additional use of the materials, the Client agrees to seek permission from the Designer and make such payments as are approved by the parties at that time. Where alterations or retakes are necessary, the Designer will be given the opportunity to make such changes at an agreed additional charge.

Electronic Files

If the Client has requirements for how the project is to be prepared electronically, the Client must communicate this to the Designer before the project begins.

Electronic files and software documents related to the Client's project are the property of the Designer and must not be copied, altered, or modified without the written permission of the Designer.

Reimbursable Expenses

Any budget figures or estimates for reimbursable expenses or implementation charges, such as out-of-pocket expenses, typesetting, printing, fabrication, or installation, are for planning purposes only. The Designer will use his or her best efforts to work within stated budgets but will not be liable if these expenses exceed budgets. When possible, no expenses in excess of the budget will be incurred without the Client's written or initialed approval in advance.

The Client will reimburse the Designer for all out-of-pocket expenses incurred by the Designer on this project. These expenses are listed in the attached estimate/proposal and will be billed at cost plus any surcharge indicated in the attached estimate/proposal for account handling and supervision. Upon the Client's request at the start of the project, records for out-of-pocket expenses will be retained by the Designer and will be made available to the Client upon completion of the project.

Credit

The Designer will have the right to include a published credit line on the completed designs or any visual representation. This same credit will be included in any publication of the design by the Client.

Samples

The Client will provide the Designer with samples of each printed or manufactured design. These samples will represent the highest quality of work produced.

Payment Schedule

Upon approval of this document, the Client will make all payment installments, as scheduled and outlined in our estimate/proposal. The Client will pay interest on all overdue amounts not exceeding the maximum amount allowed by law.

Third-Party Contracts

The Designer may contract with other individuals or companies acting on behalf of the Client to provide additional services such as writing, photography, illustration, printing, and fabrication. The Client agrees to be bound by any terms and conditions, including required credits and usage rights, with respect to reproduction of the materials that may be imposed on the Designer by these third parties.

Cancellation

In the event of cancellation of this assignment, a cancellation fee will be paid by the Client and will include full payment for all work completed, expenses incurred, and hours expended. The cancellation fee will be based on the prices outlined in the estimate/proposal. Any initial payments that have been received will be credited against any amounts due.

Miscellaneous

This document and the attached estimate/proposal represent the entire agreement between the Client and the Designer and may be changed or modified only in writing and with the approval of both parties.

The Client and the Designer represent that they have full power and authority to

enter into this agreement and that it is binding upon the Client and Designer and enforceable in accordance with its terms.

This Agreement will be governed by the law of the state in which the Designer's
principal place of business is located.

Negotiating the Key Issues
for Web Site Design

By Caryn Leland

Many think cyberspace is a realm much like the Wild West where one is free to take and claim for one's own any material found. Do not be seduced by this fantasy. Though there may not be a Wyatt Earp to bring law and order to this domain, the laws applicable to traditional media of books, visual arts, and music apply equally to the Internet. Web content providers, servers, and users must take particular notice of this situation.

The mistaken belief, for example, that copyright law does not apply to works posted on the Net, probably owes its origin to a distortion of the original spirit of the Internet. Its inventors created the Internet to be a scientific research tool to encourage and propel the free flow of ideas and information through unfettered electronic discourse—with an emphasis on "free." As commercial industry began to shape the Internet, practices of offering shareware or posting work on the Net and inviting users to download the programs or work for free fostered a user expectation that all work was, indeed, free. The hacker's ethos of "Why pay for anything on the Net if you can download it for free?" prevailed.

However, once advertising and business interests comprehended that the Internet was a medium in which goods and services could be advertised and sold, this laissez-faire approach could not continue. One's investment, that is to say, content, and specifically the originality of expression embodied in the advertisements and solicitations, had to be protected. Which is where we are now, and why contracts and copyright principles have assumed such importance in the area of Web site development.

The same criteria apply to the Internet as to other media when determinations of ownership, usage rights, or violations of the rights of privacy are made. And, as with these other media, materials which are in the public domain may be used on a Web site without risk of copyright infringement. However, the materials may still be protected against unau-

thorized use through trademark or unfair competition laws. If the rights for the use have not been secured or the use does not constitute a fair use as defined by U.S. copyright law — that is, a permissible use — the use will be held to be a copyright infringement, subjecting the Web site owner (the client), Web server, agency, and designer to liability for damages. Remember, there is no substitute for tracking down the owner and receiving written permission from the creator of the downloaded materials.

The typical Web site deal involves a computer graphics designer being hired by a company or by the company's advertising agency to create the site. Those who engage designers to create Web sites for their clients or themselves have to know that the image, text, or sound being incorporated into the site is free of claims from those who may own the rights in those materials. But, the company has no way of knowing whether the designer unlawfully downloaded images from the Internet and incorporated the materials into its site. Note, a defense of innocent use will not shield a company against an infringement action. To protect itself against the risks discussed above, the company must rely on contract law. The contract between company and designer will require the designer to promise, as follows, in what has become standard in these types of agreements:

> Designer represents, warrants, and covenants to company the following: (a) any information or materials developed shall not rely or in any way be based upon confidential or proprietary information or trade secrets obtained or derived by designer from sources other than company unless designer has received specific authorization in writing to use such proprietary information or trade secrets; and (b) except to the extent based on the content supplied by the company, the Web site content does not infringe upon or misappropriate any copyright, patent right, right of publicity or privacy (including but not limited to defamation), trade secret, or other proprietary rights of any third party.

Notice, subparagraph (b) excludes from its scope content supplied to the designer by the company. Such exclusion is appropriate, as the designer should not be legally responsible for checking rights clearance of materials supplied to the designer. If a designer is unable to have these materials excluded, it is recommended that the company be required to give the designer a reciprocal representation of the work that does not violate third parties' rights and to exempt the designer from liability thereof.

The enforcement of the warranty provision is achieved by requiring the designer to compensate and cover the company from any loss if the designer violates the warranty. This is known as the indemnification or hold harmless provision. By agreeing to such a provision, the designer contractually assumes the liability inherent from the covered situation (i.e., damages and attorneys' fees from lawsuit arising out of a breach of the warranty) and compensates the company for all of its losses and expenses. Designers can expect to be presented with a contract which contains a broadly worded indemnification provision like this one:

> Designer agrees to indemnify, hold harmless, and defend company, its directors, officers, its employees, and agents from and against all claims, defense costs (including reasonable attorneys' fees), judgments, and other expenses arising out of or on account of such claims, including without limitation claims of: (a) alleged infringement or violation of any trademark, copyright, trade secret, right of publicity or privacy (including but not limited to defamation), patent, or other proprietary right with respect to the Web site content to the extent developer has modified or added to the materials, if any, provided by the company; and (b) the breach of any covenant or warranty set forth [above].

Because of the difficulty of knowing with any assurance which of the thousands of images or pieces of music posted on the Net may be used safely without securing and paying for the permission, it is easy to run afoul of the above-quoted warranty and trigger the indemnification provision. As a result, indemnification provisions have become heavily fought over in contract negotiations and have become one of the most carefully scrutinized provisions in these types of agreements.

It is recommended that designers try to limit the breadth of the indemnity. This can be accomplished by agreeing to indemnify not for alleged cases but proven cases; by limiting the potential dollar exposure of the indemnification to the amount of fees the designer received from the company for the assignment; and if the company carries errors and omissions liability insurance for such claims, by agreeing to be responsible for damages up to and including the company's deductible under the policy, if it is a reasonable amount.

Not only do companies want to know that their Web site will not violate the rights of others, as a general rule, they also want to own the developer's work. This is accomplished by having the designer acknowledge and agree:

the Web site content, including but not limited to images, music, and any documentation and notes associated with the Web site are and shall be the property of the company. Title to all property rights including but not limited to copyrights, trademarks, patents, and trade secrets in the Web site content and documentation is with, and shall remain with, the company.

The company will also require that the designer transfer and assign all rights in the content as though it were a work made for hire:

> Designer agrees to transfer and assign, and hereby transfers and assigns to company its entire right, title, and interest worldwide, if any, including without limitation all copyright ownership therein, no matter when acquired, in the Web site content and documentation. Designer hereby waives any and all claims that designer may now or hereafter have in any jurisdiction to moral rights with respect to the results of designer's work and services hereunder.

Inclusion of provisions like these should be resisted firmly and rejected. The combined legal effect is to strip the designer of any control over the present and future use of the work as a Web site or otherwise. With such provisions, the company would be free to modify the site any way it chose. It may also prevent a designer from creating a Web site for another client with a similar look and style under an analysis that to do so would be a violation of the company's copyrights in its Web site!

Alternatively, a designer should insist in retaining all rights, including copyrights, in and to the Web site and grant the company (or the ad agency and its client) rights as follows:

> Designer shall retain ownership of the content, and all rights, including the copyrights, therein and hereby grants to the company an exclusive license to use the content in the form delivered as the company's Web site. The company may include its copyright notice on the Web site.
>
> Company shall have no right to edit, revise, alter, adapt, modify, or otherwise change, or cause others to edit, revise, alter, adapt, modify, or otherwise change

the content from the form delivered without designer's prior written consent, except to make minor changes. The determination as to whether a proposed "minor change" as this term is used herein shall be in designer's sole discretion.

Thus, by vigilance and appropriate use of traditional laws, designers can protect themselves from the uncertainties and vicissitudes of working with the Net.

CHAPTER 7

Payment
Strategies

by Emily Ruth Cohen

It's the nature of working in a creative industry; each job and client has unique characteristics, requirements, and needs. Although the professional flexibility can be rewarding, devising a consistent payment strategy can be another matter altogether. What may work for one client, may not be quite right for another. Your best strategy is to approach your payment schedule as you would any design project, personalizing your methodology with forethought, research, and creativity.

Several proactive measures and precautions to define your payment schedule can help prevent future obstacles to a successful relationship with your client.

Start with the Paperwork

Before starting a project, provide your client with all necessary project documentation. This includes proposals, estimates, letters of agreement, contracts, schedules, and change orders. Where applicable, get your client's signed approval. Although oral agreements are legally binding, they are harder to prove. If all written documentation is clear and appropriately detailed, you'll establish a professional relationship from the start, allowing for any potential disagreements and stumbling blocks to be ironed out beforehand.

Up-Front Payment

Establish a standard policy that requires partial payment from clients prior to the start of the project and before any billable work is incurred. This strategy, termed up-front payment, is becoming a common procedure within our industry and is usually based on a percentage of the total project fee or estimate. For this up-front payment strategy to work

effectively, it is crucial that you enforce it consistently, firmly, and without apology for all of your clients.

Be cautioned. This simple request can often become a time-consuming struggle. Clients may give you objections ranging from the reasonable, "Our corporate procedures preclude me from processing any up-front payment without either receipt of work or an approved, internal purchase order," to the plausible, "As a small business, our cash flow is tight and overhead payments, such as rent and utilities, may need to take priority," to the red-flag, "Why should I pay for work I haven't seen yet?" or "We don't have any money right now, but are expecting a large check in soon." Respond to these scenarios calmly and creatively.

First, emphasize that up-front payment is a reasonable request and a common procedure within the design industry. If you do not receive any up-front payment, then you are, in effect, incurring billable hours and extending the client credit. This reasoning can also apply to asking for a deposit or retainer against out-of-pocket expenses.

Also, without up-front money, it may appear that you are working on spec with payment promised only upon acceptance. Like other professionals, such as architects and lawyers, you're hired based on experience. This means that you're entitled to be paid regardless of whether your work is accepted or approved—provided, of course, that your services follow the client's initial creative direction and are of the same quality and creativity you were initially hired for.

Managing Invoices

Familiarize yourself with your client's payment policy and keep your invoices in manageable increments. Many corporations and businesses will not pay unless an approved purchase order (PO) has been processed; the absence of a PO at the time of invoicing will delay payment.

For large expenditures, your client may have to go through several rounds of time-consuming approvals, often involving upper management and accounts payable, before a PO will be issued or an invoice processed. As a rule of thumb, smaller invoices are often easier to process. Ask your client how much is too much before an invoice or PO gets delayed because of internal processing and approval procedures. Once you know the cutoff amount for a large expenditure, you can adjust your progress payments accordingly.

When you do receive a PO, read it carefully. Clients will often include special,

standard conditions or descriptions that may or may not be applicable to your project and relationship.

Typically, a client will compensate you for only up to 10 percent of the PO; check with your client for the exact percentage he or she can pay. If the scope of the project changes and additional fees are incurred that exceed 10 percent of the PO, inform the client and request a revised or additional PO.

Many clients have an established policy for how soon they pay invoices and have timetables that range from thirty to ninety days. It is important to find this out in advance and invoice accordingly. For example, if a client pays all in "net 60," and the project can be completed within two or three weeks, you may want to issue all invoices at the start of the project. This will help shorten the approval and processing time, and ensure payments are made closer to the project's completion, rather than three months later. If this isn't possible, you can ask for a large percentage of your total costs to be paid up front, thereby reducing your financial liability later in the project.

Get It in Writing

When establishing a job contract, negotiate a written and equitable payment schedule, including a due date for each payment and your specific responsibility or presentation to be delivered or completed by that date. Don't use vague terminology that can be misinterpreted such as, "Payment due midway through the project." Another important strategy is to indicate that payment is due upon completion and delivery of the specified presentation or responsibility, *not* upon client approval. Such approvals can get delayed by several days or weeks for reasons beyond your control, or the project can get put on unlimited hiatus.

Don't rely on client-defined target dates that reflect client objectives since these may get delayed for reasons beyond your control. For example, one designer I know who was responsible for a comprehensive identity project for a store opening was asked to delay the last invoice until the store opened. Unfortunately, the opening was delayed several months after the target date. Luckily, the designer based the final payment on the date when her client first anticipated the store was to open, rather than agreeing to a too general statement, "Payment to coincide with the opening of the store."

Check It Out

During the negotiation process, ask the client for credit references, three names are standard, and call the references to confirm credit history. The references should include, if available, a contact within a related industry like a photographer, copywriter, or illustrator. Then run a credit check on your client through a company like Dun & Bradstreet. Keep in mind that a credit report can't predict either your client's continued dependability, reliability, or ethics. The report simply provides a useful credit history on the client.

Include a termination or cancellation clause in your agreement or estimate like, "In the event of the cancellation of this assignment, a cancellation fee will be paid by the client and will include full payment for all work completed, expenses incurred, and hours expended. The cancellation fee will be based on the prices outlined in the estimate/proposal. Any initial payments that have been received will be credited against any amounts due."

Trust your instincts. Gut reactions to a client or project can often guide you in the right direction in formulating a payment plan—or working with the client in the first place.

Establishing Your Schedule

Once you complete your research and fully evaluate the unique needs of each client and project, you can develop an effective payment schedule that includes several progress payments. Progress payments are based on a percentage or portion of your estimated costs. As mentioned earlier, each payment should be due at a specified, defined project phase and encompass defined deliverables and responsibilities.

An advantage to receiving incremental payments throughout a project versus one lump-sum payment at the end of a job is that your financial liability throughout the project will be greatly reduced, especially if the client delays payment later on. Of course this advantage is contingent upon you effectively managing and enforcing the payment schedule.

The following payment schedule is commonly followed: the first third of the estimated project total due prior to the start of the project, a second third due midway through the project, and the final third due upon delivery and completion of all responsibilities. Typically, out-of-pocket expenses and unanticipated costs, like additional responsibilities and client revisions or AAs, are either billed upon completion or billed incrementally throughout the project.

Each project or client may require different solutions and options. For smaller projects with quick turnaround, two payments of one-half of the estimated project total may

be more appropriate. However, a lengthy, multileveled project will require several payments due either on a monthly basis or at specified dates for each project phase. Progress payment can be the same amount (determined by a percentage of the project total) or can be different amounts (determined by the specific costs estimated for each project phase).

Depending on your business goals and cash flow, you may be able to negotiate less common, but sometimes viable, alternative arrangements. Although it's less popular, bartering can be an acceptable alternative for a cash-starved client offering an exciting creative opportunity. First check with your accountant, barter arrangements may be taxable. When bartering, make sure you negotiate, in writing, an equal value exchange. For pro bono and nonprofit work, or for projects you accept at a reduced rate, you can also ask for full creative control and compensation for all out-of-pocket expenses. If you decide to negotiate such nontraditional agreements, treat them like your other professional relationships and have them approved, in writing, by the client. Also, always emphasize that you're posing a nontraditional, onetime agreement that may or may not be applicable for the next project. The downside is that you risk establishing a reputation for these types of arrangements, possibly lessening the perceived value of your services.

Once you've negotiated a payment schedule, don't assume the client will follow through. After you mail an invoice, follow up with a friendly phone call to confirm its receipt and then, a few days before it is due, call the client to remind them of the upcoming payment deadline. This last call may be more effective if you can couch it within a project-related conversation. Most importantly, discuss payment and collections in a win-win scenario, maintaining a proactive position. For example, ask if there's something you can do to expedite payment. You can also offer a discount to clients for invoices that are paid early, although this option may not be advantageous for firms with tight cash flow and should be first discussed with your accountant. Once you have received payment, follow through with a note or phone call to show your appreciation.

If All Else Fails

Even if you follow every precaution, there will be clients who won't pay for various reasons. In those cases, you have several choices. You can accept the loss as part of doing business and learn from the experience, or seek help through arbitration, collection agencies, claims court, or, at last resort, civil court. A clause in your project documentation clarifying how potential conflicts will be handled can help. For example, if you prefer arbitration,

the American Arbitration Association recommends including the following clause in your contract: "Any controversy or claim arising out of or relating to this contract, or the breach thereof, shall be settled by binding arbitration in accordance with the rules of the American Arbitration Association and judgment upon the award may be entered in any court having jurisdiction thereof."

In general, payment strategies, and the processes you go through to develop, negotiate, schedule, and collect payments should be flexible and adapted to the needs of you and your client. Just because you're in a creative business doesn't mean that your finances can't be straightforward.

The Design Firm and
Its Employees

by Roz and Jessica Goldfarb

Successful business administration includes overcoming the challenges of a plethora of employment matters. From determining staffing needs to interviewing, hiring, maintaining constructive relationships, and firing, this process presents a constant struggle for all companies. For design firms, those problems are increased by the need for balance between creative and business goals and personalities. In this creatively-driven business, the essential fact is that the firm's people are its greatest assets and they walk out the door every night. The key ingredients to a successful employment relationship, therefore, are communication and respect between employer and employee.

First, the design firm, large or small, just like any business, must put into place fair business practices and develop standardized employment policies. The problem is that few design firms review or track how employment decisions are made. Nor are individuals with these responsibilities trained as to how to interview or evaluate candidates, review or manage employees, or address problems properly. Even in small firms, one person should be identified to function as a human resource administrator and given the appropriate training. It is recommended that all employment decisions include or be channeled through this person, as should all documentation concerning resumes received, dated, and action taken (i.e., interviewed, considered, rejected, etc.) and all personnel files and other employment information (i.e., policies, health benefits, employee handbooks, etc.). This way, the firm will always have at its disposal some record of people who could be possible employees for the future, as well as documentation to protect against any possible legal actions. If the firm uses a recruitment firm, these records also can be essential to tracking referrals and pinpointing possible conflicts from multiple referrals.

Second, firms must recognize that interpersonal dynamics are involved in these

matters. The employment relationship is just that: an affiliation between an individual and a company, personified by individuals given the authority to make certain decisions. Given the extent to which we in American society identify ourselves by our job, this is one of the most important relationships in life. In creative firms, the value of the product is, obviously, its creativity, which is personality driven. This means that the identification between the individual and the product and, thus, the individual and the firm can be particularly strong. Managing creativity, therefore, poses unique challenges, requiring a sensitivity to the individual and the team.

Each of us has personal wants and needs in relation to the workplace. And those running firms have a distinct vision of the type of environment they aim to create, which, not incidentally, has a direct effect on their ability to attract the quality of individual necessary to ensure success in the marketplace. Clear communication sets the right tone for a trusting, nurturing relationship in the workplace and provides a substantial foundation upon which to build the long-lasting relationship and promise of growth that both parties seek.

Job Descriptions, Interviewing, and Hiring

Respect for these priorities must be established at the beginning of the relationship. Key hiring requirements need to be identified, prioritized, and described. It is the rare design firm that goes through the effort of writing a job description. But this is an essential part of the process for it forces the clarification of the qualifications needed and establishes expectations for the future of the relationship, thereby avoiding many problems down the road. Writing a job description can also force the firm to question the realism of their requirements and expectations.

An important step toward creating a successful relationship is ensuring that the candidate understands the employer's needs and the employer recognizes the candidate's goals. Too often employers forget their own work history and the anxiety of looking for work. It may seem that the balance of power has shifted to the employer, but a savvy individual recognizes the underlying mutual dependence of the relationship.

The time to sort all of this out is during the interview process, but, unfortunately, few people are ever trained on how to conduct an interview. Common, tricky, interview questions rarely tell anything truly useful about a candidate, unless the interviewer is very cunning. And, of course, this is also a time for romancing, when some employers may gloss over important points about the firm. Others, trying to be honest, paint an unrealistically bleak

picture of the working conditions. Either way, the candidate is left with an unclear perception and, in the end, both sides often come away knowing little about each other.

Again, clarity is required. Job descriptions help the interviewer hone in on what information is crucial. Checklists of desired skills or characteristics can help the interviewer, especially when comparing candidates. Moreover, employers should instruct interviewers not to ask questions that solicit excess information that could be a discriminatory basis for making the hiring decision, or that may imply such information was the reason for that decision.

If care is not taken during the hiring process, even after a job is accepted there may be differing views of what the job entails, its requirements, role and duties, or the terms of employment, such as salary, bonus, review schedules, length of employment, and grounds for discharge. Either the employer or the employee, under these circumstances, will sooner or later become dissatisfied and the relationship is bound to deteriorate. To avoid such difficulties, everyone involved in the hiring process should take care that all aspects of the position are clearly defined and understood. For this reason, a job description is often given with an offer letter, stating that the terms laid out are intended as guidelines and subject to change.

In practice, significant guideposts in making the decision to hire or accept a position are inevitably a combination of objective criteria, such as issues of skills, title, money, and quality of the work; less tangible elements, such as the office environment, work ownership, and access to clients; and personal characteristics, such as personality, ambition, or cultural match—not to mention office politics. Some reactions are harder to identify, based on intuition, and often chalked up to "chemistry."

Candidates should always receive some feedback, even if the standard response is "it's just not right" or "it's not a fit." Understandably, designers find it hard to face these ambiguous responses. However, the word "fit" does tell a significant story. Fit means everything. But, in the last analysis, it is vital to base the decision and, whenever possible, to articulate it on the basis of objective criteria as well as fit. For this purpose, a proper job description is indispensable. And it will provide a reference during periodic evaluations and if problems arise. If a person ultimately is to be let go, this history of information is invaluable to that decision-making process.

When the reason for refusing to hire someone is not clear, an employer runs the risk of facing a lawsuit with the applicant claiming the reason was illegal discrimination. If the applicant is successful, a lawsuit can be very costly to an employer. The applicant may obtain an order to be hired and may recover compensation for foregone pay and, where proven,

for mental suffering. In instances where the discrimination was considered especially flagrant, large punitive damages may be collected. A simple statement or notation to a file can fully eliminate this hazard.

At Will Versus Contractual Employment

Many people assume that an employer is bound by law to treat them fairly or to have just cause for letting them go or to give a specific amount of notice when doing so. However, without any particular contractual commitment, employers are not obligated to do any of these things. A largely unrecognized fact is that without a written contract stating a specific period of employment, employees are considered by law to be "at will." This means the law presumes that the employer reserves the right to change the conditions of employment, or to discharge the employee at any time for any nondiscriminatory reason.

In some instances, an applicant or employee can enforce oral or written promises (in an application, job description, offer, employee handbook, etc.) made during the interviewing and hiring process or period of employment. The key is whether it can be shown conclusively that those representations were reasonably relied on to a detriment (for instance, in hiring, that another offer was rejected or that a prior job was left on the basis of those statements), that the employer is guilty of intentional or negligent misrepresentation, or that the statements were part of an express or implied contract of employment. So, again, clarity becomes a key player in determining the rights involved.

Freelance Versus Permanent Employment

When a firm is in a hiring mode, issues of workload and the anticipated flow of projects dominate and create a sense of urgency. Often the solution is to hire a flexible workforce: freelancers, project-based employees, or virtual resources. The advantages may be obvious. To the firm there are lower costs, the capacity to bring in a talent base greater than might otherwise fit within a budget, and the ability to adjust easily and quickly to current work needs. To the employee, there are benefits of variety of work, flexibility in the location or timing of work, the ability to deduct from income all business expenses, and the availability of different retirement savings options. The disadvantages, however, are too often overlooked. These employees can be undedicated or unreliable and legal and tax penalties may also be involved. Normally, these negative aspects are of little importance until the freelance has become long-term.

While an employer and an individual may agree on any work arrangement they please, for tax purposes the laws and regulations of the Internal Revenue Service (IRS) may define workers as employees and require that the employer pay social security and Medicare taxes and withhold income taxes. Independent contractor status is allowed if the firm has a reasonable basis to treat the individual as an independent contractor, and the IRS will consider industry practice as such a basis. The firm must also take care to treat all freelancers similarly; any inconsistency can result in an IRS determination that person is an employee. Part of this similar treatment requires that the firm file reporting forms, Form 1099 or 1099-MISC, for all independent contractors. The IRS also looks to issues of control, such as who has decision-making authority over the work (whether approval by the firm is required, for instance) or financial matters (whether the person is on salary or payment is made by the hour or day, and whether expenses are reimbursed).

Benefits, such as medical insurance, pensions, profit sharing, and 401(k) plans, are also affected by employment status and employers cannot extend its benefits to nonemployees. Where formal benefit plans are in effect, the Employee Retirement Income Security Act (ERISA) and other laws govern, and these matters become more complex.

A word of warning is due because in recent years, as companies have sought to reduce labor costs by using more freelancers, federal and state authorities have become more aggressive in investigating and enforcing these issues. A failure to pay proper payroll taxes can result in an order for payment with interest and a substantial penalty. So, it is safest to assume that anyone working at the design firm on more than a temporary project is considered an employee. Firms should consult with an accountant or attorney if there is any doubt and err on the side of caution.

Moreover, designers can face different levels of protection for their work dependent on their employment status. Work completed by staff designers is normally considered "work made for hire" and property of the firm. Designs created by freelancers, however, are property of the designer. Because projects are often the product of collaboration by more than one designer, there can be confusion as to who owns these rights. Whatever the circumstance, firms must take care to acquire the specific rights that are necessary to meet the needs. For example, firms can negotiate with designers to buy all the rights to the work or to license it for a particular use.

Personnel Policies and Employee Handbooks

The clearest method to establish employment policies is to set them out in written personnel guidelines, policy statements, or manuals that have been reviewed by an attorney. These should be given to employees or kept where they can be viewed. New employees should be given copies and should ask whether these policies exist.

Most employers reserve the right to determine responses on a case by case basis or make changes at any time, by simply including a clear disclaimer on all documents that these statements are guidelines only. Employees are sometimes required to sign an acknowledgment to ensure that the policy statements or manuals have been received.

In rare instances, nonetheless, oral or written promises are enforced against an employer and are usually limited to statements which appear to be definitive terms of employment, such as "guaranteed bonus," "discharge only for cause," or "our company will . . ."). Some reasonable and harmful reliance on these promises is required before any recovery can be had.

Enforcement of these policies against an employee, such as where an employee is disciplined or discharged as a result of failing to follow work conduct, or performance policies, or procedures, is usually done within the firm. These cases may be challenged if the employer has not applied the policies consistently. Whether by reason of discrimination or favoritism, all special cases for which rules are set aside create confusion, animosities, and dilute the force — and enforceability — of the rule.

Discrimination

Federal, state, and local discrimination laws do not create a general guarantee of fairness, but rather carve out particular categories for which any bias is made illegal. Under these laws, all employment decisions — including hiring, distributing benefits, promotions, or firing — must be based on objective criteria that are justified by business necessity and related to the position.

It is generally illegal for an employer to discriminate against an applicant for employment or an employee on the grounds of race, color, national origin (or that of his or her parents or spouse), religion, age, gender, sexual preference, marital status, citizenship, or disability (now including mental or physical disabilities, drug or alcohol dependency, and AIDS or HIV+ status). Additional laws protect against discrimination on the basis of union affiliation, whistle-blowing on an employer's illegal practice, or having a criminal record.

As a result, throughout the hiring process and employment relationship, employers should not seek information or comment or keep records concerning these issues. Only objective criteria such as skills, work experience, education, and work performance should be considered or included on all application forms, interviews, screening processes, performance evaluations, and personnel files. While this may seem obvious, it is not always clear which topics are permissible and which are forbidden. Therefore, employers must prevent the existence—or even the hint—of preference based on any of the proscribed characteristics.

The most common trouble arises when seemingly innocent statements imply unlawful discrimination by indirectly conveying an employer's intent to base the decision to hire on a particular illegal ground. So, for example, questions or casual comments concerning certain physical characteristics may be taken as evidence of an employer's intent to discriminate on the basis of some physical disability. Jokes or off-color remarks on these issues also may lead to these misperceptions.

Promotions, Titles, Salary, and Profit Sharing

Of all the possible incentives toward employee retention, the award of increased earnings and position with the company is the most powerful. How this is done and the relationship between staff in an organization is complex and dependent upon the variables within each organization. The following is a partial listing of issues that must be addressed by the firm in structuring these policies:

- Existing organizational structure: Is there a system of grade levels and titles? The premise is that a system of grade levels and titles is necessary and has to be defined. In larger organizations, titles, job descriptions, and salary ranges are often tied to a point gradation system. For example, entry-level administrative positions might be classified as a grade 1; grade 8 might be an assistant manager, whose salary would be in the $47–58,000 range; grade 10 might be a manager earning $55–65,000; and grade 12 might be a director earning $62–75,000. While smaller design firms may be able to use a simpler plan, they should still connect titles to a salary range.

- Has any time frame or length of service been deemed necessary to attain a promotion? Have accomplishments been defined to justify a promotion such as excellence in performance or advanced education? Who should be moved up through this system and when? These three questions relate to a difficult judgment, evalu-

ating objective standards that have been established—some that should be outlined in personnel guidelines or manuals—and personal, highly subjective factors. They also depend on the quality of communication established between the employer and employee, especially during scheduled and ad hoc employee review sessions. While in most businesses experience is given primary weight, performance or talent can supersede issues of longevity in creatively driven businesses. The inherent danger in promoting a junior over a senior person is the possibility of friction and the implied message to the senior members that it may be time to seek another position.

- Maintaining parity with other staff members: basic equality of salary, title, and relationship to the length of term of employment. A rule of thumb is that there are no secrets in organizations, so the importance of parity cannot be over emphasized. Parity is an issue pegged to the necessity of an established structure to link titles to salary ranges. Each new hire by a firm offers the opportunity to review the existing salary structure to see if it is current with the marketplace.

- Establishing a financial cap to a defined position. It is recommended that a cap on a salary range for a specific title be established. If the employee is with the firm long enough to outlive the nominal increases allowed for the position and cannot be promoted, the employer should consider the other alternative compensations outlined under Employee Retention.

- Should a title change necessarily mean increased salary? In a word, yes.

- Considering profit sharing/stock/equity alternatives to annual salary increases. Many companies use an annual system of bonuses and/or profit sharing as a way of sharing the benefits of business growth, as well as increasing employee incentives to motivate the perception that they are a part of the process. Most employees recognize that these monies are not guaranteed, but the benefits of shared involvement and loyalty to the firm are substantial. Pension plans that are tied to years of tenure and vestment are very successful in bonding the employee to the company. For some firms, the bonus and profit sharing plans supersede the emphasis on raises allowing for lower annual salary increases. The inherent value in this case is to lower fixed overhead in favor of sharing concepts for "good years." Generally, issues of equity only come into play when the individual has become a key member of the firm. There are two key hallmarks of this form of reward: (1)

Does the individual participate in the administration of key decision-making processes of the firm? (2) Would the individual's contribution (creative or business) mean a significant loss of business if that person were to leave? If the employee is responsible and controlling a substantial portion of revenues and is part of the firm's management, then some portion of equity should be a just consideration. A recent trend has been to offer equity at earlier stages as an enticement to join new ventures.

Employee Retention

Employee turnover is a significant and costly problem for many design firms. Retaining valuable employees, therefore, becomes a priority. Techniques for employee retention can include offering increased financial rewards and incentives, as well as finding new, creative challenges for employees to stay fresh and interested.

Standard incentives, such as salary increases, promotions, change of titles, and increased vacation, work in the early years of the relationship. However, the employer's capacity to increase these benefits decreases in direct proportion to the length of tenure. Profit margins do not expand in proportion to the prospect of increased overhead and, in fact, the margins may be decreasing as the design field experiences a shakedown from the influences of technology. There are solutions for those who wish to avoid the problems and costs of turnover, restaffing, advertising, retraining, continuity issues with clients, and disruption within the firm.

The following list represents options for incentives. Some are often negotiated at the time of hiring—a time when the focus is on the short-term needs of attraction and not the long-term issues of retention—but perhaps are better left for later when expanded incentives are advantageous.

- Increased insurance benefits: expanded health, dental, optical, life, and disability insurance
- Health club memberships
- Leave of absence or a sabbatical
- Defined expense accounts
- Transportation to and from work
- Increased participation in pension plans, if company wide
- Education and professional improvement reimbursement

- Seminars and conferences
- Bonuses, company stock options, equity or profit sharing
- Child or elder care
- Flextime or job sharing

Some employees are content with maintaining a singular role within an organization. The employer must be creative in managing these people by finding ways to sustain the creative momentum to stimulate them and avoid staleness. Keeping up-to-date on esthetics, design trends, and technological advances is both the employer's and the employees' responsibility.

Others, who desire professional growth, can face a glass ceiling, where internal organizational structures and overhead restrictions tie the employer's hands. The reality is that certain people will leave for these reasons, and some will need to leave because the organization may have outgrown them as well.

While employee retention can be an important goal, there are advantages to turnover that offer creative growth and financial stability to a design firm. This includes the option to replace individuals with less experienced talent that is perhaps newer and fresher, and offer savings to the firm. The overriding challenge to the firm is to know when to pursue which of these directions.

Termination, Resignation, and Firing

In the best of circumstances, an employment relationship will end relatively amicably, quietly, and with a mutual sense that it "just didn't work out" or "it's time." In many of these cases, the employee simply outgrows the position and no longer finds it challenging. In others, the employer's needs were either not evident or changed over time, and it becomes impossible to give the employee the type of role or responsibility that is commensurate with his or her background and experience.

Sometimes employment is terminated by the employer because of matters unrelated to the specific employee, based on a business or economic reason. These are generally called layoffs rather than firings and can be precipitated by the general business climate, a downsizing, a company reorganization, or the closing of a division or business. Layoffs are governed by specific legally required procedures.

Under more unfortunate circumstances, the relationship ends by one party only and

is a disappointment, if not complete surprise, to the other. Unwelcomed resignations, stemming from employee discontent, often occur when there is lingering confusion over job duties, differing expectations concerning the growth of the position, or simply poor work conditions. Firings are caused by employer discontent when there is unsatisfactory performance, unacceptable behavior, or insubordination.

All too often, the pertinent complaints have rarely, if ever, been communicated before the surprise announcement to end the relationship. These regrettable situations should be addressed quickly, in open discussions so the problem can be corrected. The firm is, of course, in the best position to establish policies and procedures to address each situation. For the employee, this may be trickier, and battles must be chosen carefully and handled diplomatically. Whatever the reason, the best manner to deal with these matters is by taking the time for quality communication. Most situations can be solved through a straightforward discussion; usually it seems that the practical route for all involved is to move on. But without an adequate resolution, the end of an employment relationship is often marked by blame, denial, anger, and insecurity, which may lead to an unnecessary ongoing dispute.

The best practice is to establish voluntary, clear, written rules of conduct for the workplace and expectations for work performance in statements and personnel manuals. These should include specific penalties for noncompliance and internal procedures, if any, to review any problems as they arise. Employees should routinely be given copies or notices of these policies so that they are aware that they will be held to them. Employers can reserve their right to change these policies and to determine their responses on a case by case basis by simply stating this right on the document.

Employers should also avoid treating any one employee differently than others by exempting him or her from policies covering work conduct or performance. These so-called special cases only create confusion as to what is required and resentment among the staff based on perceptions of favoritism. Ultimately, special cases dilute the force—and enforceability—of the rule.

Regular, periodic, performance evaluations will ensure clarity in the employment relationship by giving all involved the opportunity to communicate. Written evaluations provide the best documentation and should be discussed at the reviews and included in personnel files. These efforts put the employee on notice of problems and provide the chance to respond or defend against any charges and raise his or her own questions or problems. It is always preferable to give an opportunity to correct the problem and a follow-up evaluation.

These steps also set the groundwork in case there is a need to discipline or fire the employee.

An employee may behave in a manner that is unacceptable and requires a response. Common misconduct is lateness, absenteeism, on-the-job drug use, foul or abusive language, or disruptive behavior. Nonperformance or insubordination can also be a failure to follow rules regarding appearance or dress or a refusal to follow an employer's instructions in fulfilling the duties of a job. These matters should always be investigated and addressed quickly.

Firms should, whenever possible, use progressive discipline or disciplinary measures that become increasingly more severe as the employee continues to engage in misconduct or fails to improve. Generally, employees are first given a verbal warning with a written memo added to the personnel file. As the behavior continues, a warning is given, followed by suspension from work without pay, and, ultimately, the employee is fired. Also wise are meetings with the employee to discuss the discipline and methods for correction and to provide notice of steps that the employer will take if the problem continues. This way, the employee has been treated fairly by having several chances to correct the behavior.

Some misconduct or performance delinquencies are sufficiently severe to warrant an immediate suspension or discharge. These may include insubordination or engaging in illegal activities such as theft, falsification of records, or sale of drugs on the employer's premises. But, typically, the employee will be sent home while the employer investigates the matter and determines the appropriate penalty.

Of course, once circumstances have reached a certain level, the employee must be fired. Many employers require approval from a neutral manager or a human resources specialist before the action is taken. Firing, while never pleasant, can be eased by a few simple procedures. Advance notice allows an employee time to tie up loose ends and find alternative work. Notice may be given at home, the end of a working day, or the end of a pay period to give the employee time to deal with the situation before spending time in the office. In some cases, however, it is necessary to take measures to ensure that the employer's property, including business files or documents related to trade secrets, is not taken.

A final meeting or exit interview should be held in all cases to give notice of the termination and/or to discuss separation issues, such as the effect on benefits, as well as reviewing any previous disciplinary actions or poor performance appraisals. At this time, the firm may offer letters of reference or letters can be requested by the employee. Copies of the letters should be included in the employee's personnel file.

It is always helpful to be very clear about the reason for the termination, without

being insulting or inflammatory. Here, as always, glossing over the truth leads only to confusion over the actual cause and resentment at the decision. If this information is not forthcoming, the employee may want to request it at a meeting or in a follow-up letter. Written notice of the reason can be given where possible; this documentation should be kept in a personnel file and could be helpful in case of a challenge or to counter claims for unemployment insurance if the termination was for cause.

In extreme instances, employers have tried to dodge firing someone by forcing him or her to quit. However, if an employer establishes work conditions which are so unbearable that a reasonable employee would quit, such as extremely abusive treatment by a supervisor or sexual harassment, that termination will be deemed under the law as a constructive discharge caused by the employer rather than a voluntary action of the employee. The employer would then be liable just as if the employee had been fired—so, no one wins.

Most employees will choose not to protest a termination because it requires a significant investment of time, money, and emotional energy to deal with complex litigation. The employer's vulnerability here may be prevented or limited by the employee's at will status or the lack of any other specific legal right. To be binding, employment commitments must be contractual, established in a personnel manual or by law, such as in the case of discharges related to discrimination. These rigorous requirements can be overwhelming to the individual who may decide that litigation is just not worth it. Of course, if there is significant cause to believe that there was wrongdoing by the employer—or sometimes, if the person fired is just angry or hurt enough, even if wrong—a legal action may be filed. And whenever action is taken, it is costly and time-consuming for all involved. That is why firms should always remember the ancient adage that "an ounce of prevention is worth a pound of cure."

Termination, Severance, Nondisclosure, and Noncompete Agreements

Sometimes an employer and employee may enter into a contract to set the terms for the termination of the employment. These terms may be negotiated in advance, at the initial hiring, or after the decision to end the relationship. These contracts may cover grounds for dismissal, a means for disputing the termination, such as alternative dispute resolution, and severance payments or other benefits.

Severance payment agreements usually depend upon the salary of the position or the length of service with that employer. Severance pay is given for a specified period and may end when the employee is hired elsewhere. In some cases, the amount of severance pay

is conditioned upon the signing of a release of claims against the employer. Termination and severance agreements often contain a provision requiring that the terms of agreement be kept confidential and be revealed only to those with an established need to know. Special issues concerning severance arise for reductions in force (RIFS) and older workers.

These agreements vary widely and can also govern the behavior of the parties after termination. They may include a so-called nondisclosure agreement that restricts a former employee against divulging trade secrets; things not generally known by the public or discovered through other means. They may also contain so-called noncompete agreements, which prohibit a former employee from soliciting the clients or staff of the employer or from otherwise competing against the employer. To be enforceable, these agreements must be limited in scope, geographical boundaries, and duration so as not to unduly limit one's ability to earn a living. Additional limitations include prohibitions against publicly disparaging the employer or cataloging specific grounds upon which the termination may be contested or the employer may be sued or the methods for these disputes. Nondisclosure or noncompete agreements also can be entered into at any stage of the employee's tenure with the company. If these are included in separation agreements, however, they should be accompanied by some additional benefit to the employee in order to be enforceable, such as requiring that a specific person at the design firm answer all reference requests concerning the employee, or by giving additional severance pay.

Assigning Work Credit and Use of the Company's Portfolio

Industry practice dictates that a designer should be credited for his or her creative role on a project, especially if the work is published. In recognition of the designer's contribution, access should always be given to samples of the work, including team based projects, to use for a portfolio. The only exception to this rule should be for projects with confidentiality restrictions, such as products that have not yet been released to the public. While some employers can make it difficult, and while there are no legal regulations per se with the exception of proprietary or confidential projects, common past business practice indicates this system of accreditation for creative roles.

It is the designer's responsibility to present the work accurately, indicating the level of the designer's responsibility and giving the proper credit to the design firm and other team members. If a person leaves a firm and starts a new company, prior work may be displayed

in a portfolio as a demonstration of his or her past experience. The ethical issue is always how the credit is assigned.

Closing

Design firms have grown in sophistication over the decades. Today, in an ever more competitive marketplace and with an educated pool of designers and marketers, design firms of all sizes must function as structured businesses. Remaining sensitive to their creative cultures, firms need to develop systems allowing them to function as an organizational unit. Smoothing out these processes will eliminate many problems, ease morale, and cultivate an environment with the freedom to create.

As we have noted, businesses with a creative product have distinctive requirements. The quality of employee relationships is the nucleus around which all else revolves. Communication, equality in the workplace, identifiable structure, planned decision making, and, finally, the balance between the objective and the subjective are day-to-day concerns facing these firms. Although too frequently left to the bottom of the pile in the face of client demands, taking the time to handle these matters thoughtfully can save everyone time, costs, and the emotional hardships that can adversely affect workplace morale. Most importantly, an emphasis on these priorities and decisions will create the positive synergy needed between employer and employee for successful, long-term relationships.

The Design Firm and
Its Suppliers

by Don Sparkman

In this age of ever-changing design, what applies to one kind of company may not fit another. If you are involved in print, you'll have an entirely different group of suppliers than those supporting a design firm specializing in Web pages or multimedia. Some design firms are part advertising agency and part direct marketing company. Some are corporate or government in-house design groups using outside design consultants.

One common denominator links us together: high ethical standards. Business ethics aren't as easily taught as selling techniques because ethical questions are often complex and vary from one situation to another. In selling, there are tried and proven approaches that work for any business, whether it's graphic arts or insurance. An ethical problem, on the other hand, doesn't always offer a clear solution and each needs to be approached on a case by case basis. Because two cases are never alike, each needs to be analyzed carefully. If you feel you don't know the correct answer to an ethical question, call a respected peer. This will usually provide you with the right solution.

Your Suppliers Are Your Company's Life Blood

A company without suppliers is like a person without food and will starve. As people need nourishment, designers need businesses that support them. We must realize that, because they support us, they are no less important than we are to our clients. There is an old saying, "We are only as strong as our weakest link." If our suppliers let us down, we will let our clients down and, ultimately, we become the real losers.

It is important to forge a strong relationship with each of our support businesses. The most successful companies include their suppliers in their successes. Many companies use holidays to send gifts of appreciation to their suppliers. They feel that this is as impor-

tant as sending gifts to clients. If you think about it, clients come and go, but suppliers are always there for you.

The Food Chain of Design

When we think of our suppliers, we often take a lofty position in the food chain of design. After all, we're the important folks. We make it all happen. The buck stops with us, or does it? Aren't we suppliers to our clients? The U.S. government labels designers as vendors. Our clients often see us as a necessary evil—suppliers with an attitude.

As a rule, we abhor spec work. We are in disdain of any client that stalls in paying us for services rendered. We want to lynch anyone reselling or reusing our work without due compensation. In essence, we feel we must be treated fairly for work we have produced in good faith and through due diligence.

Unfortunately, we don't always see our suppliers in the same light. We think to ourselves, "They're there to make us look good or they won't get anymore of our valuable work." It's human nature to view things from our own perspective.

Successful designers realize that they must be respected as good business people. If we are anything less, we will lose the respect of our clients. After all, if we can't control our own bottom line, how can our clients trust us to help them control their bottom lines? In this age of "partnering," clients don't want vendors. They want a more interactive relationship with design and their designers.

If we are a part of our client's team, then our vendors must be part of our team. We need to know the rules of doing business the right way. If we don't, we may end up with a bad reputation among our suppliers that will be irreversible. To think they don't communicate with each other is to forget how much we communicate with other designers.

Rules for Working with Suppliers
Never falsely represent yourself or your needs.

Asking for a low price to receive potential work is a prime example. You hate it when this carrot is dangled in front of you by a potential client. If no lucrative work follows, you'll only make this request once because you will have lost the respect of the vendor. And, more than likely, lucrative work won't follow. Even if made in earnest, this promise is a jinx.

Don't ask for speculative work.

Asking freelancers to do what you would never do—speculative design—plays on their need for work. Some design firms will only pay a freelancer if the work that is done is accepted by their client. No other industry would think of asking a worker to do this.

Asking a printer for free work for future projects is an example of "work for ransom." For example, you ask a printer to print your company brochure because of a big project in the offing or the promise of an account you really don't have control over. This is just another form of asking for spec work.

Never ask for under-the-table remuneration.

An example of this is a finder's fee. This fee should be a onetime commission agreed on in advance and paid to you for work you've brought to a supplier. Let's say you are purchasing printing for a client or referring a client directly to a printer. You tell the printer that you expect a commission for finding this project. The fee should be agreed on in advance, not brought up after you've referred the printer to this account. You also should not expect a finder's fee to be a continuing royalty for future work. Just like it sounds, it is a fee for finding a client, not for keeping your client happy.

We all know the names for unethical commissions given: under-the-table kickbacks, payola, hidden commissions. Ethical commissions are added to the top by the supplier or taken as a markup by you, if you are purchasing the service for your client. A good rule to follow is, "If you can't explain your commission to your client, it's wrong." And, you shouldn't always expect a commission; suppliers don't have margins of profit large enough to make sure there is always something in the job to pay you a commission.

Don't take unfair advantages of a supplier in a captive situation.

An example of unfair advantage would be a design firm coercing an inexpensive printer into a team situation on a design and printing project. For instance, a magazine is sent out for bids to three designers and three printers. The design firms are all competitive in pricing and caliber of work. Two of the printers are known to be expensive and the third will most certainly be low. One of the design firms controls a substantial amount of work done by the inexpensive printer. The design firm forces the printer to agree not to offer a quote to the magazine publisher without including a quote for its design work. Other design firms and

printers bidding separately stand less of a chance of staying competitive. The "combined only" bid makes the design firm look good, but severely limits the printer.

Don't prepare vague Requests For Quotations (RFQs).

This is deliberately asking a vendor for a price, knowing that you have room to get more from the vendor than it would normally give. An example of this is confusing a photographer or illustrator by minimizing the actual assignment which, for them, will mean more time than they've included in their estimate.

If you are sincere in your RFQ, do your homework so there are no loose ends. We as designers are often given vague specifications by clients out of ignorance. Creativity is hard enough to price, but open-ended specs can be disastrous. A good example is an RFQ for the design and production of a publication with no mention of the number of pages. The bidding firms aren't mind readers and, unless the scope of work is defined by the client, a bid is useless.

Don't ask suppliers for materials that you know won't lead to a sale.

Stock photography is often a victim of cavalier designers. For years, advertising agencies would use stock photos as images for major campaign pitches without paying for them. They would order the images for consideration, use them for layouts, and then return them. Now, stock houses charge a research fee to protect themselves from unscrupulous designers. Other unscrupulous design firms scan the images right out of the catalogs, or know that if they use the actual images they can lie about the extent of use.

Paper merchants are often also victims of misuse. Typically, a designer will request paper samples or dummies and make up a layout for the client. The finished work is then turned over to the printer, which is when the problem can crop up. Paper mills typically let more than one merchant carry their products, which allows printers to shop price. The friendly merchant who helped the designer may never get the final sale. Designers can do several things to alleviate this situation. One is to let the printer know that a certain merchant has been a great help, and you would like them to be considered. Another is to let the paper merchant know who the printer is. This at least gives them a chance to approach the printer. The optimum is to make the paper merchant part of the bid process. This can be done by simply including the merchant within the printing specifications. In your RFQ, tell the bidders that your paper merchant will be the only supplier used on this specific job. You may get some

disgruntled printers, but at least they all have the same restriction. While you may be in the minority of design firms doing this, you'll have the undying gratitude of the paper merchants.

Don't mislead suppliers in billing procedures.

When it's always been assumed that you'd be invoiced, telling the supplier to bill your client at the end of a project is taking unfair advantage of a situation. The better your relationship is with the vendor, the worse the sin. If you know your client is slow in paying, this procedure is unforgivable.

Don't provide false schedules.

The opposite of building in time so that there will be a cushion for both you and the supplier, a false schedule is one that you know you will have to compress later on. If the supplier knew the real schedule, overtime would have to be a factor in the quote. Clients often provide false schedules to designers to get a quote for a normal turnaround, after which they compress the schedule. Doing this to your suppliers is not fair play.

Never establish new credit terms after a job is completed.

If you know you can't live with thirty-day terms, be up front about it. Your suppliers are not in business to finance your business. Never agree to credit terms you know you can't adhere to. This is false representation and will come back to haunt you when you need this supplier. Your word is your credit and vice versa.

Don't reject work to elicit corrections of your own mistakes.

Printing is often a vehicle for this type of abuse. The scenario is: a printing job is commercially acceptable, but the designer or client has made a mistake. Because of a minor printer's error, the designer then demands a reprint and asks for additional changes or corrections. Most printers will not make any changes other than correcting their own mistakes, and designers should not ask them to correct more than that. In fact, because reprints are often a way for a customer to correct their own mistakes for free, printing trade customs specify that printers should only correct their own mistakes. Unfortunately, some printers may be hungry enough to break this rule. Fortunately, most won't.

Protect yourself, know your liabilities.

Take proper precautions when the property of suppliers is in your possession. Some materials won't need to be returned while others may be originals that require insurance coverage on your part. Stock photography is a good example. If lost or destroyed, an original transparency from a stock house is worth $1,500, and you are responsible for insuring it.

A designer I know once ordered stock photos on different subjects from several stock houses. The eager stock houses sent the designer more than 500 transparencies. When all was said and done, the designer had $1,500,000 worth of original material with his normal business insurance covering one-tenth of that amount. A small fire, a disgruntled employee, or an unfortunate accident could have wiped the designer out. By calling his insurance agent, the designer was able to get a rider on his business policy that would increase and decrease as the transparencies were accumulated and then returned.

The best way to cope with unforeseen loss or damage of materials like stock photography is to list every scenario and every type of valuable paper in your possession, or that could possibly be in your possession. Then find out from your insurance agent what coverage you need.

Treat your suppliers as you would like to be treated.

We will get far more positive response when we offer our suppliers the professional respect and consideration we expect from our clients. If we don't, we'll get more than just bad service, we'll also acquire a bad reputation, which may be irreversible. Think about the suppliers you've been warned about and remember, word travels quickly.

These are some, but hardly all, of the ethical abuses that may tempt designers as well as their clients. To better understand business ethics and liabilities, ask questions first. Every facet of design has experts available to answer your questions. While you can't go to jail for abusing ethics, you can ruin your reputation with your suppliers and impede your ability to compete successfully.

Part II.

Management

Legal Structures for the Design Firm

by Leonard DuBoff

Every graphic design business has an optimal structure that will provide it with the maximum possible benefits. These may include tax benefits, protection from liability, continuity of existence, and the like. It is important for small business owners to determine which business form will best serve their needs and whether their business objectives can legally be achieved.

Sole Proprietorships

The simplest form of business is a sole proprietorship. This is the name given to a business that is owned and controlled by a single individual. Little need be done to create a sole proprietorship. All you have to do is obtain a business license if it is required in your jurisdiction and, if you are using a name for your business other than your own, register that as an assumed business name or fictitious name. This simple business form has a major downside, though. Sole proprietors have full personal liability for all debts of the business. This means that your house, car, personal bank accounts, and the like will be exposed to the risks of your business. Certainly you can obtain insurance, but insurance policies have limits and some risks are not insurable.

If a sole proprietor hires an employee and the employee commits a wrongful act within the scope of the business, then the sole proprietor will have full personal liability for the employee's wrongful conduct. In addition, if the employee contracts on behalf of the sole proprietorship business and the contract is within the scope of that business, the sole proprietor will be liable on the contract, even if it was not authorized or approved.

Sole proprietors pay income tax on their earnings at their individual rates. While most sole proprietors segregate their business bank accounts from their individual bank ac-

counts for a number of reasons, the IRS lumps all of the sole proprietor's earnings together for tax purposes. That is, the sole proprietor's personal tax return will reflect business earnings as well as investment or bank interest.

Partnerships

When two or more individuals join together for purposes of engaging in a business, then the relationship between them is known as a partnership. No formal acts are necessary to form a partnership, although it is always a good idea to put all of the parties' understandings regarding the business into writing so misunderstandings can be avoided.

A partnership is defined as an arrangement whereby two or more persons act as co-owners and engage in a business for profit. Note that the individuals need not be equal partners, although, if they have not specified a particular relationship, the law presumes that they are equal. Because there are numerous presumptions which attach to the relationship under state laws, it is important for individuals who become partners to specify the terms of the partnership with some particularity in order to avoid confusion.

Each partner has full personal liability for the debts and wrongful acts of any other partner when they occur within the scope of the partnership business. In addition, partners have full personal liability for the acts and the contracts of all partnership employees. For example, if one partner engages in acts of copyright infringement, all partners will be liable for the wrongful conduct, even though only one of the partners was the wrongdoer.

Each partner pays tax on his or her distributable share of partnership profit and may deduct his or her share of partnership losses. Note that tax liability is imposed on the partner even if there is no actual distribution of profit. If, for example, two graphic designers have an equal partnership that earns $50,000 per year and decide to retain those earnings for purposes of expansion, then each partner has a tax liability of $25,000, even though the money was not distributed.

Limited Partnerships

A type of partnership that can afford some partners' limited liability is known as a limited partnership. This business form is a partnership comprised of one or more general partners who have full personal liability and one or more limited partners who may enjoy limited liability so long as they are not actively involved in running the business. A limited partner may receive financial information and, in some states, retain the right to elect or

remove general partners, but the limited partner may not, under any circumstances, conduct the day-to-day operations of the business.

If a limited partner becomes actively involved in determining policy and running the partnership's business, then the active limited partner will have full personal liability as if he or she were a general partner.

Partners in a limited partnership, whether they are general or limited partners, are taxed on distributable profits and may deduct distributable losses. The limited partnership entity is not taxed as such, though an informational return is filed; rather, individual tax returns of the partners reflect partnership profits and losses. The partnership does file an annual return, but it is for informational purposes only.

One method by which business owners may be shielded from liability for business obligations is to have the business structured as a corporation or some other business form with limited liability.

Corporations

One of the most popular business forms is the corporation. It is considered a separate legal entity apart from its owner(s), even if the owner is one individual. The corporation is responsible for all of its business activities and the owner generally is not. If an employee engages in wrongful conduct within the scope of the business or if the employee involves the corporation in an unfavorable contractual arrangement, the corporation, not the owner, will be liable. With few exceptions, the owner's only exposure when engaging in business in the corporate form is for the assets placed in the corporation.

A corporation is a taxable entity, and it must, therefore, file its own corporate tax return. There is, however, a special type of corporation which may elect, for tax purposes, to be treated as if it were not incorporated. This is the so-called "S" corporation. Unfortunately, "S" corporations do not truly pass through profits and losses as if the business were unincorporated, and there are a number of restrictions imposed on businesses with an "S" corporation status. This form of business is unavailable if any of the shareholders are not American citizens or are other for-profit corporations. Until just recently, if there was more than one class of stock, the "S" form was then also unavailable. In addition, the number of shareholders was limited. However, new legislation has expanded the applicability of "S" corporations. Certain tax-exempt organizations will now be permitted to hold stock, and the number of permitted shareholders will be increased from thirty-five to seventy-five.

Those who conduct business in the corporate form and desire to provide medical, dental, or prepaid legal insurance for employees may do so by adopting a plan permitting them to fund these benefits with pre-tax dollars. In addition, the benefits are not taxable to the employee recipients. This is available only for corporations that are considered taxable entities, not "S" corporations. A properly structured contract between the corporation and its shareholders could provide for a tax-deductible life insurance program. This type of arrangement is also available only for regular or "C" corporations, which are taxable entities.

A "C" corporation must retain its losses and carry them forward until it has earned profits. The individual owners may not personally net those losses against their individual earnings. In addition, if money is paid to shareholders on account of their stock interest as dividends, then that money will be taxed to the recipient and may not be deducted by the corporation. Essentially, then, this money is taxed twice.

There are a number of methods by which a business attorney can structure a graphic arts business in order to maximize liability protection while minimizing tax. If, for example, the parties have conducted their business under a particular name or logo, then they can protect that trademark and continue to use it when they set up their business form. The trademark could be owned by the business, or a more sophisticated plan could be implemented. For instance, if the owners personally retain ownership of that mark and register it in their own names, they can license the mark to their graphic design business and obtain some benefits, including royalty payments. Royalty income is known as passive income and is exempt from certain income-related taxes. There are, thus, some tax benefits in having a licensing arrangement between the business owners who are also owners of the trademark of the business they own.

It is common for owners of small businesses, including graphic design businesses, to be employees of their businesses. The money paid to employees is known as earned income, and that income is subject to all employment taxes. Earned income is also deductible by a corporation, which is a taxable entity. This means that even though the corporation earned considerable money, it may pay that money out in reasonable salaries and payroll withholding expenses so long as the salary is reasonable, and, thus, have no taxable income at year-end.

Limited Liability Companies

There is a new business form known as a limited liability company (LLC). This business form allows the individual owners to achieve the same kind of liability they would have in a corporation, while the business organization is ignored for tax purposes. Essentially, the owners of the graphic design firm would be taxed as if they were sole proprietors or partners, even though the business organization could not qualify as an "S" corporation.

"S" corporations and LLCs are not taxable entities, and the owners must pay tax on their distributable profits and may deduct their pro rata share of business losses. It would, therefore, be important for you to determine whether your graphic design business is likely to lose money during the formative years. If so, it may be in your best interest to create an "S" corporation or an LLC. In this way, your business losses may be netted against your personal earnings from other sources.

If a corporation retains profits of up to $50,000 for purposes of expansion, it will be taxed at 15 percent on that $50,000, while sole proprietors, partners, or those who conduct business as "S" corporations or LLCs that retain any money in the business for expansion will be taxed on those retained profits at the individual's rate of 15 to 28 percent. (See table below for more tax rate information.)

Single Individuals

TAXABLE INCOME				
OVER	BUT NOT OVER	PAY	% ON EXCESS	OF THE AMOUNT OVER
$ 0	$ 24,650	$ 0	15.0%	$ 0
24,650	59,750	3,967.50	28.0%	24,650
59,750	124,650	13,525.50	31.0%	59,750
124,650	271,050	33,644.50	36.0%	124,650
271,050	——	86,348.50	39.6%	271,050

Corporations

TAXABLE INCOME				
OVER	BUT NOT OVER	PAY	% ON EXCESS	OF THE AMOUNT OVER
$ 0	$ 50,000	$ 0	15.0%	$ 0
50,000	75,000	7,500	25.0%	50,000
75,000	100,000	13,750	34.0%	75,000
100,000	335,000	22,250	39.0%	100,000
335,000	10,000,000	113,900	34.0%	335,000
10,000,000	15,000,000	3,400,000	35.0%	10,000,000
15,000,000	18,333,333	5,150,000	38.0%	15,000,000
18,333,333	—	—	35.0%	0

There are numerous other considerations that affect the determination of what business form will best serve your interests and maximize your business security. A skilled business lawyer can assist you in making that determination and helping you realize your objectives.

Principles of Design Firm Management

by Shel Perkins

Professional design firms present unusual organizational and management challenges. How do we support something as intangible as creativity? How do we stabilize something in constant motion? What sort of valid comparisons can be made between things that are unique? How can personal needs and business needs overlap to a great extent yet not be identical? What happens when we have to make a decision that's good for the business but perhaps not for us personally? Each creative organization must meet these challenges in its own way. Organizing and nurturing a design studio means not only challenging, motivating, and rewarding the individual staff members, but also perceiving and meeting the needs of the firm itself, while maintaining a strong and consistent client orientation.

I'd like to share some thoughts about appropriate organizational structures and management approaches. These ideas are presented in fairly broad terms, and some important topics, such as marketing, will only be mentioned in passing. My emphasis here is on the vision of the firm and how that is expressed in the business structure and supported by daily operations.

In order to successfully launch a new firm, the founders must have several things. First, they must have experience in producing quality design. They need to have a vision for what they want to accomplish and what the focus of the new firm will be. This vision must be supported by a detailed business plan that includes an analysis of the market demand for the kind of services that the firm will offer, an accurate evaluation of the competition, and a realistic budget of the revenues and expenses that can be expected during the first year of operations. Preparation of a business plan is important because it is a declaration of mission—a narrative of who the firm is and what it cares about—and it establishes the standards for success.

It is important that the new firm be adequately capitalized. Exactly how much capital is required is a matter for discussion. A conservative advisor would say that it's not unusual for a new business to take two years to break even, so it should have enough cash and financing available to cover overhead for twenty-four months. My approach is less conservative because it is based on the assumption that a studio should not be opened until it already has client work lined up. Each new firm must have at least one major client account, plus a step-by-step plan for winning additional accounts in very short order. Having a major account from day one means that we are doing billable work that will be invoiced in the first thirty to forty-five days and payment from the client will be received thirty to forty-five days after the invoice has gone out. If we are certain that our billings will be enough to cover our overhead, and if we are certain that it will take no longer than ninety days for us to turn labor into cash, then the firm could start with enough money on hand to pay for start-up costs and at least the first ninety days of expenses.

I want to emphasize that founders need good advice from professionals outside of design: An attorney who can help with legal requirements and contractual issues, both with clients and with employees; an accountant who can advise on general financial management and tax issues; a banker who can assist the growing firm with financing and cash management; and a business insurance agent who can offer guidance on risk management. These advisors should be consulted well in advance of opening the doors. In particular, the accountant and the banker can be of great service in evaluating plans and advising on capital needs.

In observing the growth of new firms, I would suggest that there is a pattern. The first three or four years are the start-up phase, and those years are often quite turbulent. It takes that long for a firm to establish its client base and reputation, and to evolve its own internal organizational structure and culture to the point where projects can consistently be completed in a profitable way.

In the graphic design profession, firms that have successfully graduated from that start-up stage often find themselves to be midsized, with a staff of somewhere between eleven and twenty-five people. Continued success will create continued opportunities for growth. However, growth is not something that happens automatically. It is a conscious decision that is made in response to each opportunity that presents itself.

Decisions about growth must be tied into the overall business plan. There are positive aspects as well as risks. If a large new project or client account is accepted, how many new employees will be needed to service it properly? If and when that account ends, how

many others will be required to keep the expanded staff busy? On the other hand, a small studio that is largely dependent on one main account is vulnerable. What happens if that client goes out of business or their industry goes into a slump? A larger studio can consciously develop new business relationships that allow it to diversify with multiple clients in multiple industries, so that all of their eggs are not in one basket. Related to that, the firm must choose whether to expand its offer to include a more complete range of services or to concentrate in one special area where they can be perceived as a clear leader.

If the firm decides to grow, that continued expansion will lead to a second period of turbulence as the organization learns to manage larger projects, larger teams, and higher stakes.

Objective

The overall objective is to evolve a structure that meets client needs and supports the creative process. There is no cookie-cutter solution to the challenges of establishing and growing a creative firm. There is no off-the-shelf solution that works for one firm that is going to be a custom fit for another. Each firm provides different services to clients in different markets. Each firm has a different mix of people. The work situation is very fluid and constantly evolving. Over time, each successful firm must evolve a flexible structure that is appropriate for its own activities and that supports coordination of its many commitments.

If the basic objective is to evolve a structure that meets client needs, we need to start by thinking about what those external needs are. Essentially they have to do with quality, efficiency, and service.

External Needs

Clients want design firms to bring a new perspective to their business challenges and add value to client enterprises through innovative thinking. They come to design firms for a competitive advantage. So, adding value is at the top of the list of external needs. Clients need creative firms that can understand the context of a particular problem as well as provide a depth of understanding on larger issues. Clients want to hire firms that know them, their business, their market, their competitors, and that can help them create and profit from opportunities.

Clients need studios to provide fast response. I know we've all been there. We need to produce proposals quickly, and then more often than not the projects themselves need to move along as fast as humanly possible. Fast response is definitely an issue for creative firms.

Clients want to have no confusion about the work that is being done for them. There needs to be clear communication, clearly stated objectives, a shared road map, and frequent updates on progress. Clients need to have one senior contact within the studio, a decision maker who receives their project information and answers their questions.

Clients need to be included in the process so that there are no surprises. Different clients have different comfort levels for how much they want to be included, but my personal feeling is the more they are included the better. An inclusive process features work sessions with the client, discussion documents, and signed client approvals at the end of each interim phase. It is important to note that, from the client standpoint, the studio structure is not an issue. I don't believe that clients really care how the creative firm is organized internally, as long as the work is good and client needs are being met.

Internal Needs

Complementary to these external needs are the internal needs of the studio itself. Obviously, the studio needs to be doing great design. Quality of design must be a given right from the start and design excellence must be an ongoing priority.

Within the studio, there needs to be a sense of continuity, a sense of history. Information about what the firm has done in the past needs to be available. Project types, professional tasks performed, resources needed, successful schedules, patterns of client activity, these are the design-specific measurements that are important to build into studio management systems.

New proposals need to be informed by past history. What we've done for the client before, how long the project really took, what materials really cost. The studio needs to have a memory. By drawing on cumulative history, new projects have a better chance of being priced correctly and structured to succeed. The firm may be traveling fast, but it needs to remember where it has been. Reinventing the wheel and repeating past mistakes is wasteful and demoralizing.

In order for a studio to consistently provide fast response to clients, it must have sufficient internal resources. It's important to recognize that this is always going to be a moving target. We need to have the right kind of resources to do the sort of work that we have committed to do, but the work changes constantly. We must continually reevaluate the services that we are marketing and the core competencies of our staff, and get feedback from clients about how well they are being taken care of.

In order to work as effectively as possible, there needs to be excellent ongoing communication within the studio, and a clear understanding of individual responsibilities. Especially in small firms, where each team member wears a number of different hats, it's important to know who's wearing which hat at any given time. Sorting the hats and doing some honest self-assessment will identify gaps in skill sets that can be addressed through future hires.

Each firm has a range of needs and must hire staff members with core competencies in each area. Together, they comprise a spectrum of complementary skills. Small firms will out-source more of those skills, and larger firms will bring more of them in-house. I believe that every firm needs to hire the best across the board and create an all-star team. Let each of the players succeed in their particular area and make sure that there is excellent communication between them all. Distributing responsibilities to the most appropriate staff members will allow the founders of the firm to focus their own energies and prevent their attention from becoming scattered, as well as keep their personal workload manageable.

Active projects should be led by senior people who are good collaborators. Within design firms, these project leaders are often the primary contact for the client, as well as being a manager and mentor to their coworkers. A senior person is experienced in coordinating the activities of a multidisciplinary team. He or she must be well organized and able to set priorities and achieve results in a sometimes stressful environment.

A successful studio needs to establish and maintain a culture of cooperation and concern; a culture that supports negotiation and management of the network of commitments necessary to satisfy both internal and external needs. In addition, the internal structure and business practices need to support the creative process without getting in the way of it. From the point of view of the client and the larger business community, it is primarily the creative work itself that should be visible.

Project after project, year after year, is important to build these values and concerns into the structure of the firm in such a way that success is sustainable.

Make It Sustainable

Despite the fact that client services will evolve and there will inevitably be staff turnover, high standards have to be set and maintained in all areas. We need to bring the same commitment and quality to all activities within the studio, both business-related and design-related. This includes selecting and developing good relationships that are mutually beneficial, and making sure all staff members are learning and growing—that we have created a learn-

ing organization. To remain in business, there is an obvious need to be consistently profitable. Another need is to have fun. Enjoyment of our work motivates us and contributes to the freshness of our creative solutions. If the fun ever drains away from what we do, it will be time to close the doors.

At the risk of stating the obvious, we need to be careful about managing the workload to make sure that we haven't taken on too much at any given time. We need to have the right amount of time and the appropriate resources to successfully deliver on our commitments. This requires effective coordination between all of the activities within the firm. The right hand needs to know what the left hand is doing.

Making the firm sustainable over time means that each individual project has to be structured for success. There are many aspects to a successful project.

Structuring Projects

It's important that the projects be well-defined, that we really do understand the scope of the work, that we're treating the base situation and not the symptoms. Key information may come from the client in a request for proposal, but that needs to be fleshed out by the studio into a comprehensive project definition that states the business objective, the market positioning, the competitive environment, the expected business results, and all relevant specifications. It is necessary to establish common goals with the client right at the start and clearly define the deliverables. Then we need to manage the client's expectations as the project unfolds, particularly if the definition of the project shifts. It is vital to identify those shifts and communicate them in an effective way.

Occasionally a project will be downsized. If the scope of the work is reduced, adjusting the billings downward is an easy matter. However, it is more typical for project changes to expand the scope of work. The studio needs to be diligent about letting clients know the implications of expanded requests by sending change orders that spell out the additional effort that will be involved. There should be no surprises. A change order not only documents who requested what and when, but it gives the client an immediate opportunity to reconsider and renegotiate. The process clarifies the studio's commitments and how those commitments will meet specific client needs.

Project schedules and budgets obviously are tied to detailed specifications. Appropriate pricing cannot be determined until realistic specifications have been agreed upon. Not only do budgets need to account for all costs, but they must also contain an expected profit

margin for the studio. Beginning a project without sorting out all of these issues is a recipe for failure. The process of clarifying these issues strengthens the design brief and actually leads to better work. At the end of each project, we need to assess the client's satisfaction, refine our offer accordingly, and position the studio for additional work. It is an important practice to close the loop in this way. An ongoing series of well-managed projects with great design solutions spells success for the firm. Reliable fulfillment builds strong relationships with clients who value our professionalism and the competitive advantage that we provide.

Design-Centered Organization

From an organizational standpoint, the design of client projects is at the center of the firm, supported by various kinds of support and feedback: marketing activities, traffic, financial management, network administration, and other administrative tasks. The design process is supported by these other kinds of expertise.

Within the design function, different studios have different job titles and sometimes describe the process in different ways. There tends to be senior level design and creative direction. There is the design staff, production, project coordination, and project management. This is the majority of what is taking place in the studio, and often represents about 70 percent of the total number of employees. To support these activities, the combination of administration, finance, network management, and marketing is usually no more than 30 percent of the staff. If we look at that with X-ray vision, what we are seeing is the differentiation between billable and nonbillable labor.

Since the client work that is performed is primarily tracked and measured in terms of hours, time management is critical to the profitability of any design firm. An appropriate range of billable time needs to be established for each staff position. All hours need to be recorded, both billable and nonbillable, and staff members need periodic feedback on where they stand in relation to targets. Realistic goals must have some relation to past levels of performance, which must have been measured in a comparable way. For these and other indicators, it's important to capture complete information, and the system for tracking activity must be current and consistent. Over time each firm will develop a sense of norms, like temperature or blood pressure. Real activity will never be an average, but once we have defined acceptable ranges for each indicator—high and low, best case and worst case—we can watch actual performance within these parameters without becoming too alarmed.

Billable Time

For the studio to be profitable over time, we need to maximize the billable time. If we look at this more closely, the time that people actually spend in the office is not going to be 100 percent billable. There is a certain amount of built-in downtime: vacation time, sick time, staff meetings, and various studio activities that will not be billable to clients. When these have been subtracted from the total, about 80 percent may be the maximum billable percentage for a creative firm with a standard forty-hour work week.

Enough staff members need to be near the maximum billable percentage to support the few people who are primarily nonbillable. Marketing is probably going to be largely nonbillable, and definitely financial management and administrative support will be primarily nonbillable. As we structure the staff, we are creating a weighted average of the various billable percentages. Company wide, at least 60 percent of all regularly scheduled hours should be billable to clients. See example below:

	PROJECT TIME	STUDIO TIME
Creative direction	80%	20%
Design	80%	20%
Production	80%	20%
Project coordination	80%	20%
Marketing	30%	70%
Administration, finance, network	10%	90%
OVERALL	60%	40%

The following information is from the Association of Professional Design Firms (APDF). Sixty percent as a benchmark for billable time is supported by survey information that the APDF has compiled for each of the last five years. The APDF collects, in confidence, and analyzes complete financial statements from a large number of independent design consultancies in the United States and Canada. Over the past five years, the median billable percentage has ranged from 59 to 62 percent.

In the APDF survey, two different methods of determining the billable percentage have been reported by firms. Most studios calculate billable time based on actual hours reported by each staff member. In contrast, a few firms look at job titles only; for example, creative director 100 percent billable, or administrator 100 percent nonbillable. Job titles are not reliable indicators. Actual hours should be the basis of this calculation.

On a related note, it's important to remember that recording time as billable on a time sheet is not the same as actually invoicing a client for it.

Staffing

Over time more people will be added, and new positions will be created in the various categories of the organization. Though the size of the organization will be getting larger, we want the proportions to stay roughly the same. Each time the workload dictates that someone be added, we'll want to be aware of how he or she will fit into the mix. If administrative staffing outweighs project staffing, then the firm will not be able to pay for its increasing overhead. An example of staff for small and large design firms follows:

Total number of employees

	SMALL FIRM	LARGE FIRM
70% of staff		
Creative direction	1	3
Design	3	9
Production	2	6
Project coordination	1	3
30% of staff		
Marketing	2	6
Administration, finance, network	1	3
TOTAL	10	30

Questions about structure arise in every firm that experiences growth. Various types of internal organizational structures are common for both midsized and larger creative firms. One is a corporate-style pyramid—a hierarchy of responsibility with a single authority at the top. This is often seen in firms where one person's name is on the door. Another structure has multiple segments that meet at the center, like a flower or star, allowing several principals to each manage a separate staff without too much overlap. Regardless of the geometry, the need is to evolve an appropriate system based on the combined personalities involved and the range of services provided to clients. An appropriate system will facilitate the daily work being done, respond well to change, and support future growth. These issues are addressed in terms of teams.

Teams

As a studio grows and more people become involved in the creative process, the loop of communication becomes quite large. If there are fifteen or twenty people involved in the creative process, it's appropriate to begin to think of them in dedicated teams of some sort. This is an important organizational issue that all growing firms face. Decisions about organization can either facilitate growth or prevent it.

There are a lot of ways of organizing creative resources. Everyone in the studio is involved in different projects, so each person is probably on multiple project teams. But if we step back a bit, we might think about client teams. Perhaps there are certain teams that service certain client accounts. Perhaps that is how designers are hired—you are hired to join the client E team or the client R team, and you know that most of the work that you will be doing is for that particular client.

It's also possible to organize resources around certain industries; that some industrial design firms and some consulting firms are organized in this way. If we have a depth of understanding in a particular area such as software development, hardware manufacturing, biotechnology, or financial services, then that might be a way of organizing internal resources.

There are also creative firms that are organized by design discipline, by the creative service that is being offered. We might have a corporate identity team that does its own hiring and manages its own activities. We might have a brand identity and packaging team. Maybe there's a team that does a three-dimensional work and creates retail environments. It's possible to organize resources based on various disciplines.

Different disciplines sometimes have different pricing and contractual conventions. Fixed-fee agreements are typical for small graphic design projects, whereas time-and-materials contracts and royalties are more common for industrial design projects. For work in some disciplines, it may be appropriate to negotiate amounts not to exceed per page or per square foot. For some deliverables, the frequency and scope of use will determine the scope of creative fees. Clients purchasing identity work need to receive full rights and ownership, but with some interactive projects perhaps only a licensing arrangement is appropriate. Teams organized by discipline may have different norms in these important respects.

Finally, we might also consider sorting design and production staff based on personalities. That is to say, selecting complementary personalities with a range of skill sets for a team led by a strong senior person that they respect. Team building based on personal chemistry as well as professional competencies can reinforce communication and facilitate cooperation when pressure builds on projects. The downside might be that ego could get in the way of effective coordination, and that clients could develop a loyalty to an individual rather than to the firm.

The choice of team structure will have an impact on marketing strategies and the way that the firm describes itself to clients. There will be a need to keep the different teams equally busy with appropriate assignments. We will also have to think about whether an optimum mix of disciplines or categories exists for the firm, and whether future growth needs to be proportional in that respect.

Once a growing firm has sorted a large pool of creative resources into teams, the hard part is to make sure that everyone stays challenged—that everyone has new work, and no one feels that they've been pigeonholed into a narrow area. What is the best way of coaching, challenging, evaluating, rewarding, and encouraging personal growth? How do we make sure that this structure remains open and flexible? Addressing these issues involves a lot of trust and effective communication between team members.

How do we maintain a shared vision across the teams, to reaffirm and clarify the purpose that unifies the group, to restate the company's mission and put individual activities into context and explain their relevance. In a busy studio, with resources being used in shifting configurations and individuals playing multiple roles, competing priorities can cause confusion and stress. To prevent burnout, there is an operational challenge to maintain cohesion and direction, rather like a flexible background grid that the various client projects play across.

Financial Targets

In reviewing monthly financial statements with an accountant, it becomes clear that much of the financial information is not industry-specific. Certain comparisons and standard ratios can reveal the general financial health of any business. The best indicators, like percentages and multipliers, are scalable and are not affected by the size of the company.

Beyond the standard measurements, creative firms have a need for measurements that are more specific to our activities. External benchmarks that are design specific are not always easy to come by. Many firms develop their own internal measurements over time with the help of their accountants. When looking at a profit and loss statement, one important way to gauge revenue is to divide the billings for a period by the total number of employees during that period. There are two ways of doing this. One way is to look at fee billings (labor billings) only. The other way is to look at total billings, which includes labor and all other revenue, such as materials, third-party costs passed through the studio, and markups. Revenue per employee can be used as a way of setting personal targets for employees. It can be used to estimate future sales based on staff size or, conversely, to estimate staffing needs based on expected sales. If the studio is organized into teams, personal targets can be used as a modular way of constructing team targets.

Revenue is measured in currency, so it will change over time due to factors like inflation. Currently, annual fee billings per employee tend to range from $85,000 to $91,000 according to the APDF survey. When we add in billings for project materials, total billings per employee range from $122,000 to $124,000, with materials comprising 27 to 30 percent of the total. Thus total income for a firm of ten people might range from $1,220,000 to $1,240,000 per year, whereas a firm of thirty might range from $3,660,000 to $3,720,000 per year, assuming the right client relationships are in place. An example of figuring total income follows:

EXAMPLE	SMALL FIRM	LARGE FIRM
Number of employees	10	30
Total billings per employee	$124,000	$124,000
Total annual billings for firm	$1,240,000	$3,720,000
Less annual materials billings		
at approx. 27% of total	$330,000	$990,000

Fee billings for firm	$910,000	$2,730,000
Fee billings per employee	$91,000	$91,000

Another way to analyze our profit and loss statement is to look at individual cost categories as a percentage of total sales. For example, rent might be equal to 3 or 4 percent of total sales. Total salaries might equal 34 to 38 percent of total sales. Thus total income for any given period might be approximately three times our salary expense. This multiplier is affected by the number of billable hours being reported, and the billing rates that we charge to clients for those hours.

One reason for tracking billable and nonbillable hours is to split salary costs into direct labor and indirect labor categories on the profit and loss statement. Direct labor contributes to the cost of goods sold along with other project-related expenses, such as materials and freelancers. Indirect labor goes into overhead along with items like rent, utilities, and employer taxes. In each accounting period, the cost of goods sold is subtracted from total revenue to calculate the gross margin. The gross margin must be large enough to cover all overhead and leave a profit. A gross margin equal to 45 or 50 percent of the total revenue is probably typical for graphic design firms. For many design firms, pre-tax profits might vary from 4 to 10 percent, depending on how much money is disbursed through retirement plans and discretionary incentive programs.

These are a few of many possible measurements. Percentage indicators, ratios, and multipliers can be expected to stay within certain ranges despite the size of the firm. Real activity will never exactly match our plan, but over time we'll develop a good sense of the acceptable range for each indicator. The right combination of key measurements can provide us with a multidimensional picture of our financial situation and help us identify and respond to trends. It is important to revisit the business plan quarterly to review and adjust targets. The ongoing business plan should include the establishment of cash reserves the firm can draw on in an emergency and specific plans for the most productive use of cumulative profits produced by successfully completed projects.

Ongoing Issues

Over time, basic management issues remain fairly constant in terms of finance, marketing, and human resources. Individual responsibilities for those issues will no doubt shift

based on changes in staff and personal workloads, but ongoing concerns will include: maintaining the right mix of people and resources, maintaining a healthy financial and cash flow situation, and guiding new business efforts so the firm identifies and pursues the most appropriate client relationships. There will continue to be operational issues around the planning of sustainable schedules, and an ongoing need to find scalable solutions for studio organization.

If the organization grows, that growth must never obscure the underlying mission of the firm. Whether small or large, every studio is part of a unique service industry. Design is really about people and communication. It's about quality relationships and respect; within the design team, between the design team and the client, and with the client's customers in the world.

CHAPTER 12

Transition

by Colin Forbes

Most design firms whether graphic, product, or architectural, have grown from the creative and entrepreneurial energy of an individual or two or three partners. Historically, only one or two out of thousands of firms have ever continued into a second generation. The design-driven offices of George Nelson, Charles and Ray Eames, and Eliot Noyes disappeared with the death of their founders. Practically the only design firms to survive beyond the first generation have been marketing-driven companies like Lippincott & Margulies and Walter Dorwin Teague. Yet if you consider dominant names in other service industries, Arthur Andersen or Peat Marwick in accounting, for example, or McKinsey or Deloitte in management consultancy, they have all reached their second or third generation. The size and success of these organizations make it hard to relate their experience to relatively minuscule design firms, but I believe we still have something to learn from them. The challenge is to run what we believe to be an excellent design-driven firm into a second generation.

As the first generation of the Pentagram partners, including myself, start to think about retiring, there are critical transitional issues facing our firm. In my opinion these issues are our constitution, personalities, and critical mass, and of these, by far the most important are constitution and personalities. There are two quotes, one from a management consultant and the other from a venture capitalist, which at first glance are contradictory but in fact support my view. The first is: "An above average person will fail in a poor structure where an average person can succeed in a good structure." The second is: "I would rather back an A man with a B idea than a B man with an A idea."

The Pentagram Constitution

Pentagram's constitution is based on the equality of its partners. Although we are incorporated, we use the term partners because that conveys the spirit of the relationship. The idea of equality goes back to our first company, Fletcher/Forbes/Gill, where the three partners decided on equal equity and equal incomes. However, each partner's profitability was openly decided, which contributed to a competitive element.

During these early years, the partner who worried first about cash flow, the need for more studio space, or what might happen in five years, got the job of planning the progress of the firm permanently. That happened to be me. We were fundamentally a roundtable organization, but I was the one who led efforts to develop the shareholder agreements and the constitution with lawyers, to refine the financial reporting with the accountants, and to map out a five-year plan.

Our London lawyer was instrumental in drafting the agreements between LIS. He said at one of our early meetings, "You must be generous towards an incoming partner. The talented thirty-five-year-old that you need to help the business continue to thrive will not be able to buy in at ten times earnings." Therefore, we agreed that incoming partners would buy shares at asset value only, with no allowance for good will, and that the firm would assist with financing over an extended period. The lawyer also said, "You must create adhesion—the advantage must go to the remaining partners and not to a leaving partner." Therefore, a partner leaves with the auditor's valuation of the current asset value only; retirement pension schemes are our individual responsibilities. We have always taken the attitude that partners should be financially self-reliant because the variety of ages means that the requirements vary too much.

My position was further entrenched when, with the addition of two more partners and the formation of Pentagram in 1972, I instituted our six-monthly partners' retreats which eventually formalized into our policy meetings. It seemed natural that I would chair all of the partners' meetings, and I continued to do so for eighteen years. Through these meetings we have learned to communicate with each other (although never enough) and to connect with the community. I believe the meetings are one of the major reasons the partners have stayed together. They have been part of our continuing education because they provide a forum where we can learn from one another and from our guests. They have taken place at remarkable venues such as Leeds Castle, the American Academy in Rome, and the St. Francis Yacht Club in San Francisco.

By 1978 two more partners had joined in London, and I moved to New York to establish the office there. In 1986 the San Francisco partners joined and introduced a new location. As we have continued to grow, our democratic philosophy stood us in good stead, but my role in all of this had been concentrated for three major reasons. First, I was unique in having strong relationships with the U.K. partners; second, I had negotiated the entry of each one of the U.S. partners; and third, I had always chaired all of our meetings. I should credit the fact that I have been blessed with exceptional mentors and consultants, but, maybe without undue modesty, I could say that I have had the good sense to choose and to listen to them.

When I announced in 1991 that I wanted to resign my long-term chairmanship, a number of interesting observations immediately arose from my partners. The most important seemed to be that one learned through leadership, and there were a number of partners who felt that they had been excluded from that experience. I had been advised that I should go on as chairman until the last minute and that the issue would resolve itself when I left. But I didn't accept that; I felt we needed a transition period during which we should agree on a Pentagram constitution to carry us through the next decade. I had also been advised that the chairman's tasks had to remain in one hand and that rotation of leadership would be a disaster. Whereas that may be sound advice for a conventional corporation, in my opinion, it did not take into account the personalities and motivations of my partners, and indeed, designers in general.

The following describes the structure that I proposed after listening carefully to my partners and which has been accepted. The basis is the division of responsibility to allow the chairmanship of the meetings to rotate and to establish permanent elected committees to be responsible for the major functions.

The real authority for policy decisions remains the full assembly of the partner-shareholders, however, we have had to establish executive committees to get things done. One partner is elected to be policy committee chairman to organize and lead the six monthly policy meetings and to deal with any matters affecting the whole group that are not included in the roles of other committees. This position rotates after three meetings (eighteen months) by tenure such that each partner shall, in turn, serve as policy chairman. Therefore, by definition the policy chairman will always be a senior member who has fully become part of Pentagram's culture.

Through our experience we had learned to divide nonprofessional work into three

distinct areas: accounting, communication, and administration. The first two have impact on the offices internationally, but the third is primarily local. We therefore established two international sub-committees, a finance committee and a communications committee, each comprised of one representative from each of the three offices. In order to channel information and simplify meetings with outside advisers, we have also elected a chairman for each of these committees.

The committee members are nominated locally by each office and then approved by the group. In order to minimize rotation, there is no limitation on the term of membership, so unless someone is patently incompetent or uninterested, the committee appointments are virtually permanent.

The finance committee has the task of coordinating the financial affairs of the group with our financial advisers and lawyers. They discuss the details of matters like profitability by each partner and office, the distribution of our income and major capital investment, and then report to the full partnership when decisions need to be made. Likewise, the communications committee coordinates our substantial publishing program including the books, *Pentagram Papers, Pentaspeak,* and other initiatives pertaining to public relations and business development.

After the first six months with this structure in place, some partners still had concerns about leadership of the group as a whole; it seemed increasingly difficult to get the partners internationally to develop both working and social relationships. A group of partners met on an ad hoc basis to address this problem, and they proposed that there should be an elected steering committee to be responsible for long-term strategic planning for Pentagram as a whole and for finding solutions to internal conflicts. Like the others, the steering committee has one elected member from each of the three offices, and they elect a chairman for that group.

Although the structure appears to be complicated, it provides a necessary balance of involvement in leading the firm and yet ensures that the specialized jobs are done by the right person. The transition has not been simple. With changes, one is bound to make mistakes; things have fallen between the cracks, and we have had to arrive at new definitions of responsibility. Even though the policy committee—the full partnership—has ultimate power and can change or decide anything, it is very difficult to keep each partner at the same level of understanding of complicated legal and financial issues. Therefore it is perceived, and may be in reality, that the executive committee members have more power than the other partners.

It is an understatement to say that most designers are not naturally good managers and there is a necessary learning curve. Designers must learn to be managers and to take executive responsibility, or their company policy will be set by administrators.

Personalities

The next big issue is personalities: who we will choose to elect as Pentagram partners and how they fit with and use the organization. Seventeen people cannot be the same or even truly equal, however, there are four criteria that are important in my view.

1. A partner must be able to generate business. Other partners do not want to become salesmen. Help is available on a collaborative basis, and the advantages include an expanded depth of work to draw from, the knowledge and expertise of other partners, and shared central support, but there should be no doubt as to where the ultimate responsibility lies.

2. A partner must have a national reputation as an outstanding professional in the chosen discipline. This is a subjective decision, but the partners have a sense of their standing in the field and the quality of work with which they wish to be associated. It is too easy to "water the wine."

3. A partner must be able to control projects and contribute to the profits of the firm. There is considerable generosity about difference of earning because of different contributions in other areas. However, one cannot share income with a person who does not have similar potential and, probably more important, a similar attitude towards desired income. Nor can one share with a person who cannot manage a project or a team.

4. The last, and certainly not the least, is that a partner must be a proactive member of the group and care about Pentagram and the partners. We spend our working lives together; we should like each other.

It sometimes helps to mix metaphors to make a point: I often say that this is not a shopping list; it is necessary to fire on all four cylinders. As stated by the venture capitalist, you need A people.

Our traditional source for new partners remains successful independent designers with small practices. However, we have established a precedent of developing new partners through an associate program. This additional route provides training in a way that is not

available elsewhere and may suit the needs of a larger organization. Maybe Pentagram will also need partners in disciplines other than design. I do not know the answers, but I do know there will be change.

Critical Mass

The last factor which I believe helps an organization survive is a critical mass. We have grown to a count of seventeen partners with more than twenty years' history. There comes a point when a sufficiency has been invested in building an international reputation, developing management skills, and a fund of case histories so that the organization has a value beyond the individuals. Growth will enable Pentagram to reinforce its traditional way of doing business: maintaining the balance between commercial and cultural and our aspiration to be the "thinking designers."

A larger firm has greater prominence in a crowded marketplace of hundreds of small design firms. This is evident when projects are on a national or international scale. For example, even a design enthusiast in Japan probably only knows of the six largest or most prominent western firms. A firm the size of Pentagram also has the resources to support a sophisticated and varied communication and publication program. The collective financial resources of a large group make it possible to invest in better facilities and resources or enter into new ventures.

These are the same reasons that bring the international service firms like McKinsey & Co. or Price Waterhouse. I believe that Pentagram's new structure will provide an opportunity for us to adapt to our larger size. Ultimately, if Pentagram is to fulfill its potential, there is a need for the members of the group to have a vision of what the organization should be — not only within the design industry, but also in the larger international business community.

Napoleon was once asked to comment on what quality he most valued in his generals. "I want them to be lucky," he said. There are changes to be made, risks to be taken, and conflicts to be resolved, and Pentagram needs to be lucky.

Principles of Managing the Corporate Design Department

by Peter L. Phillips

"Why don't I get any respect?" This is not only a phrase made famous by comedian Rodney Dangerfield, but also the common lament of thousands of managers of corporate design departments worldwide. "Why doesn't management value what I can offer?" "Why is the design function considered a service group rather than a team member?" "Why are there very few vice president's of design?" "Why is my budget always the first to get cut?" These are routine questions I am asked as I meet with design managers at my client companies.

Design managers spend a lot of time lamenting their lowly position on the corporate totem pole. Frankly, they also wish they could get paid more for what they do. After all, they understand how important design is to the success of the enterprise. The problem is they don't work hard enough to make others understand how important the design function really is.

Design managers have to stop saying, "ain't it awful," and work at repositioning themselves in the corporate hierarchy. They need to demonstrate that they understand the business of *business.* They need to demonstrate that they know how to contribute to operating the business. They need to learn how to ask probing business questions and then how to solve the business problem with design thinking. They must learn how to talk about design, without talking about "design."

The worldwide market for graphic design services is upwards of $34 billion, according to James Woudhuysen, associate director at the Henley Centre for Forecasting in London and professor of design management at De Montfort University, Leicester, England. Woudhuysen suggests that design managers become more proactive in this large and growing international marketplace. The interesting thing is that the expenditures for design are probably the least understood in boardrooms worldwide. I would suggest that senior manage-

ment has little awareness of how much it all costs. It gets buried in other budgets. Design managers must make management aware that they are dealing with enormous budgets that could have incredible pay backs if managed properly. The design manager must position himself as an asset manager.

Woudhuysen's statistics place the design market fourth on the list of marketing services expenditures, after sales promotion, media advertising, and direct mail, and ahead of ten other categories including public relations, market research, and audiovisual communications.

Woudhuysen argues that "It is a marketplace which, in my view, will grow in the future, given the continued importance of graphic design to the maintenance of product, service, and especially corporate brands. The need, as never before, is to 'think big' in graphics and to recognize the political and cultural influence which the graphic design profession can bring to bear. The need is thus to get serious and to get real in design; to seek genuine and universal benefits by its application."

What's Wrong with this Picture?

In order to illustrate some of the most common problems faced by design managers, let me describe three situations which I have encountered in the past few years.

Vignette #1

Harry is the head of design for a major manufacturer of low-cost consumer products. Although the company's headquarters is in Asia, their single largest market is in the United States. The company built an enormous share of the market by focusing on the low-end. Their products were among the least expensive in their categories. They also sold heavily through mass-market discounters. Although the products were inexpensive, they did function in a satisfactory manner.

But the world changed. Due to increases in manufacturing and selling costs it was no longer profitable for the company to produce products at their traditional low price to the consumer. The dilemma management faced involved changing consumer perception to assure the new higher prices at retail would be accepted.

Senior management held countless high-level meetings to try to develop a strategy for effectively repositioning the company in the marketplace. They hired a well-known management consulting firm to help them write the plan.

Harry, the intrepid head of design, was aware of the dilemma and the high-level meetings, but he was not a participant. He anxiously awaited the results so he could determine how the new positioning would affect his design organization.

What would you advise Harry to do?

Vignette #2

A major, global, high-tech company, in the race to keep competitive and still be a market leader, acquired a smaller company to create a new division and offer some innovative new products. As part of the purchase agreement, the smaller company's founder and president was made president of the new division and promised a great deal of autonomy in running the division. He was a brilliant engineer and manager and knew that he had only one year to show a profit or be replaced.

The new division head went to a former college classmate of his who ran a small design firm and commissioned him to develop a division logo, product logos, packaging, and communications collateral material. The design manager of the parent corporation did not find out this work was going on until after it had been completed. The new division's materials bore absolutely no relationship to the parent corporation's house style and, frankly, were outstanding examples of mediocre design.

The corporate design manager had a meeting with his boss and complained that the new division's material was not acceptable and that his group should have been involved from the beginning. The design manager's boss patiently explained that the new division president had to move quickly, was promised autonomy, and had no time or budget to go back and do the work over again. He suggested that the design manager just let the whole thing drop.

What went wrong?

Vignette #3

Clarence is the design manager for a U.S. based company that has been expanding into the international marketplace over the past five years. Nearly all of the company's design work was done by Clarence's corporate design group, made up entirely of American designers. About the only design work not under the corporate group's control was the look and feel of the advertising, which was handled by a New York ad agency.

Company sales and marketing people, based in Europe and Asia, were expected to implement all design work created in the corporate headquarters without question. There

were no trained designers on staff in the countries and the U.S. ad agency's work was the only advertising they could run. From time to time, when sales and market share did not grow as planned in the countries, high-level meetings were held with the country managers. They often pointed to both the advertising as well as the design of packaging and sales collateral materials as being inappropriate for their countries. Management looked at this as a weak excuse at best, but agreed to invite Clarence in to hear their complaints and other issues regarding design. They also invited the account manager from the advertising agency to attend. Both Clarence and the advertising agency were convinced their design work was excellent, strong, and compelling. Management agreed that there was probably nothing wrong with the design work and so were supportive of both Clarence and the agency.

As the day of the meeting approaches, how would you prepare yourself if you were Clarence? How would you handle this situation?

These three vignettes illustrate the most common mistakes corporate design managers make in the design function; recognizing the role of design in the business, establishing and maintaining mutually valuable relationships, and implementing efficient work with processes.

As a first, proactive step in repositioning your corporate design function, consider the model outlined on the next page.

The Value You Offer

Let's start with you—the design manager. All managers of corporate functions need to periodically do a self-assessment. Make a list of your strengths and your weaknesses as they relate to your ability to manage the resources of people, money, time, and materials to accomplish the primary mission of your company. Rate yourself on your skills in planning, organizing, coordinating, and communicating. How are you at establishing job objectives, motivating people, and making and communicating decisions?

If you have been objective, and honest, you will have a clear picture of the areas in which you might improve. If you sincerely want to reposition the design function, first you have to understand how you and the function you manage are perceived today.

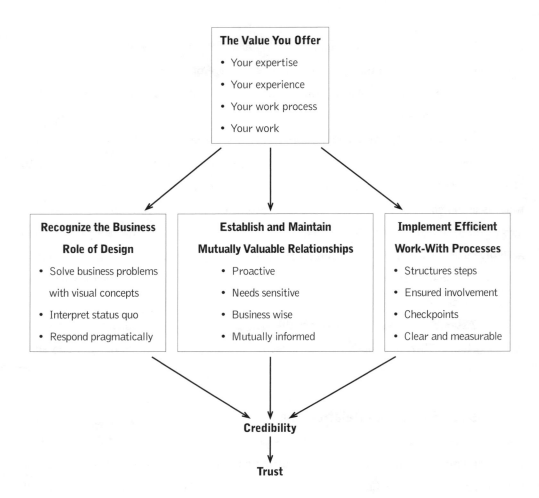

The Value You Offer

- Your expertise
- Your experience
- Your work process
- Your work

Recognize the Business Role of Design

- Solve business problems with visual concepts
- Interpret status quo
- Respond pragmatically

Establish and Maintain Mutually Valuable Relationships

- Proactive
- Needs sensitive
- Business wise
- Mutually informed

Implement Efficient Work-With Processes

- Structures steps
- Ensured involvement
- Checkpoints
- Clear and measurable

Credibility

Trust

Recognize the Business Role of Design

When I was managing corporate design departments earlier in my career, the first thing I would do is change the name of the group. Invariably, the department had been traditionally known as the Art Department. I believe art and design are two different things. I think of art as the free expression of an artist. Design is a problem solving discipline, not free expression. The term "art department" conjures up a group of nice enough people who draw well. Corporate design group has a more professional, business-like aura. As I used to tell my colleagues, artists create beautiful pieces of art, but you need a designer to tell you where to hang it! The point is to focus on problem solving, not aesthetics. Vice president's of sales, marketing, manufacturing, or any function are not kept awake at night worrying about which typeface is best for their printed material or the colors, imagery, layout, etc. They are

worried about making deadlines, manufacturing and moving product out the door, making their budgets, and keeping their jobs. Become very aware of the business needs of the company you work for, and then step forward with solutions that involve the considerable skills of your design function.

In vignette # 1, Harry, being aware of the crises, should have developed a plan that: (a) demonstrated that he understood the problem, (b) offered options to control costs by altering the design and production of product graphics and collateral materials, (c) explained that his group could effectively translate the new positioning strategy, whatever it might be, into a compelling visual manifestation of that identity. In doing all of this, Harry should not actually show design work or use too much technical jargon in talking about cost containment. The strategy is to not be the "art guy." The strategy is to be a valued partner in solving business problems.

Assemble your key staff. Identify the most critical business problems your company is facing today. Then develop a plan to present to management that shows you can solve business problems with design.

Establish and Maintain Relationships

Take a hard look at your company's organization chart. Identify the most critical people and make an effort to get to know them. Visit other departments. Learn as much as you can about their operations, their worries, and their methods. All of this knowledge will be of enormous help as you move forward. You will also begin to be recognized by your peers. When you visit other departments resist the temptation to talk about your group. Listen to them as they tell you about their function.

Read everything written about your company. Know your company as well as the CEO knows the company. After you visit other departments, develop a profile of each group and make an assessment of how the design function could help them, and then offer that help.

In vignette #2, the corporate design manager did not take the time to get to know the new division president. He neglected to see that the man had a short time frame to prove himself and keep his job. He didn't make any effort to understand the perceived needs for design of this new division. As a result of all this, the company not only ended up with mediocre design from one division, but the design manager also lost credibility as a valuable contributor to the corporation.

Implement Efficient Work-With Processes

Establish some cross-functional work groups. By involving key stakeholders in the work of the design function, you become partners and allies. These groups do not design or get involved in design direction, but rather give you valuable input concerning business problems they are facing. Cultivate support from the highest possible management level. This will help you open doors to a variety of other senior managers. Establish, and publish, a strategic objective for the design function that maps to the corporate mission statement. Use the company newspaper or bulletin boards to inform the enterprise of your various activities. Above all, be a valued contributor, not an obstacle.

In vignette #3, Clarence clearly had not implemented any work-with processes with non-U.S. operations of the company. He was satisfied with his group's work in the United States and failed to recognize potential cultural or national issues in other parts of the world. Instead of being called to defend his work, Clarence should have taken the time to contact the country managers and ask for their input early on.

The most common mistake design managers make is to become too focused on design rather than how design can support the corporation and add to the bottom line. Design managers must position themselves, and their departments, as business partners. They must talk about design as an asset of the corporation. An asset that they manage. Perceived as a well-managed corporate asset, the design function gains credibility and trust throughout the organization.

Departmental Management Is Also Critical

So far, I have been talking about positioning the design function within the larger organization. But management of the function itself is equally critical. Once you have made a promise, you must be prepared to deliver on that promise. In general (there are notable exceptions) the most talented and creative designers working in a corporate environment today have had little business training or experience. The leading design schools seem to never include in their curriculum any management or business education. As a result, designers tend to not think about bottom lines, production efficiencies, return on investment, and marketing. It is the design manager's responsibility to impress upon his or her staff the importance of learning more about business and design's role in helping that business be profitable. The best design managers I know spend a considerable amount of time researching and identifying appropriate professional development programs for their staff. They lobby to be sure

their staff are included in key business meetings concerning the design projects they will be working on. The design manager must also take the time to discuss each project at length with each designer prior to work beginning on the project, and help the designer understand the business objective and the business constraints. Returning to the vignettes, the staff designers also need to understand the business crises the corporation is facing, the need to be proactive in recognizing emerging business problems, and the needs of various cultural and regional operations. A design solution that works brilliantly in the United States might be a disaster in Asia or Europe.

Many design departments are woefully understaffed relative to the number of projects the group is expected to execute in any given year. This condition leads to well-meaning design managers who try to take the burden of going to endless meetings away from designers. This can be a fatal error. If a designer is to solve the business problem through design, then the designer has to understand the problem in great depth. The designer also needs to focus on developing critical work-with skills. Especially important is to help the designer learn how to tactfully keep his or her internal client out of the aesthetic aspects of design. Design by committee never works, but nearly all internal corporate clients I have ever met cannot resist the temptation to make comments like, "what if we made the logo bigger, put it in the bottom center and change the color!" Designers must be trained to keep the discussions focused. The design manager must help by making it clear that designer-client meetings are not group meetings to design the artifacts. The internal client has the business need, the designer has the skill to use design principles effectively to meet the need.

One technique I have found successful is to agree to a simple norm at the outset of meetings with internal clients; no one present can use the phrases "I like" or "I don't like." I might like brown and you like blue, but the point is that neither of our personal preferences has anything to do with the business problem or need. Rather, each person must argue with points that can be substantiated, such as "Brown will work best to solve the business problem because . . . ," or, "Blue will not work as well as brown because. . . ." Once you get people away from their personal likes and dislikes and focused on the merits of various design elements in addressing the real business problem, you have a much better chance of being successful and of being recognized as a credible and respected partner.

Following all of the corporate downsizing of the past decade, design managers have been increasingly forced to utilize independent, external design resources. The principles of working with these agencies are the same. Agencies must be selected not only on their cre-

dentials as producers of good design, but also for their ability to interact with internal corporate clients as business problem-solving partners.

Unlike accounting, law, purchasing, or many other corporate functions, design is viewed as subjective. The design function must counter this view with hard, objective, factual arguments. Design functions and design managers will not earn the respect they are looking for or be truly valued in the corporate environment if they continue to ignore the real role they should be playing in the business. Their contribution will ultimately be measured on their success at helping the business to grow and prosper, not on the number of awards they win for beautiful design.

CHAPTER 14

Large Project
Management

by Eva Doman Bruck

The greatest challenge in producing a complicated and long-term assignment is finding ways to manage it so that there is enough time left to design it. Considering the overall span of time for the project, the potential need for more people, equipment, and outside resources, as well as systems for tracking and reporting information, materials, and costs that such projects generate, it is a formidable challenge.

Michael Bierut, a principal in Pentagram's New York office, says, "A large project is basically a series of interrelated small projects. The end users don't relate to the epic sweep and grandeur of the effort; they usually only see a few items at a time." Deborah Sussman of Sussman/Preja in Los Angeles suggests, "You need to have the 'gut' for large projects. There are so many people who have an impact on what you do. In our environmental projects, there are usually architects, engineers, landscape architects, interior and lighting designers, fabricators, builders, and, of course, the client, which may include the state, city, local, private sectors, and all the layers of people in each."

Proposals, Progress Reports, and Minutes

However, before you need to worry about how to administer a large project, you will be required to prove that you are capable of doing so to the prospective client. Large projects imply large budgets, lots of people, many meetings and presentations, a complex process of production, fabrication, and installation, and serious record keeping requirements.

In addition to the description of deliverables, working methodology, and conceptual framework that are usually included in any proposal, a large-scale project document should outline information concerning numbers and types of personnel that will be dedicated to the project, including designers, production artists, writers, project/client managers, fabrication

specialists, and so on. It's always reassuring to include related project experience, especially if of similar scope or scale. Outside resources such as researchers, photographers, illustrators, and other design and nondesign specialists that will be brought in to work on the project should be named, and, if possible, include brief professional descriptions for each of them.

Schedules and timetables for individual project tasks, presentations, targeted completion dates, and project billings need to be identified. Knowing that no one reads long-winded proposals, charts, and graphs can be very effective in illustrating this kind of information.

While it is not necessary to list equipment and resource allocation in a proposal, you will want to have the appropriate computers, printers, scanners, software, and other necessary tools dedicated to the project.

Proposals usually do not include a description of the project documentation you plan to provide, but such information is essential to a well-run assignment. The purpose of providing the client with regular updates is not to make you a slave to paperwork; it is actually an effective way to communicate to your client matters which are irksome and obstructing the project's progress, but which you may be reluctant to voice—particularly if your client contact is the source of the difficulties.

Progress reports are also a good place to identify items due from the client, such as add-ons, extensive changes, and delays. A clear, concise, and regularly disseminated status report is easy to produce using a word processing program. Column headings may be as simple as "Item," "Status," "Next Steps," "Due Date," "Who." Everyone associated with the project, including your contact's supervisor should be sent a copy. Naturally, confidential information should be treated carefully and disseminated discreetly.

Large projects tend to be sponsored by government agencies or institutions, and their record keeping (and showing) requirements are usually intensely demanding. Depending upon how the deal is structured—flat fee or on a cost/use basis with a cap (i.e., not to exceed . . .) the budget report usually includes line-by-line listings of personnel, materials, services, etc., as well as columns showing amounts for "Budget," "Actuals," and "Variance." Even if line itemization is not routinely required, always be prepared to have your books examined. Keep time sheets, job sheets, and accurate backup for vendors and all outside resources.

Meeting minutes are an additional form of project reporting and, while it may seem an added burden, it is often useful to have the chance to interpret events from your point of

view. If there is ever a serious misunderstanding during the course of a project, thorough documentation may be your best protection.

Sussman recounts, "We try to be as organized as possible, but projects can be so unpredictable . . . we do block out and schedule at least three months ahead to get a sense of how things may unfold. Ironically, we often find that we produce design faster than clients are prepared to respond." She continues, "We have weekly meetings with our five associates to go over operations and managerial issues, and then talk about key events and problems of current projects. While we don't usually write meeting minutes, we do always try to issue work change orders for significant items."

Leslie Smolan of Carbone Smolan in New York City says, "Meeting minutes and progress reports are found to be useful when the client is missing deadlines. Sometimes we are pushing them as hard as they are pushing us. There are financial consequences for us as well as the client if turnaround is not quick enough. We do issue change orders, with or without numbers, when additional work is requested. Also, we put things in writing because we know that no one remembers details after the fact."

Day-to-Day Management

Once you have spent the time and effort preparing the project proposal, you will begin to have a sense of just how big this bread box is going to be. Now is the perfect time to figure out how you are going to get your arms around it. Perhaps the most crucial decision to make at the onset is who will be selected to manage the day-to-day aspects of the project.

If you are a principal with marketing, creative, and client responsibilities for other projects as well as this one, a project manager will become necessary for you to continue to run your firm and oversee a variety of projects. Some design offices place project management responsibilities on the project's chief designer, usually a senior level designer who reports directly to a principal. Besides cost savings, there are significant advantages to this arrangement. It provides the client with a central design and management contact, it places comprehensive responsibility (design, schedule, budget) on one person, and it is also a way of identifying candidates for the firm's future management. Be sure to provide administrative assistance for scheduling appointments, meetings, cost tracking, word processing, and so on, so your chief designer doesn't get bogged down with minutiae and unable to fulfill design responsibilities.

There are some disadvantages to combining the design and project manager roles. Great designers are not always great administrators. A senior level designer may be able to handle several projects if not too thinly spread because of time-consuming administrative tasks. It may be cheaper to hire a project manager than to have a top level designer fulfill the role. That is not to say, however, that the senior designer of a project should be relieved of all administrative responsibilities. There needs to be strong communication between the project designer and the project manager. Since designers are usually most privy to the intricacies of the design process, they must be accountable for information that is to be transmitted to the project administrator.

"While I oversee entire projects," says Smolan, "a selected design director has the day-to-day responsibilities for the assignment. There is a level of discussion about design where, with a nondesign manager, something gets lost in the translation." She adds, "If necessary, we prefer to bring a junior level designer into the role of project manager, which we call production coordinator. . . who can also spec and set type, proofread, and manage production traffic. We are wary of keeping on a single skilled person because of the inevitable downtime which is endemic to most long-term projects."

Formerly of Lewin/Holland and currently creative vice president of a large cosmetics company, Cheryl Lewin recalls, "When I had my own studio, I had always been the manager and designer on all of my projects. Clients tended to come to me for design services and I always made sure to make the project management side invisible. Unfortunately, doing that much by yourself can become all consuming. Now, I am more involved with managing the process, organizing people and resources, and communications between departments. While I am no longer on the boards, I see my work being applied to a larger arena in a much bigger business. I find it very satisfying."

At Sussman/Preja, "We have five associates—all with design backgrounds who, with a design director, both design and manage projects. It is necessary to have a team with the skills and experience to design projects, but you also have to provide the necessary administrative staff to help manage them."

When affordable and appropriate, a professional project manager or coordinator can be a tremendous asset to a large project. They can relieve design professionals of most administrative chores, thereby allowing the greatest efficiencies of skills to tasks. Scheduling, tracking vendors, cost accounting, correspondence, status reports, and all other project communications are the responsibility of the project manager.

An experienced manager may even be able to locate and screen freelancers, vendors, and other outside resources. The manager should be able to do most of his or her own writing. With the right technical information, the manager should be able to build and maintain spreadsheets for cost accounting and scheduling and communicate effectively with the design team and the client's team. A project administrator must have good judgment, self-motivation, and organizational skills. He or she also needs to be endorsed with enough authority to gather information and carry out decisions.

Quirks and Tips

"We find that we have to resell the project over and over during the course of the assignment. It seems to become our periodic role to convince the client to move forward," notes Leslie Smolan.

Keep clear lines of communication on both sides. Sometimes there are bottleneck people — those who seem incapable of moving projects forward; work around them. It helps to understand the political processes at work, all the players, and their roles in obtaining approvals. The bigger the project, the less it is about design, and the more it is about moving through an organizational and political process.

Break down the project step-by-step and component-by-component. Analyze it in small pieces for personnel requirements, equipment, scheduling, and other items. Consider a customized accounting software package that links project scheduling, labor allocation, and cost tracking via network. This should help minimize additional bookkeeping.

Michael Bierut's observation cuts to the essentials and final conclusion of this topic, "I had always been involved in large projects, so I never thought they had any particular mystical qualities. At Pentagram, we manage a book cover about the same as a large project. In both instances, depending on the clients' behavior, intelligence, and commitment to the work, they can either make a project a dream or a nightmare. It is really a joy when someone with sufficient authority has decided to trust the designer and is capable of accepting some elements of unpredictability — and I'm not talking about novelty — but in those thoughts that might make the design memorable or breakthrough."

CHAPTER 15

Audits and the Design Firm

By Aubrey Balkind

Audits are taxing; the laws are complex, each tax auditor has a different interpretation, they take lots of time, and are emotionally stressful. No matter how hard you try to implement constructive policies, each audit often results in some financial exposure.

Before I get to the audits, you need to understand my perspective. I am the CEO of Frankfurt Balkind, a hundred and fifty person multidisciplinary strategic communications agency. We design traditional print projects where the deliverable is a physical product like an annual report or an identity program; we undertake strategic consulting projects where the only product is a report similar to those created by a "McKinsey"; as an advertising agency, we create broadcast, print, and radio campaigns; we build Web sites with sophisticated backend technology like software companies; and we function as a publisher or an entertainment production company when we develop content properties. Each of these business categories has its own industry idiosyncrasies with differing tax regulations that also may vary by state. When you combine these businesses under the umbrella of one company, which many of you do, the complexity increases. And, please, remember that my perspective is not as a lawyer but as a creative/business person. Do not rely on my interpretation of the laws which are dependent on precise factual circumstances. You must get a professional opinion from your own lawyers and accountants.

There are two audit categories that give the communications industry the most difficulty: sales taxes and employment taxes.

Sales Taxes

Sales tax laws are complex, ill defined, and can vary from state to state. They are imposed by the city and state and have two main components: sales tax on revenues and use

tax on certain purchases. While a project may be exempt from sales tax, some of its purchases may not be exempt from use tax. And paying one doesn't always preclude also having to pay the other (see the example product models below).

In making sense of sales tax laws, I find it helpful to categorize different types of projects or businesses into four models: (1) professional; (2) advertising; (3) product; and (4) software. This enables you to implement a clear and comprehensive tax policy that is appropriate for each specific job.

1. The Professional Model

Designers like to think of themselves as professionals, and their tendency is often to run their businesses much like architects, accountants, consultants, or lawyers. In order for you not to charge your client sales taxes on your fees, you must disassociate your services from any physical product (e.g., the printed piece or even the mechanical). This could be a risky model to follow because of the close tie between service and physical product, and because of ownership. Accountants and lawyers don't have a physical product, and architects seldom pay for the construction of a building, making it more appropriate for them to follow this model. One way might be to keep ownership of the mechanicals and transfer to the client only the right to reproduce, print, from the mechanicals. This position is dependent on the ownership rights negotiated between the client and the designer. In some cases, and with increasing frequency (another business problem), clients are specifying contracts that are ''work for hire'' which makes using this model difficult.

2. The Advertising Model

Most advertising agencies treat sales taxes in a way that is similar to the professional model by maintaining a principal-agent relationship. To establish a principal-agent relationship, you must: (1) have a clause in your client contract stating agent status; (2) disclose the name of the client to the supplier; and (3) bill the client the same amount paid to the supplier with any commissions or markups broken out on a separate line. Agencies do not charge clients sales tax on creative fees incurred in the creation of advertising or markups on purchases. They are often compensated not on time spent, but on media commission. With expenses, they pay sales taxes to their suppliers, thereby, eliminating the need to charge their clients a sales tax on the reimbursed revenue. Because the advertising industry is well-

organized and powerful, it has lobbied and succeeded in having special sales tax laws passed. So, be familiar with these laws.

This model does not automatically apply to their nonmedia advertising services or what is commonly referred to as "below the line," such as the design of collateral brochures, videos, etc. For these services you may need to pay taxes much like in the product model.

3. The Product Model

Design firms often fall into this model because they have difficulty separating their services from a physical product. When you act as an independent buyer and seller of goods and services and deliver a physical product, the agency has a vendor-vendee relationship. Sales tax is due on the total client invoice and fees and expenses, excluding minor reimbursable expenses such as telephone calls and travel, which you generally don't mark up and where you pay your suppliers' sales tax.

In most states, you can issue your suppliers a resale certificate so they need not charge you sales taxes. However, you must be careful not to use your resale certificate for the purchase of equipment (including computers and software), furniture, and consumables, such as paper and supplies, or nonbillable purchases. Also, there is a tricky definition of consumed. For example, some tax auditors have maintained that reragging type bought from a supplier or retouching a photograph is consuming that item and, therefore, does not fall under a resale definition. This situation makes it necessary to pay your supplier sales tax and then charge sales tax again to the client.

4. The Software Model

Web site development is a large and growing industry, and sales tax issues are not yet fully resolved. This area is unique because, although you are producing a product, personal property might not be transferred. Some states are considering Web sites nontaxable, provided they are transferred to the client electronically and not delivered on a disk. Since this is still a new and evolving area, interpretation can change so tread carefully. Also, what does this interpretation mean for print mechanicals that are transferred to a client or printer over a modem and not on a disk? Confusing? Yes.

Exemptions

There are times when you need not charge your client sales tax. The most common is when the product you created will be delivered and consumed out-of-state and you do not have a branch office in that state. This is not as simple as it seems. For example, you design an annual report for an in-state client and also buy the printing. Then, sales tax on the total invoice is calculated only on the proportion of books remaining in your state after distribution to shareholders and other offices. If, however, you do not buy the printing, then sales tax might be due on all your services and expenses.

There are also other situations when your client is exempt from sales taxes, such as being not-for-profit. In these cases make sure your client issues you a tax exempt certificate.

Employment Taxes

Today, the most common employment audit relates to freelancers, independent contractor versus employee. The government, federal, state, and city, is concerned about the withholding of taxes, benefits, and unemployment insurance. They define freelancers not by how long or how permanent they are, but by whether you have control of where, when, and how they work. We employed what we thought was a freelancer for a two week project. Because she worked on our premises and we controlled when and how (supervised) she worked, the government claimed she was on staff, making us liable for her taxes, entitling her to benefits, including unemployment. They also then expanded their audit to include all of our freelancers.

As an additional protection, your freelancers should not be employees under the "where, when, and how" categories. They should sign an independent contractor agreement reviewed by your attorney and accountant. Your protection is enhanced if they are a corporation, and if they simultaneously work for you and others.

Audits

When an audit begins you probably have to decide whether you want an audit of the entire period or just a sample of a few weeks or, if your books are computerized, a statistical sample. Generally, you should accept a test period as it is much less onerous on your time (cost) and theirs. The more time they spend, the harder they look to find revenue to justify their time. However, be aware that if the period scheduled is, say, three weeks out of a thirty-six-week period, then any mistake you may have made during that period is magnified twelve times even though the mistake may only have happened once. Also, when they assess you for

unpaid taxes they also add interest to those payments and can impose penalties. Thus mistakes or misinterpretations can escalate into large numbers.

When you are finally assessed, while you might not agree with the assessment, you need to decide whether it's worthwhile to fight it. If the amount is close to your costs of fighting, including time, accounting, and legal fees, and the aggravation, then you might decide to pay, though you believe it's not due. This is called a nuisance cost.

Remember, auditors are people; the outcome of an audit is dependent not only on their interpretation of how you adhered to the law, but also on how easy you are to work with and the completeness of your records. My advice is to be represented at the audit by your accountant, err on the safe side in interpreting laws, and maintain clear policies and complete records so you can spend time creating without worrying that someday an assessment could hurt you or put you out of business. And, of course, good luck!

CHAPTER 16

Valuing the Graphic
Design Firm

By Ed Morris

At some point an owner will probably have to determine a value for his or her business. Valuations may be compelled by a variety of reasons, among which are:

- Sale or purchase of all or a partial interest of the firm
- Divorce
- Gift, estate, and inheritance taxes
- Obtaining financing
- Determining damages for breach of contract or business interruption

Although value seems like a fairly simple term, its determination can be complex due to the factors to be considered and the various methodologies that can be employed.

Definition of Value

"Value," or more precisely, "fair market value" is generally defined as the price at which property would change hands between willing parties (buyer and seller), neither being under any compulsion to trade, and both having reasonable knowledge of the relevant facts. Such value is always determined as of a specific date and is based on all pertinent facts and conditions which were either known or reasonably anticipated on that date. This definition is commonly used by the IRS and the courts. It assumes a hypothetical arm's-length sale.

The determination of fair market value should take into account such factors as:

- The history and nature of the firm. The history will show past stability (or lack thereof), diversity, product development, investment in plant facilities, and other considerations.
- The prior earnings record of the practice

- The financial condition of the practice
- The fair market values of similar practices, if known
- Economic outlook, in general, and the condition and outlook of the specific industry
- The value to the practice of goodwill or other intangible assets

The departure of the present owner could have a severe impact on the value of a firm. Given such an eventuality, some dispersion of clientele might occur, and the valuation may have to be modified accordingly. The buyer of a firm may wish to have a covenant not to compete put in place if the present owner will not be staying with the firm after the purchase.

Valuation Methodologies

Various methods of calculating value may be employed depending upon the specific circumstances and the purpose for which a valuation is required. Some of the more prominent methods are as follows:

Discounted Future Earnings

This approach may be used if future earnings can be reasonably estimated and are expected to differ significantly from current operations because of factors such as changes in business structure, or changes in economic conditions (e.g., the firm will be developing a Web page for a large new client). To apply this approach, earnings, as preliminarily determined by averaging prior year data, are projected over a certain period and discounted to present value using an appropriate interest rate. The discount rate represents a hypothetical rate of return that an investor would require given the risk involved. Benchmark rates such as the U.S. Treasury obligation yield (minimal risk) or junk bond yields (higher degree of risk) might be used to establish an appropriate discount rate. (The application of a higher discount rate [higher risk] produces a lower present value and the converse in lower risk situations.)

Capitalized Returns Approach

This approach may be used if future earnings are not expected to change significantly from current operations, or where future earnings are expected to grow at a predictable rate. To apply this approach, current earnings are divided by a capitalization rate to estimate value. The capitalization rate is derived from the discount rate, as follows:

Discount Rate – *Expected Growth Rate* = Capitalization Rate.

Determining a growth rate generally requires a great deal of judgment. The rate should be based on such factors as the firm's past performance and projected future operations. Expected average growth rates should be used as opposed to just selecting the next year's rate.

Comparative Data

Purchases of comparable businesses can be used to approximate the value of the subject business. For example, the purchase price for a design firm may be based on the most current year's gross annual revenues, or based on average revenues over several years. Contacts with other business owners are useful to develop transaction information and rules of thumb.

Value of Underlying Assets

In many industries the value of a business's underlying assets is regarded as a highly critical factor. Under a net asset value method, assets and liabilities are adjusted to their appraised values under the assumption that the firm's value will be realized as part of a going concern. Under a liquidation value method, the hypothetical proceeds from the sale of assets and payment of liabilities are discounted to present value under the assumption that the value will be realized through either a forced or orderly liquidation of assets, instead of as a going concern.

Discretionary Cash Flow

This method is commonly used to value small, owner-managed businesses. In particular, it is useful for businesses where the salary and perks of the owner represent a significant portion of the benefits generated by the business. In these situations, owners think of earnings in terms of the net to the owner or to the family rather than after-tax or pre-tax earnings. Discretionary cash flow is defined as earnings plus owner's compensation and benefits (e.g., owner's life insurance, pension, medical benefits, value of company provided apartments and cars, etc.), interest expense, and noncash expenses, less the amount of anticipated capital expenditures. The value of the practice is determined by multiplying the discretionary cash flow by an industry accepted multiple.

Federal, state, and local income taxes should be factored into the analysis. Valuations involving practices conducted as nontaxable "S"corporations or limited liability companies give consideration to tax effects by using the top individual tax rates, currently 39.6 percent for federal purposes. Variations on this method may be appropriate given the unique circumstances of the buyer or seller.

The information in this article, presented in general terms, may not apply in all situations and should not be acted upon without specific professional advice.

Insurance Basics for
the Designer

by Ray and Scott Taylor

This article discusses the types of insurance coverage that graphic designers should know about. Purchasing insurance is similar in theory to purchasing a car. When you set out to purchase a car, you start with a basic, stripped-down model. Then you may add options, such as air conditioning, power windows, and automatic transmission. These added options improve the quality of the car you buy. Insurance is similar in that you start with a basic policy that excludes many types of losses. As with a car, you can add coverage by purchasing different types of endorsements, or options, and thereby improve the policy that you end up purchasing.

Business Owners Policies

The list below highlights the benefits offered by various business owners policies:

- Office Contents pays for the replacement cost of office contents lost due to fire, theft, water damage, smoke, lightning, hail, mischief, or an automobile or aircraft crashing into your building.
- Business Interruption covers the actual loss sustained for up to twelve months as a result of direct damage to the premises listed in your policy by a type of loss listed above. Payment is given for continuing overhead expenses during the period of business interruption.
- Valuable Papers covers the cost to restore the design work to the state it was in just prior to loss by fire, theft, or water damage. It is designed to cover a current job, and you must reproduce the job in order to collect. Coverage is usually limited to your office location.
- Electronic Data Processing protects your hardware and software in the event

the equipment is damaged by fire, theft, or water. Coverage can be expanded to include any extra expenses needed to recreate the lost data in the event of a covered peril. Coverage is usually limited to your office location.

- Bailee protects property damage to other people's property in your care, custody, or control. There is usually a sublimit for jewelry, furs, fine arts, antiques, and no coverage for breakage, scratching, and marring.

- Portfolio covers the cost of duplicating twenty-five images at a cost not to exceed $100 each in the event your portfolio is destroyed, lost, or stolen. The coverage is worldwide. Please note, this does not cover stock photographs.

- Commercial General Liability protects your legal liability against lawsuits for bodily injuries or property damages that occur within the United States and Canada to other people or other people's property. Important exclusions are listed below. (Rest assured the actual policy contains many more exclusions):

  - Damage to those people considered to be employees covered under your workers' compensation

  - Damage to those people eligible for disability benefits under a state statute

  - Damage to anything pertaining to an automobile, watercraft, or aircraft

  - Damage to other people's property in your care, custody, or control

  - Claims resulting from an improper model's release, invasion of privacy, infringement of copyright or trademark, infringement of patent, or libel or slander

  - Claims occurring outside the United States or Canada

  - Any damage pertaining to pollution

  - Any intentional act or criminal act

  - Discrimination or sexual harassment

  - Claims by someone other than an employee to recover damages paid to or sought from a former or existing employee

- Nonowned and Hired Automobile Liability protects the employer for bodily injury or property damage claims that arise from use of a hired, borrowed, or rented automobile. This coverage will respond only after the policy insuring the vehicle involved in the accident has paid its limit. There is no coverage for damage to the vehicle being driven, for the graphic artist to whom the vehicle belongs, or for damage to property belonging to the graphic artist. Coverage is limited to the United States, its possessions, and Canada.

Workers' Compensation and Statutory Disability Benefits

There are other insurance options that should be purchased in addition to the business owners policy or its equivalent. They are: workers' compensation and employers liability insurance, and statutory disability benefits in the states of New York, New Jersey, Rhode Island, California, Puerto Rico, and Hawaii.

When you purchase workers' compensation and employers liability coverage, you are eliminating two important exclusions in the standard commercial liability policy. A workers' compensation policy will protect you for the benefits required under a state statute in the event your employee gets hurt on the job. Most state statutes cover an employee for his or her medical expenses and a portion of his or her income for disability. If you have not purchased this coverage, you are personally responsible for this benefit. Failure to provide workers' compensation is punishable by a fine, and the shareholders of the corporation will be personally liable for any benefits.

Oftentimes, the graphic designer will hire temporary workers in order to save money and paperwork. Because the designer considers temporary workers to be freelance, he or she will not withhold taxes or buy workers' compensation. However, the IRS and the Workers' Compensation Board are two different administrative agencies. In the eyes of the Workers' Compensation Board, freelance workers can be determined to be employees. In the event of an injury, the courts will go to great lengths to protect an employees' workers' compensation benefits. For example, a written agreement between an employer and employee where the employee signs away his rights to workers' compensation benefits will not be upheld.

Furthermore, it is far cheaper for an insurance company to pay the state mandated workers' compensation benefits than to pay the same claim under the commercial general liability coverage. This is because a large portion of the damage awards are for pain and suffering and there is no jury to award these damages in the workers' compensation. Since the structure of the benefits is set by the legislature, a commercial general liability insurance carrier will usually try to have a claimant categorized as an employee to lower the payout. The employers liability coverage will protect you for claims brought by someone other than an employee to recover for damages paid to or sought from a former or existing employee. Workers' compensation benefits are determined by the state in which an employee is hired, and most state insurance policies offer a discount to the policy holder if there are no claims. The major disadvantage to these policies is that they only provide the benefits of the state in which they are located. Policies offered by the private insurance carriers will usually

provide benefits of all states except the six monopolistic ones. Therefore, coverage is not available for employees hired in Ohio, Nevada, Wyoming, West Virginia, Washington, North Dakota, or any state in which your insurance carrier is not licensed.

Lastly, it is important not to hire children in violation of their working papers. When such a worker is injured while on the job, the standard policy will only pay a single workers' compensation benefit. Some states require that multiple benefits be paid as a penalty in such cases. The difference between the standard compensation benefit and the penalized benefit is the responsibility of the employer.

When you purchase statutory disability coverage you are eliminating an important exclusion in the standard commercial general liability policy. Coverage is mandatory in New York, Hawaii, Rhode Island, Puerto Rico, California, and New Jersey. The statute renders an employer responsible for a set dollar amount should an employee get hurt or sick while off the job. In New York and Hawaii, coverage is usually purchased directly through the state or payroll deducted and transmitted with your other taxes.

Additional Options

Options that should be considered in addition to the business owners policy or its equivalent, workers' compensation and statutory disability benefits include:

- Umbrella liability—which covers the insured sums that exceed the underlying liability limits of the commercial general liability, auto liability, nonowned and hired automobile liability, etc.
- Foreign commercial general liability, foreign nonowned and hired automobile liability, foreign workers' compensation
- Stock photo library coverage
- Coverage on a per job basis for jewelry, furs, antiques, silverware, and objects of art
- Nonowned and hired watercraft liability and/or physical damage
- Nonowned and hired aviation liability and/or physical damage
- Nonowned automobile physical damage
- Errors and omissions—to cover an improper model's release
- Pollution liability
- Coverage for improvements and betterments to studios
- Glass

- Boiler and machinery
- Employee dishonesty
- Monies and securities inside and outside premises, for petty cash
- Pension plan liability
- Business automobile policy

Loss Payee Versus Additional Insureds

People are always asking about the differences between a loss payee and an additional insured. A loss payee is a person or organization that has a financial interest in property given or leased to you and for which you have agreed to provide the insurance. By adding a loss payee endorsement, both signatures are needed on a claim check in order to cash the check. The loss payee thereby maintains control of the insurance claim proceeds.

An additional insured endorsement extends your liability policy to cover a person or organization other than yourself. You are sharing your insurance limit with this other party. Since the insurance carrier is now protecting more than one business, there is an added premium for this coverage.

Deductibles

All property insurance coverages carry deductibles that provide no payment for claims that are less than $200, less than $500, or less than $1,000, and the deductible clause serves to lower the premium that needs to be paid for the coverage and eliminates the costly expense of adjusting minor or small claims. Higher deductibles can be obtained from the insurance carrier, particularly when the items or property insured are much greater in value and, therefore, greater in cost. With higher deductibles, the cost can be reduced substantially.

Valuation

In buying property insurance, one should insure as close to actual value or replacement value of the property so as to be able to replace the property in the event of a loss. Liability limits should be adequate or high enough so that if there is a serious bodily injury or property damage claim caused by use of vehicles or ownership of a business or property, there is enough insurance coverage to prevent your personal assets from being used to satisfy a judgment or debt obligation.

In buying insurance coverages, the graphic designer should try to purchase as much coverage from the same brokerage company and insurance carrier that he or she can, since various discounts are available when all insurance coverages are maintained through the same agency or insurance carrier.

Personal Insurance

In addition to the business property and liability insurance discussed above, the graphic designer should simultaneously maintain adequate personal insurance coverages. Obviously, if the graphic designer owns a house or an apartment, home owners' insurance should be kept in force. If the designer owns valuable personal belongings such as fine art objects, cameras, and jewelry, he or she should have them insured under a floater to cover them in the event of burglary, theft, fire, or related losses. The graphic designer should also have adequate levels of disability income to enable the payment of continuing overhead expenses and to replace lost income during periods of disability. Consideration should be given to purchasing adequate levels of life insurance to protect the designer's family or combine with savings that can be used with a retirement plan. The designer should give consideration to creating pension plans such as a SEP (Self-Employed Pension), Keogh Plan, 401(k), or IRA (Individual Retirement Account), and the form selected should be what best suits his or her needs. The AIGA can provide Association group disability income insurance at favorable rates, as well as hospitalization and major medical coverages.

This article is a general description of business insurance coverage for a graphic artist, and discusses coverage that is in effect and available as of the date of this printing. Each individual must refer to his or her insurance policies for an exact description of coverage provided.

Managing Health and Safety
in the Design Studio

by Monona Rossol

Graphic designers combine photos, type, and illustrations to make pages, posters, packages, or textile design. Processes used in graphic and commercial art include computer graphics design, illustration, and photo processes, and paste up of mechanicals.

Recently, an illustrator friend of mine was working on a job for a major university press. She called the head graphic designer at the press about a problem that could be easily fixed if he would cut and paste a section of photostat. To her surprise, she found that this was not possible because the graphic designer had never cut and pasted anything in his life!

This story demonstrates the incredible change that has occurred in the graphic design field. Computers have taken over. They have made skilled paste up and mechanical production workers an endangered species. They also make it possible for small studios and home-based freelancers to compete with established studios.

Some people see a certain coldness in computer generated graphics. They prefer to use the old methods in the same way that some music lovers are rejecting CDS and returning to vinyl. This chapter will cover health and safety issues of the old methods as well as the new.

Traditional Graphic Art

Traditional graphic art is an industrial process. Its workers, like other industrial workers, use toxic chemicals to create their product. Included are aerosol spray products, toxic pigments and dyes, lead-containing sign and artists paints, and toxic solvents. Hazardous equipment may be used such as eye-damaging xenon and quartz light sources, ammonia producing diazo copiers, and ozone-emitting photocopiers and laser printers.

Hazardous Products Used in Traditional Graphic Art

- Toxic/Flammable Solvent Vapors: rubber cement thinner, some glues and adhesives, felt-tip markers and pens, turpentine propanol, and other solvents
- Toxic Dyes and Pigments: air brush inks and dyes, textile dyes and paints, touch-up colors, color correction products, gouache, oils, water colors, sign paints, and colored pencils
- May Contain Lead and Cadmium: sign paints, artists paints, metal primers, boat and auto paints
- Toxic/Flammable Aerosol Mists: spray adhesives, spray fixatives, aerosol spray paints
- Photo and Photo Print Chemicals: black and white processing, color developing chemicals, imaging and proofing systems, typography, photostats, etc., blueprint chemicals, and ammonia
- Ozone-Emitting Equipment: copy machines, laser printers, bogus air purifiers, and old carbon arcs

Hazards of Traditional Materials

Dyes and Pigments

Dyes and pigments are used in airbrush colors, textile processes, and paints. Most are synthetic organic chemicals. Historically, the first synthetic dyes were made from a chemical called aniline which was derived from coal tar. Now there are dozens of different chemical classes of dyes. Most dyes and organic pigments are members of these chemical classes.

The vast majority of dyes and pigments never have been studied for long-term hazards, such as cancer and birth defects. However, when several members of one of the chemical classes are tested and shown to cause cancer, it is wise to assume that the rest cause cancer too. Under current labeling laws, untested dyes and pigments can be labeled "non-toxic" even when they are closely related to chemicals known to cause cancer! It is best to treat all dyes and pigments as potentially toxic.

It is suspected that the cause of elevated incidences of bladder cancer in industrial and art painters is related to their use of such dyes and pigments. Some dyes and pigments also are hazardous because they contain highly toxic impurities such as cancer-causing PCBs.

Another class of pigments are the inorganic metal-containing pigments. Included among these are pigments containing lead, cadmium, cobalt, chrome, nickel, manganese, and

mercury. The toxic effects of these pigments are better known. Lead-containing colors are especially toxic and are banned in consumer wall paints. Paints that still are allowed to contain lead include artists' paints and printmaking inks, sign paints, boat paints, automobile paints, and metal priming paints.

Solvents

The term "solvent" is applied to many different liquids used to dilute paints, inks, marking pens, adhesives, aerosol sprays, and the like. All common solvents are narcotics at some level of exposure. Glue sniffers have proven that they can get high—even die—from inhaling vapors from any solvent-containing product, including glue, gasoline, or spray paints. Even abuse of correction fluid killed three people in 1985!

There are no safe solvents. All solvents, natural or synthetic, are toxic. Exposure may occur either by skin contact with the liquid or by inhalation of the vapors they emit into the air. Solvents also can damage the skin, eyes, respiratory tract, nervous system, and internal organs such as the liver and kidneys. These kinds of damage can be acute, from single heavy exposures, or chronic, from repeated low dose exposures over months or years. In addition, some solvents can cause specific diseases such as cancer.

Studies of one of the least toxic solvents—grain alcohol—have shown that babies born to drinking mothers may be of low birth weight and have varying degrees of mental retardation. Since most solvents damage the brain and nervous system, cautious doctors counsel both men and women planning families to avoid solvents.

Photographic Chemicals

Vast numbers of substances, many of them complex organic chemicals, are used in photographic processes. Many of these are known to be hazardous, while the hazards of many others are unknown and unstudied. In addition, manufacturers add new photochemicals to their products regularly. For these reasons, it is impossible in the scope of this chapter to discuss all photochemicals. But in general, these chemicals cause occupational skin and respiratory diseases.

Skin Diseases

Many types of dermatitis have been seen in photographers including hyper- and hypopigmentation of the skin, contact dermatitis, lichen planus (rough scaly itching patches),

and more. Developing chemicals probably are primarily responsible for these skin conditions since so many are strong irritants and sensitizers. Skin burns can also occur from contact with acids such as glacial acetic acid for stopbaths and caustics, such as sodium hydroxide, intensifiers (bleaches), and oxalic acid (in some toners).

Respiratory Diseases

Allergic asthma, increased susceptibility to colds, and respiratory infections are associated with photographic developing. These effects can be caused by irritating and sensitizing gases and vapors emitted by photochemicals. Emissions from common photochemicals include sulfur dioxide, acetic acid vapors, and formaldehyde.

Photoprinting Chemicals

Many photographic processes have been adapted to printmaking uses. Included are photolithography, photoetching, and photo silk screen processes. These processes require precautions since the chemicals used are similar to those used in printmaking.

High intensity light from sources such as halide, xenon, or quartz bulbs are needed for these processes. Historically, carbon arc lamps were used; these also emit highly toxic gases and should be avoided.

Photoetching uses solvents to etch plastic. Some of these solvents, called glycol ethers, are highly toxic to male and female reproductive systems. Photolithography uses solvents and dichromate solutions. The dichromates cause allergies and cancer.

Photo silk screen processes include both direct and indirect emulsion methods. Direct emulsions usually use ammonium dichromate as the sensitizer. Indirect emulsions use presensitized films developed by concentrated hydrogen peroxide and cleaned of emulsion with bleach. Concentrated hydrogen peroxide and bleach can cause severe eye and skin damage on contact. When used to remove emulsions, bleach emits chlorine gas which requires ventilation.

Precautions for Traditional Graphic Design
The Safe Studio

- Never use toxic chemical products in home studios. Working at home can result in contamination of eating and sleeping areas. Workers are exposed longer peri-

ods of time at home than in workplaces. Children and pregnant women must not be exposed to even low levels of toxic substances.

- Plan studios that can be cleaned easily. Shelving and floors must be sponged and wet-mopped.
- Install ventilation systems appropriate for the work done in the studio. For example, provide a spray booth for air brushing. Provide ventilation at a rate of roughly twenty room exchanges per hour for small darkrooms, ten room exchanges per hour for large darkrooms.
- Separate electrical equipment from sources of water and wet processes as much as possible. Install ground fault interrupters on all outlets within ten feet of sources of water.
- Install eye wash stations if chemical corrosives or irritants are used. (Emergency showers also are required if large amounts are used.)
- Mark exits and fire evacuation routes. Provide a fire suppression system or fire extinguishers that are approved for the type of chemicals stored and the equipment used. Know how to use the extinguishers.

Personal Hygiene

- Do not eat, smoke, or drink in studios, shops, or other environments where there are toxic materials. Dust settles in coffee cups, vapors can be absorbed by sandwiches, and hands can transfer substances to food.
- Wash hands carefully after work, before eating, using the bathroom, and applying makeup.
- Wear special work clothes and remove them after work. If possible, leave them in the workshop and wash them frequently and separately from other clothing. Wear aprons for photochemical work, and other protective clothing as needed.

Storage of Materials

- Purchase materials in unbreakable containers whenever possible. Do not transfer materials to other containers unless all the label information is transferred as well.
- Apply good bookkeeping rules to storage of flammable or toxic materials. Keep

a current inventory of all the materials and post locations of flammable or highly toxic materials.

- Apply good housekeeping rules to chemical storage. Have cleaning supplies and spill control materials at hand.

- Organize storage wisely. For example, do not store large containers on high shelves where they are difficult to retrieve. Never store hazardous chemicals directly on the floor or above shoulder height.

- Store reactive chemicals separately. Check technical advice from the manufacturer of each product (e.g., the Material Safety Data Sheet, MSDS).

- Keep all containers closed, except when using them, to prevent escape of dust or vapors.

- Storage of flammable chemicals should conform to all state and provincial fire regulations. Contact your local authorities for advice. Store large amounts of flammable solvents in metal flammable storage cabinets or specially designed storage rooms.

Chemical Handling and Disposal

- Do not use any cleaning methods which raise dust. Wet-mop floors, or sponge surfaces frequently and empty waste cans daily.

- Dispose of waste or unwanted materials safely. Check federal and local environmental protection regulations. Do not pour solvents down drains. Pour nonpolluting aqueous liquids down the sink one at a time with lots of water. For large amounts of regularly produced wastes, engage a waste disposal service.

- Do not store flammable or combustible materials near exits or entrances. Keep sources of sparks, flames, ultraviolet light, and heat, as well as cigarettes, away from flammable or combustible materials.

Substitution

- Avoid solvents and solvent-containing products when possible. For example, use glue sticks (some glues now allow artists to reposition copy) and waxers rather than rubber cement or spray adhesives. Choose water-based or latex paints, inks, and other products over those containing solvents.

- Choose products that do not create dusts. Avoid materials in powdered form such as dry photochemical, powdered dyes or pigments, or soft pastels.
- Avoid air brush or aerosol products whenever possible to avoid inhalation hazards. If they must be used, install a spray booth or other local exhaust system that captures and removes the spray mists.
- The most comprehensive substitution is to replace chemical processes with computer generated graphics.

Computer Graphics

Computer generation of graphics is certainly a safer method than traditional chemical processes. However, this method is not entirely free of hazards. For example, computers and their monitors emit radiation in the form of visible, infrared, and ultraviolet light and electromagnetic frequency radiation. Video display terminals are associated with eye strain. Keyboard and stylus use may lead to physical overuse injuries and stress.

Light

Natural light contains a wide spectrum of visible, ultraviolet, and infrared rays. Artificial light contains a more limited array of light waves. It is well known that ultraviolet rays can damage the skin and eyes, and even cause skin cancer. Both sunlight and unshielded fluorescent lights have been implicated in causing cancer. Inadequate lighting, glare, and shadow-producing direct lighting can cause eye strain.

Electromagnetic Radiation

Computers and monitors emit low-level, pulsed, electromagnetic frequency (EMF) radiation. EMF radiation is emitted from all electrical appliances and was thought to be harmless for many years. Now some studies show an increased risk of developing cancer among children, workers, and animals who are exposed to EMF radiation. However, there still is no conclusive evidence that these effects are due to EMF radiation.

To be on the safe side, pregnant Canadian government workers have been given the right to transfer from video display terminal jobs without loss of pay. This is a humane and reasonable strategy in the absence of definitive data on EMF radiation.

Exposure can also be reduced by remaining out of the high-dose areas immediately

adjacent to the back and sides of the computer. And many new computers produce less EMF radiation than older models.

Overuse Injuries

Repetitive tasks such as typing from the keyboard and using a mouse or stylus put artists at risk of developing special types of injuries called cumulative trauma disorders (CTDs). These usually affect tendons, bones, muscles, and nerves of the hands, wrists, arms, and shoulders. Common injuries include tendinitis and carpal tunnel syndrome.

Ergonomics is the study of ways to prevent CTDs. Ergonomics is the science of making the best use of human capabilities by designing work environments using data from engineering, anatomical, physiological, and psychological principles. Today many tools, machines, and office and shop furniture have been redesigned with ergonomic principles in mind.

Precautions for Computer Graphics Studios

Overuse Injuries

- Prevent CTDs by paying careful attention to your body for signs of fatigue, pain, changes in endurance, weakness, and the like. Use good work habits to resolve early symptoms, including: good posture, frequent rest breaks, every fifteen to thirty minutes, alternating tasks often, or varying the types of work done; warming up muscles before work; moving and stretching muscles during breaks; easing back into heavy work schedules rather than expecting to work at full capacity immediately after holidays or periods away from work; and modifying technique and equipment to avoid uncomfortable positions or movements.

- If your symptoms of CTDs do not respond quickly to better work habits, seek medical attention. Early medical intervention will cause the majority of overuse injuries to resolve without expensive treatment or surgery. Delaying treatment can leave you disabled for long periods or even for life.

Room Lighting

- Provide good lighting, especially for close work. Use diffuse, indirect, overhead lighting combined with direct light on the copy and tasks.

- Keep room lighting levels at a comfortable medium level. This can be more easily facilitated if the walls are painted a neutral color like gray rather than bright colors or white.
- Use incandescent lights. Avoid fluorescent lights whose flickering and incomplete spectra can tire and irritate some people.
- If there are windows, use Venetian blinds, translucent curtaining, or other methods to avoid glare on the computer screen.

Screen Lighting and Use

- Use monitors that have accessible contrast and brightness controls for easy adjustments.
- Use maximum brightness and contrast only for mixing colors. When working on an image, lower contrast and brightness to more comfortable levels.
- Avoid background colors that are light and bright. Use black, dark, or neutral colors when possible.
- Get your eyes and your prescription glasses checked frequently. If you wear glasses, have one pair that focuses your eyes at between two to three feet and keep the monitor at this distance. Get lenses that block ultraviolet light. If you need a colored lens, use a neutral gray that will not interfere with color perception.
- Take breaks every fifteen minutes or so to look away from the screen and focus on a more distant place.
- Avoid using a one-pixel brush when possible. If you have to use the one-pixel brush, increase the scale.
- Use light tables lit by incandescent bulbs of low wattage. If you make your own light table, remember to provide a vent for the heat created by incandescent bulbs.

Equipment

- Place computer backs toward a wall to reduce exposure to EMF radiation. Never face the back or sides of a computer or monitor toward yourself or others.
- Purchase monitors that can swivel and tilt easily.
- Chairs should adjust easily for height. Those that can be pneumatically raised and lowered with a foot lever are easiest to operate. Arm rests are desirable.

- Tables or keyboard shelves should be adjustable. Keyboards should be positioned so that hands and arms are in a relaxed position when typing.
- Using a stylus can cause repetitive motion problems. Modifying their shape can be helpful. This can be done by putting the handle into a hole drilled in a rubber ball, or placing a lump of warm, hard plasticine or casting material on the stylus and squeezing it into the shape of your hand.
- Drafting boards should be adjustable, even to a vertical position. Select work tables that are at a comfortable level for your height.

Ventilation

Windows should provide enough ventilation for small studios and home studios in which computer graphics are the sole method of work. Larger studios require ventilation systems.

The American Society of Heating, Refrigerating, and Air-Conditioning Engineers estimates the amount of fresh air required for comfort and health at twenty cubic feet per minute per building occupant. Many office and commercial buildings do not provide this much fresh air. And no office building ventilation system is capable of providing proper ventilation for control of chemicals from traditional graphic arts processes.

Should you suspect there is poor air quality in an office or commercial building, a ventilation engineer or industrial hygienist may be needed to identify the cause. This may involve a survey of the system, tests of temperature, humidity, carbon dioxide levels over time, and others. If the ventilation system is at fault, fixing it may involve rebalancing the system or modification of the existing equipment.

Temporary relief from poor air quality can sometimes be accomplished with air purifying devices. But advertising claims for air purifiers often grossly overestimate their effectiveness. Before purchasing one, obtain professional advice from someone who is not selling the equipment.

Occasionally, people will experience air quality problems when new computer equipment is installed. Computers outgas small amounts of plasticizers and solvents used in the plastic casing, wiring, and circuit boards when they are turned on and get warm. Most people do not even notice these chemicals, but others will have symptoms that will only resolve after months or years when the computer stops outgassing.

Graphic Art Workplaces and the Law

Whether traditional chemical processes or computers are used, graphic design studios are just another workplace as far as the laws are concerned. Employees in these studios, like any other industrial workers, are protected by the Occupational Safety and Health Administration (OSHA). OSHA requires that employers provide graphic art workers with work and a workplace that is "free of recognized hazards."

OSHA only has jurisdiction over employees. Some graphic studio owners try to avoid the OSHA rules and paperwork by giving their jobs to independent contractors. But if these people work under the employer's direction, and especially if they work on the premises, it is likely the IRS will consider these people employees. Many an employer has found this out after a laid off or fired independent contractor has filed for unemployment benefits.

Should an employee become injured or ill on the job, workers' compensation usually provides benefits for the employee. At the same time, workers' compensation protects the employer from being sued for damages by the employee. There are only a few states in which employees can sue employers for workplace injuries under limited circumstances.

Some employers also allow nonemployees to work in the studio. These might include students, interns, volunteers, or worker's children. Should these nonemployees incur injuries or illnesses in the studio, they usually can sue the shop owner.

While nonemployees are not regulated by OSHA, the liability of the employer can best be protected by extending to nonemployees the same rights OSHA accords to workers. This means that all the required protective equipment, training, and access to hazard information should be provided to all workers paid and unpaid.

What Are Your OSHA Obligations?

The OSHA regulations apply to every phase of workplace safety such as walking surfaces, lighting, electrical equipment, air quality, fire safety, and much more. OSHA requires employers to provide a workplace free of "recognized hazards." To determine what these hazards actually are, you need to consult the regulations. The OSHA rules are found in the Code of Federal Regulations (CFR) Section 29 from numbers 1900–1910. Information about obtaining these regulations can be obtained from your local OSHA office (see the blue pages of your telephone book).

If hazardous chemicals and products are used in the graphic studio there are three rules that apply specifically to their use:

1. Hazard Communication (29 CFR 1910.1200)

2. Respiratory Protection (29 CFR 1910.134)

3. Personal Protective Equipment (29 CFR 1910.132)

The fewer the number of chemical products used on the premises, the easier these rules are to follow. In fact, one of the greatest benefits of conversion to digital and computer-generated graphics is that they do not involve chemicals that apply to these rules.

Hazard Communication

The Hazard Communication Standard (29 CFR 1910.1200), or Right-to-Know law, requires that employers develop a program to inform and train all full- and part-time employees about the hazards on their jobs. Failure to comply can result in OSHA citations and fines. The following items are required:

- A written hazard communication program detailing how the provisions of the rule will be met. A prototype plan for small businesses can be obtained from OSHA.
- A written inventory of all potentially hazardous products on the premises must be developed.
- Material safety data sheets on all potentially hazardous materials must be on file.
- Labels on all containers of chemicals must be in compliance with the Hazard Communication Standard rules.
- Formal training by a qualified person must be provided for all employees who are potentially exposed to toxic chemicals.
- Ready access to MSDSs and all written elements of the program must be given to workers during all working hours.

Canadian graphic artists are protected by a similar law called the Workplace Hazardous Materials Information System (WHMIS). It also requires collection of MSDSs and formal training of workers.

Respiratory Protection

Respirator use must comply with 29 CFR 1910.134 which requires employers to establish a respirator program. 29 CFR 1910.134(b) provisions (1) to (11) list the "Requirements for a minimal acceptable program." These include:

- A written program explaining how the employer will meet the requirements and how respirators will be selected
- Formal fit testing of workers by a qualified person using one of the approved methods done at least annually
- An annual check on the employee's medical status to assure that they are physically able to wear a respirator and safely tolerate the breathing stress caused by masks and respirators
- Procedures for regular cleaning, disinfecting, and maintaining all respirators. Respirators that are shared must be disinfected after every use.
- Procedures for formal, documented training of workers

Personal Protective Equipment

In 1996 OSHA changed the rules for personal protective equipment (29 CFR 1910.132, 133, 135–138). OSHA now requires a written program, documented worker training, and regular review of the effectiveness of the program. These requirements are not as onerous as they sound. A short statement about why protective equipment is needed and a list of things the worker needs to know about the equipment takes care of the written materials. Then checking each point off as it is explained to a worker and having the worker sign and date a copy of the list should suffice for training about gloves, goggles, etc. These procedures also protect the liability of employers and supervisors.

Summary

There are scores of other OSHA regulations affecting employees in the workplace. However, self-employed workers who work alone do not come under OSHA's jurisdiction. The fact that home workers can bid on jobs without factoring in the cost of worker training and OSHA compliance programs is likely to make them even more competitive in the graphic design business.

Yet, home workers need safety training and precautions, too. Homes are often less than ideal workplaces. Space, lighting, ventilation, and other studio requirements must be provided at home. And unless great care is taken, the chemicals home workers use, such as those in spray adhesives, markers, paints, airbrush dyes, and the like, will put children and other family members at risk.

Whether in a large graphic design studio or a home office, safety and health must be the graphic designers first priority.

Source of Help

For advice on safety or regulatory issues, contact Monona Rossol at Arts, Crafts and Theater Safety, 181 Thompson St. # 23, New York, NY 10012-2586; (212) 777-0062; *www.caseweb.com/acts/*.

Marketing

Discovering America
(Or Someplace Close Enough)

By DK Holland

A new client confided in me recently, "When we called around to talk to designers, we were shocked at the response we got. Some firms never even called us back, others said they were just too busy to talk to us." This cosmopolitan, thoughtful professional had brought us one of the more energized, interesting projects for children I'd seen in a long time. I responded, "You know, designers get very emotionally involved with projects. So they can only handle so many at one time." This felt like a really lame apology for my colleagues' rude behavior. Then I added, "We're one of the only firms I know of that has a specialty in children's products." This may have been true, but I was still not addressing the issue. I caved in, "They should have taken the time to listen to you."

Designers who have all the time in the world to design have none left to deal with the core issue of business—business. And they may not see this problem as a threat to their livelihood. But if they have no business strategy, they are letting their capabilities become defined by the work that comes their way. This client, like many others, went on a methodical hunt to find graphic designers. She looked in books and magazines from publishers like *Communication Arts* and *Graphis*. Of course this didn't lead her to any good fits, only work she liked and names to call.

Back in the late sixties, we were told by our teachers at Parsons School of Design, "When someone comes to you and asks 'Can you do this?' you answer with a resounding 'Absolutely!' even if you have no clue. Then, after you get the job, find out how to do it!" We eagerly awaited the day we, too, could meet the challenge and tell a client, "Yes, I can. I can fly to Mars. Yes, I can. I can find a cure for cancer. For I am a de-sigh-ner. What's more, I am an American."

This "can do" attitude is a phenomenon of American culture, and a big part of the

appeal of working in graphic design. Graphic design is like air, it's everywhere, almost indefinable. So designers are asked to consider a seemingly limitless range of projects, which is one of the big reasons design is such an exciting and important field. (The variety also keeps our brains from experiencing atrophy.)

But being spread so thin makes it difficult for us to act as experts for many of our clients; thus causing us to take on tasks that we may not be able to fulfill, no matter how talented (and American) we are. Thus causing us to risk damaging our clients' businesses, our reputations, and the image people have of our profession.

Designers often sound alike in promoting their companies. Consider the classic graphic design firm's promotion copy: "We are visual problem solvers, tailoring our design solutions for our clients, developing each project from the beginning through to delivery of the printed piece, blah blah blah. . . ." The tone of the promotion makes it sound like this design firm is convinced they are quite unique in this approach. Perhaps this blandness is another symptom—a fuzziness, a lack of business focus that makes it more comfortable for the designer to articulate in visuals what is hard to say in words. The look of the work is what distinguishes the firm from its competition. So the promotion relies on the old adage, "The work speaks for itself."

Since the client "listening" to "the work" doesn't necessarily speak the same language as the designer, or may in fact be blind to design, the client may get little out of the visuals. Business speaks business language, not design language. And since the client may be a perfectly reasonable person to work with, a little education could make all the difference. If the client were a designer, they wouldn't be the client, and they wouldn't need a designer. Design companies bypass the discipline of marketing yet marketing may be the key to taking control.

Inching Closer to the Client

In the wild, naturalists have learned how to get close to gorillas. The naturalist finds a family of grazing gorillas and squats far enough away not to pose a threat to the head male gorilla. As the family grazes, so does the naturalist, gnawing on a small branch of an acacia tree (or whatever vegetation the family's eating at that point) inching closer to the group. The naturalist makes some familiar grunts and scratches his or her belly, just like the gorillas are doing and, as the naturalist finally comes within arm's length of the closest gorilla, he or she may be accepted as one of the family.

Taking a cue from the naturalist's example, it behooves the designer to observe the client in the client's natural habitat. The client must identify with the designer; eye contact must be made. It is up to the designer to create a comfort level for the client. Luckily for designers, the number and kind of clients is vast and growing. A large part of the comfort level is achieved by establishing respect for the client, and conversely, respect will come from the client to the designer. This respect comes from recognition and understanding of what it is each does (and does well) in business. The naturalist understands that, without the gorilla—this strange and often inscrutable creature—the naturalist would be out of work. So it is with the designer-client relationship as well. It trivializes design for the designer to stop short of a circumspect and profound understanding of the client's world.

Some of the most exciting work is done by designers who bring a fresh, new approach to a business area. And the most engaging work, for the designer, is often the freshest and newest. Again, it's the calculation of risk that leads the designer and client to a successful encounter.

The Core Business

A little of this, a little of that, is the way some design firms may describe the kinds of clients and projects they handle. And variety may, indeed, be important to the health of a design firm. All companies rely on revenue streams. Think of revenue streams as streams of light controlled by an aperture: too narrow and the light is too limited, the film is under exposed; too wide and the light floods in and overexposes the film. Right in the middle is perhaps the most comfortable setting.

We need a balance of revenue streams coming into a design firm because certain types of businesses that come to designers may wither or flourish depending on the business climate. A diversification of clients ensures that the design firm may adapt in the midst of varying business climates. In 1990, for instance, business decreased in the eastern United States. There was a lot of discussion about what businesses designers should target, if any, and quite often computer technology was mentioned. Design firms that had done work in the high-technology areas might have found it a relatively easy area to move into, while those design firms that lacked such experience had a rough time breaking in (see "The Matrix"). Of course, the health of a design firm that works solely in the high-technology area may be equally jeopardized by such a narrow focus. Remember, business is dynamic.

A marketing plan can help a firm achieve a healthy balance of clients. No one cli-

ent should represent more than 30 percent of your annual gross income. If the work comes your way, think first before you take it. Why? Because it will make your business lopsided and if that one client fails, it could sink your company by loading you down with uncollectible accounts receivable. Or if you lose that one client, the contraction could be too great to survive.

Business categories include consumer, goods and services purchased by individuals; business to business, goods and services purchased by businesses; and institutional, goods and services purchased by hospitals, universities, museums, etc. These categories include subcategories useful to consider when evaluating the marketing targets: publishing, including magazines, books, newspapers, and the Internet; and product, including packaging, promotion, and products. For most businesses to survive they must first establish the need for what they do best in a niche market, which includes the thousands of business arenas that fit into the three business categories listed above, and show how that need can be filled by their design firm.

The C Word

Designers are not, I've observed, very competitive. And they certainly are not ruthless and cutthroat like some businesses people. In fact, designers are notoriously nice. But Darwinism in design does exist and taking stock of the capabilities of the office is important to survival. Assessing the strengths and fitness of the staff and facilities as matched against those of the competition is essential. Clients size you up in this way, so it's important to take a hard look and be forewarned and forearmed.

Take a look at the principals of your firm, the size of your firm, its location, your staff or consultant technological support, and the number and type of employees you have. What is the correct ratio of nonbillable administrative personnel to those personnel working on billable projects if you keep your overhead, and your billing rate, reasonable? How do your rates compare with other firms? Check out other design firms that you compete with every six months.

Identify your core capabilities. Highlight those which you haven't developed but would like to such as design, interior, environmental, exhibition, cartography, packaging, product, and surface; and computer, including production programming; nondesign; writing; and marketing.

It's amazing how good designers always know who's out there and who's doing what.

In fact, the better a designer is, the more he or she seems to know. Match the firms that you know you are in competition with and the business category(ies) in which you compete. Then put your company alongside the competition and compare core capabilities. Identify the competition by their business persona as well. Are they known as smart and fresh? Established and reliable? Think of the principals of the firm, since that's where the persona comes from. Then define your own firm. If this is difficult to do, ask colleagues to help. This is not a dumb "If I were an animal, what kind of animal would I be?" exercise. It's important to realize that any firm that doesn't have a persona is difficult to differentiate in the marketplace. Certainly other areas of design have proven this; just consider Ralph Lauren, Philipe Stark, Donna Karan. These designers have distinctive personalities that are at the heart of their success.

From all this information, you can start to define your company, develop a reasonable focus, and institute a plan to do what you do for your clients. Create a way of differentiating your firm in the marketplace. The plan comes after soul searching and discussion.

Definitions

One of the ways to think about your firm is to define the kind of work the company does best and wants to do more of. This is an important qualification when developing a marketing plan.

- What do the principals do best? Not only are the principals the constants, and the reason the company exists, but they generally have the greatest talent and contribute the most to the portfolio, even if they don't design "on the board." It is the principals' communication with the client that creates the marching orders for the design staff. It is the approval or rejection of the work by the principals that dictate what work sees the light of day.

- What does the staff do best? Does the staff support what the principals do best? Are changes necessary to reach 100 percent efficiency?

- What do the principals want to do more of? Principals put most of their time and effort into keeping the company going. They may work a sixty-hour week. This means more risk, more hassle, and more reward. The gains are long-term and the carrot must be out there to keep the doors open and energy up. This seems obvious, but an honest look at what the principals want to do more of is important and must be distinguished from work the principals think they can get, if these aren't one and the same.

- What kind of work does the staff want more of? What work will energize the whole firm? These questions should be reviewed each year to keep the firm on track.

The Matrix

It's generally easier to get more of the type of work you are known for by referrals from satisfied clients. Conversely, it's hard to get work for which you have no track record from clients you have never worked with. So, if the principals decide to expand into new markets, the matrix below is very useful.

- Get current clients to let you work in new areas.
- Approach new clients who have a strength in the new areas in which you are interested, but begin by getting work in the areas in which you're proven.

The Watering Holes

The trade shows and magazines in the business areas in which you work can be a source of targeted exposure and information for your marketing effort. For instance, if you have just designed a great line of packaging for fancy chocolates, read the magazine *Chocolatier* and attend the annual gourmet food show. Send out feelers to get more work to build this area into a specialty for your firm. Or, to put it another way, read a trade magazine in the area you want to work in and go to a trade show. Do you see your competition there? If not, great, because you are. If yes, great, because you are too.

Remember the gorilla metaphor? Getting exposed to and informed about a business area is one of the first steps in getting work in that area. Getting media coverage about your company in a trade magazine is tantamount to a gorilla seeing you biting down on an acacia branch. It's love at first sight.

One of the biggest problems in getting new business is getting the client to come to you with a project in hand—it gets the ball rolling. How many clients come because they know some day they will need a designer, not now, but some day? Those are the clients that never return.

The best clients come with a sense of urgency. They have objectives they need to meet, and they need your help. These clients know why they need your help—not help from some other design firm down the block—and you know too. A vice president of a Fortune 100 toy company called on us at Pushpin about a year ago. This person was having a hard

time finding designers to work with. She spoke with our communications director, Ellen Landress-Bowkett, asking, "What's the difference between Pushpin and other large, well-known design firms?" Ellen replied, "Warmth." She, of course, knew that this client would not only respond to the concept of "warmth" but that we had it and the other firms didn't. The vice president responded, "That's the answer I was looking for." She visited our offices and soon became one of our largest and most favorite clients. She had found our work in a *Communication Arts* and *Graphis* book on letterhead design. The projects she hired us for have nothing to do with letterheads.

Is Your Style Your Brand?

Have you established a company design philosophy? If you don't know what you do, how do you expect your staff or clients to know? If you know, but you've never expressed it coherently, that's almost worse because your staff has probably heard bits of a philosophy spoken by you here and there and are now second guessing you.

What would Ralph Lauren, Philipe Stark, or Donna Karan do? The entourage of public relations professionals that name designers controls the word that gets out about their "talent." However, the name designers, have undoubtedly spent personal time developing their philosophies—if not in writing, then verbally to someone who has been able to articulate it to others in writing.

The brand is a promise, and the promise is fulfilled in the consistency of everything the brand delivers. Your style is your brand. And Ralph, Philipe, or Donna wouldn't seek to create new work in an area that is counter to their philosophy because it would weaken the brand. By articulating the brand, others can help nurture it.

Fuzzy Logic

In the end, work comes from some pretty strange places: people you know surprise you and bring you clients because they believe in you; books that your work is in offer you exposure, and clients give you work that pushes the envelope for your firm. And you thank God for their leap of faith.

The point is, you never know where the work comes from until it comes. And since most design firms are purposely small, they only need a few good clients, the marketing effort need not be a major investment. The statement, "Half of my money is wasted on advertising, the only problem is, I don't know which half," is a truism. All that we can do is put

our good efforts out there and be pleasantly surprised at the results. It's good to get into the habit of finding out where the inquiries about your firm come from, so that over a period of years it becomes clear which half of your money is wasted and which is well spent.

Knowledge helps open up the world, it makes progress possible. Well-informed marketing can make your thirty to fifty year voyage through the business world more exhilarating because you can take advantage of where you are and guide your firm to where you want it to go. And as when Columbus landed in the West Indies thinking he had discovered the New World, it was someplace close enough.

CHAPTER 20

Marketing the Design Firm

by Maria Piscopo

Now that designers know how to create a marketing plan and target a market, they need techniques and tips for getting the work they want. This will involve both personal and nonpersonal promotion. Personal promotion involves identifying the prospective clients to call. Nonpersonal promotion supports selling and includes publicity and networking. The two also work together to increase sales success and decrease sales rejection. Clients get to know designers through their publicity and networking. Then, direct sales contact is "warm calling" as opposed to "cold calling."

Personal Promotion

Sales Strategy

A computer database is required for the maximum effectiveness and efficiency in the search for new business. These contact management software programs are available for both Mac and PC systems. Selecting the best program is not as easy as what's on sale this week at the local software warehouse. Many designers use the database in their existing project management programs, such as FileMaker Pro, for managing client data. Some word processing programs come with their own database programs. There are two basic directions that will help decide what to buy.

One choice is to buy a program that has a preexisting client profile form and fields of information. This works great if it is the first database the designer has used, as it is simple to input client profile information from index cards into existing fields. (A field of information is anything a designer will want to retrieve later, such as addresses, phone numbers, or dates of client contacts.) This type of database is quick to set up, but generally less flexible.

The other choice is to buy a program that requires designing client profile form fields,

also called record, and laying out the form. This type takes more time to set up, but it will be exactly what the designer needs, especially if he or she changes from one program to another. Designing the form for this client profile is critically important for sales follow-up. Selling design services can be as simple as managing the information on what clients and prospective clients need and when they need it! For example, designers can imagine the following situations with the above database information. First, they can call prospective clients, sorted by zip code, so when they make appointments they're not driving from one end of town to the other. Second, they can call all current clients they talked to in March that said to call back in June. Third, they can mail new promo pieces to all prospective clients that they presented a food packaging portfolio to the previous month. Fourth, they can mail a different promo piece to magazines and manufacturers. Information management is the key to successful selling.

Researching New Clients

The more designers know about prospective clients, the better presentation they can make. The better the presentation, the more likely they'll get work! Because they research their target market, designers know what kind of client they are looking for. There are six areas of research to find new clients.

1. The daily newspaper business section always has information on new products, services, expansions, and personnel changes that provide opportunity to get in the door. For example, a news item that is headlined, "ABC Food Company Launches Six New Products" can be translated into a lead for food packaging design!

2. The office or industrial park where the studio is located will give the names and types of tenants. These may make a great bread-and-butter client base to launch a sales strategy.

3. Editorial calendars of magazines that designers want to work with list the theme for each issue. This information is valuable when approaching the publication for appointments. Instead of being just another designer that wants to show a portfolio, the designer can discuss how he or she can meet the magazine's needs on a specific topic in an upcoming issue.

4. Trade shows are still one of the best sources for new business. Not every company exhibits in their own industry trade show. The ones that do are always go-

ing to need more promotion, design, production, and printing services than the ones that stay home!

5. Awards annuals are good for clients that have a strong sense of style and are willing to take creative risks. These best of the best annual awards programs recognize clients that take chances. If a client used highly creative and stylish design once, he or she would probably do it again.

6. The bulk of the database of prospective clients will actually come from annual directories available in the local library reference section or online. Many of these are now available on CD-ROM and make the entire process of setting up a file much easier—no keyboard work required!

Turning Information into Prospects

Once designers have the basic information on the prospective client they want to work with, the next step is to identify the true client, the individual with the responsibility and authority to hire designers. The best way to approach this step is to write a script for the phone call, almost as a preproduction step. Scripts are simply preparation for any interaction with a client or potential client where there is a specific objective. The interaction must be accomplished with confidence and efficiency, and the objective is to get the name of the individual that purchases design services. A typical script might read, "Hello, this is (name) from (firm) and I'm updating the information we have on your company. Who is the person in charge of (name a specific type of design or service)?"

Getting the Portfolio Appointment

When designers identify clients based on the client's need for what the design firm wants to do, the prospective client can decide whether to meet based on his or her need at the time of the call.

A script for a portfolio appointment might read, "Hello, this is (name) from (firm), and I'm calling regarding providing your firm with (type of services). When would be a good time for us to meet?" This script prompts the prospective client to decide whether or not there is a need to meet with the designer. The approach allows a client to make an informed and efficient choice, and can save designers a lot of time and energy. If the client decides not to meet, the script asks, "When should I check back with you?" allowing the client an opportunity to schedule the next call.

The Sales Portfolio Presentations

The problem with the use of the term "portfolio presentation" is that it implies a one-way flow of information. To simply present the portfolio will not give enough information for follow-up and will probably waste the client's time. The better approach is a consultation to discuss the client's needs and the designer's ability to meet those needs.

Since this makes each appointment with a prospective client completely unique, a script isn't possible, but preparing an agenda is a great idea! Following is a checklist for a client consultation including sample scripts:

- Prepare an introduction. Even though this appointment was made the day before, the client has had many distractions since the call. While settling in for the meeting, review the agenda with the client. Is this meeting from a referral or listing in a directory or an item in the newspaper? State what items will be discussed in the meeting. This gives the client an opportunity to mention any changes in his or her needs, or the meeting's agenda.

- Go behind the scenes. When presenting work from the portfolio, be sure to discuss the who, how, and why and not the what. The client can clearly see whether it is an annual report, packaging, or a newsletter. It is the creative process and problem solving that went into the work he or she needs to hear about. Discuss who the work was for, how the client's problem was solved, and why this was the best solution. Design clients are hiring for what the designer can do for them or what problems they can solve!

- What happens next? Probably the biggest mistake designers make when presenting a portfolio is not connecting the meeting or consultation with the follow-up steps. The follow up to this appointment begins now, in the meeting, not after. The key to being persistent and not a pest is coming to an agreement as to what happens next while still in the meeting. There are three different agreements the designer and the client can choose from. First, meeting again within a specified time. Usually this is when the consultation has stimulated the prospect of a job. Second, a call to the client regarding follow-up on a specific project or need. Third, mail the client updated promotion material as it becomes available. Usually this is the lowest level of follow-up. All of the above options are decided on within a timeframe to update the database for both "type of contact" and "date of next contact."

- Ask for a referral. Before leaving the meeting, ask the prospect for a recommendation for a referral. Be sure to ask an open-ended question and not a yes or no question. For example, "Do you know anyone that should see my portfolio?" does not allow the client to take the time to think about the question. A better approach would be, "Who do you know that should see my portfolio?"

Nonpersonal Promotion

Publicity Strategy

Submitting press releases is probably the most overlooked area of self-promotion, yet for the low cost, it has high return. Like direct mail and advertising, the goal of publicity is not to sell. Only selling can sell! Press releases support the sales strategy and bring the designer name recognition. There is no guarantee of publication; however, publicity carries tremendous credibility because information must be submitted and accepted for publication. Also, the reprints of any publicity make wonderful promo pieces!

Here is a five point checklist to start or improve publicity strategy:

1. Research trade and design industry publications that hold annual creative awards. Designers get the immediate exposure on entering when, quite often, their potential clients are the jurors. When they win, they get publication exposure and get to write their own press release, further expanding on the equity earned from the entry fee.

2. Submit work to book publishers to try and be included in their compilations. NorthLight Books, for example, publishes *Fresh Ideas In Promotion*. Again, this acceptance is newsworthy enough to generate a press release.

3. Identify the media for submitting press releases to and build a media database for a mailing list. Unlike advertising, where designers would only buy space where clients can see the ad, it is appropriate to submit publicity as broadly as possible. Research magazines, newspapers, and newsletters of the three major media: clients, designers, and the community.

4. A newsworthy item to submit to the media can be generated at anytime! In addition to submitting book publication and magazine awards, here is a list of what to look for:
   - Recently opened or moved a business?
   - Added (even part time) any staff or a rep?

- Included any new or expanded services?
- Been in a juried show or exhibit?
- Completed an interesting project?
- Involved in any public service projects?
- Been elected to an association board or committee?

5. Use a standard format press release to submit the news to the media. Editors receive hundreds of press releases a week, so be sure to conform to the standard format to avoid having the release thrown away! Always enclose samples or photos whenever possible to increase the media interest and the chances of being published. Be sure to print the release on letterhead, it looks more professional than a photocopy of the letterhead.

Networking Strategy

Getting the marketing message broadcasted should also be done by the traditional word-of-mouth method. Joining trade associations in which your clients are members will bring their attention. This will also provide opportunities to buy mailing lists, advertise, submit press releases to a prequalified audience in association newsletters, and participate in public service projects. Peer association membership such as AIGA is also important to any self-promotion plan. Other designers offer professional support, industry information, and referrals. In addition, the membership is a professional credential in advertising and direct mail promotions.

Community association networking gives great access to public service projects. These projects make wonderful promo pieces, can be used for press releases, and can be satisfying to give back to the community!

Conclusion

Ultimately, the best design clients come from a plan to get the work the designer really wants. This plan includes portfolio consultations, follow-up, and sales support. No waiting for the phone to ring. Do the homework, write those press releases, plan the networking, and follow up to get the jobs. Finally, do good work to keep the client coming back for more!

CHAPTER 21

Internet Marketing Strategies

by V. A. Shiva

Consider a Web site as the electronic version of your current print brochures or materials. In traditional materials you use graphics, text, and design elements to represent yourself or your company. A Web site contains similar information that has been digitized and laid out in a format for viewing on a computer screen. All of your material is accessible to anyone who has your Web site address on the Internet.

Why Create a Web Site?

The reason to create a Web site is the array of opportunities it affords. A successful Web site can:

- Generate valuable leads and mailing lists of prospective clients
- Create awareness of your products and services among an audience you may never have reached
- Provide detailed presales information on you and your organization
- Increase your profits by attracting new customers from the Internet and World Wide Web's (WWW) twenty million young, educated professionals with household incomes above $50,000
- Create new sales channels you won't find anywhere else
- Distribute your products faster and more flexibly
- Position your company strategically for the twenty-first century
- Improve customer service
- Enable you to update your information instantaneously and often
- Collect prospective client demographics
- Find new partners and allies around the world

The cost of creating a Web site and making your address accessible to the millions of people on the WWW is pennies compared to traditional means of advertising and communication. That's why people say the WWW levels the playing field. A local recording artist in Arkansas has equal access to a Web site as a major multibillion-dollar corporation. However, that same local artist, unlikely to win a guest spot on a major television program, can reach a bigger audience on the Web.

The Basics

A Web site is only as good as the number and kind of people who come to it. Once you have spent a great deal of time getting on the Internet and building your Web site, you cannot afford to neglect cyberpublicity: the art and science of promoting your presence in cyberspace and getting the kind of exposure you need. Cyberpublicity will also serve to give you statistics on the number of people who visit your site, so you'll gain useful demographic information on your electronic prospects.

Who Am I?

The first step in cyberpublicity is to determine who you are. You should take some time to think about it. I recommend that clients take paper and pen, or word processor and keyboard, and jot down words or phrases that describe them. Most people or business owners know who they are, but they have never tried to categorize themselves in words and concepts. The end product of this exercise should be one paragraph, at most fifty words, describing who you are: twenty key words that characterize your organization and ten that describe the broad categories related to your organization.

Recently, I helped to cyberpublicize a small business owner who owns and operates an independent record label. He wrote a fifty-word statement describing the business, the mission of the label, and the kinds of musicians they serviced. Next, he gave me twenty key words: new age, music, soft, easy listening, contemporary, New York, haunting, award-winning, Celtic, musician, guitar, flute, vocal, piano, sitar, Indian, bamboo, and Grammy. These key words reflected the traits of the organization. Finally, he gave me a list of ten words describing the categories under which the business could be indexed: weddings, concerts, labels, distributors, retailer, music, awards, entertainment, Celtic, Indian.

This type of information is central to starting a cyberpublicity campaign. Take time to get the key words and categories right before proceeding.

Netiquette

Once you have taken the time to figure out who you are, you are ready to start your cyberpublicity campaign. But before taking any direct action, you need to understand the nature of your medium and the rules of the game. Users of the Internet, including the WWW and UseNet, are expected to follow a set of guidelines for their behavior, called netiquette. The complete guide to netiquette is available through another newsgroup called *news.announce.newusers*, which has articles on the latest guidelines. Before you begin to communicate your information using e-mail, newsgroups, or the WWW, I encourage you to read the articles at that newsgroup thoroughly.

One netiquette rule is that insulting, degrading, or racist comments are intolerable, unless you are in one of the underground "alt" newsgroups. It is also important to keep your communications succinct. If you are excerpting or quoting someone else's article in your communication, keep the excerpt short and relevant to your communication. Despite what newspapers and some public relations companies say, newsgroups are not for promoting business items, advertisements, get-rich-quick schemes, or other similar postings. Blatant postings to solicit customers are unequivocally condemned. It is acceptable, however, to mention a service, Web site, local store, or company in the context of the rest of the articles posted in a newsgroup. Direct soliciting is considered forbidden. Multilevel marketing schemes, form letters, and other such methods are a major breach of netiquette. While the users of the Internet may not have direct control of what you communicate, the Internet is very quick to condemn that kind of behavior.

Cross Links

Linking your Web site to other related sites and directories is the first step in your cyberpublicity campaign. The ten words you chose earlier to describe your Web site helps identify those WWW directories and indices to which your site should be linked. Post your site address to as many relevant directories and indices as possible. I always encourage clients to post their Web site address to the top five WWW search engines: Yahoo, WebCrawler, Lycos, InfoSeek, and Excite. It costs you nothing to post on these directories.

Surf the Internet to find other Web sites similar to yours. Many other sites can serve as jump sites to your own. Once you find a site that attracts a similar audience as yours, find the e-mail account of the Web master or the person in charge of running the Web site. Send an e-mail to this person asking for a reciprocal hyperlink. Explain that you will provide a

hyperlink to their site, if they provide one to yours. This is a great way to become known within your audience, by narrowcasting on the Internet. Posting your Web site at popular sites similar to yours can make your location an overnight success.

Newsgroups

The next major area for posting your Web site address is UseNet newsgroups on the Internet. These very specific groups are easy to subscribe to and post messages on. A discussion group exists for almost any topic imaginable. By analyzing the words and categories you use to describe yourself, you should be able to find relevant newsgroups. Newsgroups may reach hundreds of thousands of users every day, so make sure your postings are well thought out.

Experiment with newsgroups, and you will notice the most effective postings are well-reasoned, logical, and properly laid out, with good grammar and spelling. They don't ramble. Adopt this pattern. Remember, some users come to the Internet via some other online service, such as America Online or Microsoft Network, and pay by the hour to receive their newsgroup information. Nothing will annoy them more than paying for long and pointless postings. Keep this in mind when you write. Some subjects need many lines of explanation, but do not use up valuable space to say nothing.

Good grammar and spelling are sometimes difficult to maintain when typing quickly, but do try. Your presentation reflects the image and credibility you have worked hard to create. Construct sentences properly. An odd spelling mistake is easily tolerated; a series of them invites disdain. Make sure you post informative messages to the group. Any message directly promoting your Web site is considered improper netiquette.

In terms of netiquette, the best method of promoting your Web site is to participate in an ongoing newsgroup discussion. At the bottom of each article you post, make sure your signature has your Web site address. A signature is a several-line block of text that can be added to any article that you post on a newsgroup. Using signatures is an accepted form of advertisement that can bring many people to your site. Do not just join a newsgroup and leave a message like, "Hi! My name is——, come visit my Web site at——." You will suffer the wrath of that newsgroup. Become an active participant in the group's discussion and offer information to the newsgroup. Find ways to mention your Web site in the context of the newsgroup's discussion. You will get what you give. This kind of interaction takes more

time than simply posting your Web site address on a directory or search engine, but is well worth it.

Cross Publicize

We still live in a physical world, so market your Web site address by traditional methods too. Publicity should not exist in a vacuum; cyberpublicity is no exception. If you spend money to set up your on-line presence, protect that investment by promoting your on-line Web site address in brochures, at performances, shows, in press releases, etc. Use your new Web site address in your advertising and on your business cards.

Mention your Web site address in radio spots and magazines or newspaper ads. If you do it right, you will actually add value to your traditional publicity by enabling people to go to cyberspace to get more information about you. Such cross-publicity increases the value of your traditional advertising; it would cost a fortune to include all the information on your Web site in print, TV, or radio ads. Promoting your Web site address on traditional publicity materials offers a physical hyperlink to your cyberspace billboard.

Hold Promotional Offers

Put promotional offers on your Web site. Offer discounts on products or tickets for customers who visit your Web site. Promotional offers are a way to continue the cycle of cyberpublicity on a regular basis. It is not sufficient to cyberpublicize only once. Creating promotional offers or new features gives a reason to continue the cycle of cyberpublicity.

Guest Book and E-Mail

Internet publicity is based on feedback from your audience—a key difference from traditional publicity. Guest book and e-mail forwarding are two vehicles for transmitting feedback.

A guest book can be a simple form containing fields such as name, address, phone, e-mail address, and zip code that Web site visitors fill out when they visit your site. Most visitors will not fill out such a form unless you either offer them something, a promotion, or ask them a question that requires their input. You need to be clever and creative to get people to fill out your guest book. You could, for example, give a visitor 5 to 10 percent off the price of tickets, CDs, purchases, etc., for filling out the guest book. Their entries become a valuable resource and a mailing list of future clients.

Adding an e-mail forwarding link to your Web site is a necessity. An e-mail forwarding link will allow visitors to contact you directly. Visitors can give their comments on your Web site, as well as feedback on the service or product you provide.

Acquiring Demographics

Unlike traditional publicity and advertising, the Internet lets you know, numerically, how effective your publicity efforts are. The Internet maintains log files, which can be used to determine the number of unique visitors coming to your site. Each entry is stamped with the date, time, and address of a remote visitor. One frequent mistake is to count each entry in the log file as a unique visitor to the Web site. Each entry records everything from the user accessing text to images; therefore, a single user requesting a single document might actually result in several entries in the log file as the document and related images are being received.

Suppose you run an art gallery on the WWW. You may have done all your cyberpublicity on WWW directories, newsgroups, etc., and are now interested in knowing how many unique users are coming to your site. Ask your provider for the log file. When you receive the log file, you can either get an expert to help you analyze it, or you can make the estimates. Teaching you to analyze log files is beyond the scope of this book; however, there is one quick method to estimate the number of unique users.

First, determine how many images you have per page on your Web site. If you average ten images per Web page, and have ten thousand entries in the log file, simply divide the number of entries by the number of images. Your total is one thousand unique users to your Web site. This is an approximation. If you learn to read log files, you can ascertain which parts of your Web site are heavily trafficked.

The most accurate way to learn the number of hits on your Web site is with a page counter. This device simply increases the number each time the page is viewed by the user. Because each page on the Web site can have its own counter, you can easily see how many times each page has been accessed. You may have seen counters throughout the WWW. Page counters will also tell a user how many people have visited that site. Displaying such information builds perceived value. Implementing page counters involves special programming, so ask an expert to assist you in implementing one for your Web site.

In addition to log files and page counters, forms like guest books are great for generating demographic information. How do you get someone to fill out a form? Most obvi-

ously, you ask questions in a form that a user fills out and submits to you via e-mail. You can collate the information to use in any way you like. Many types of demographics can be solicited in this manner. You can ask questions about improving your site: is it too slow? does it provide enough graphics? too many graphics? is it easy to use? Internet users, in general, like to give their opinions. Once you get demographic information, you can use standard methods of market analysis to understand your audience. A good database system can help collate the information you received from your forms.

Cyberpublicity is both art and science. The basic information in this chapter offers a foundation for cyberpublicity and can guide your Internet and marketing promotions effort. However, the intricacies of planning effective marketing are a much broader topic.

Publicity is an ongoing part of your marketing program, not a one-shot effort you make when you launch your business. With a clear publicity plan, you have goals for how you want your company portrayed in the media over the long term, and some tactics, weapons, and targets to help you achieve those goals.

Part IV.

Rights

CHAPTER 22

Copyright and Licensing

by Tad Crawford

This chapter on copyright and licensing is an appropriate introduction to the section on rights. This section tries to cover the most important intellectual property issues that the graphic designer may confront. Copyright is the foundation for many of the rights created by the designer in the course of doing work. Whether on behalf of the designer or client, the designer must understand the attributes of copyright and how to protect and deal with copyrights. Licensing is the best way to be paid for creating copyrights—that is, to license and be paid for many pieces of a copyright rather than simply selling the entire copyright. The designer's perplexity as to when copying the work of others is a forbidden infringement is addressed in chapter 23, "Infringement, Influence, and Plagiarism," while chapter 24 on "Fair Use and Permissions" explains the guidelines for when designers may use the work of other creators without having to obtain permission. The next three chapters delve into trademarks, another important form of intellectual property which the designer may create for clients. How to avoid trademark infringement is explored in chapter 25, "Other People's Trademarks—Using Them Without Problems." Chapter 26, "Trademark and Trade Dress," offers guidance not only to the laws pertaining to trademarks but also the closely related doctrines that apply to trade dress. Finally, chapter 27, "Trademarks in Cyberspace," reviews some of the issues that the vast corporate migration to the Web has been causing in the trademark realm.

Copyright and the Graphic Designer

I have found that a significant number of graphic designers seem less interested in copyright and licensing than photographers, illustrators, and authors. While some designers feel they are not adequately compensated and are concerned about the protection of copyrights that they create, other designers believe that they are creating client-specific work

that has no other potential application. If they are paid well enough, they assume that the client should own the copyright and that is the end of the matter. This is an unfortunate attitude, because it discourages understanding the ways in which copyright may be of value to graphic designers and their clients. If some designers are paid extremely well for work that only their client could use, these designers may be satisfied to transfer the copyright to the client. However, other designers may be creating designs that can only be used by a particular client but not receiving fees sufficient to compensate for unlimited uses. In this situation, or for designs that have obvious reuse potential in other markets, the designer would be wise to license limited rights and retain rights that the client does not immediately need. If the client later wants to make additional uses, the contract between designer and client can provide for reuse fees. On the other hand, if the designer wants to license the design to other markets, such as merchandising, the designer has retained the rights and is free to do this. And, of course, what designers transfer to clients are copyright licenses. Copyright gives the designer the power to bargain; it gives the client the power to protect the client's designs.

So copyright is, in fact, immensely important for the graphic designer. While many designers seldom consider copyright, the designs they license to clients are protected under the copyright law. It is copyright that allows a designer to control whether or not a work may be copied. If the designer permits a work to be copied, it is the copyright that gives the designer the right to negotiate for fees or royalties. If the client of a designer is to be protected from the theft of designs by competitors, it is because the copyright law gives such protection. Also, an understanding of copyright is necessary if the designer is to obtain for the client appropriate licenses of copyright from suppliers such as photographers, illustrators, and authors.

What is Copyrightable?

Pictorial, graphic, and sculptural works are copyrightable. Included in these categories are such items as two- and three-dimensional works of fine, graphic, and applied art; photographs; photographic slides not intended to be shown as a related series of images; prints and art reproductions; maps; globes; charts; technical drawings; diagrams; and models. Audiovisual works form another category of copyrightable work and include works that consist of a series of related images intended to be shown by the use of a machine, such as a projector or a viewer, together with any accompanying sounds. A motion picture is an audio-

visual work that also imparts an impression of motion, something the other audiovisual works don't have to do.

Work must be original and creative to be copyrightable. Originality simply means that the designer created the work and did not copy it from someone else. If, by some incredible chance, two designers independently created an identical work, each work would be original and copyrightable. Creative means that the work has some minimal aesthetic qualities. A child's painting, for example, could meet this standard. Although the Copyright Office has sometimes shown a limited understanding of the artistry of graphic design, especially when uncopyrightable elements are arranged to create a new design, most graphic design should be copyrightable.

Ideas, titles, names, and short phrases are usually not copyrightable because they lack a sufficient amount of expression. Ideas can sometimes be protected by an idea disclosure agreement. Likewise, style is not copyrightable, but specific designs created as the expression of a style are copyrightable. Utilitarian objects are not copyrightable, but a utilitarian object incorporating an artistic motif, such as a lamp base in the form of a statue, can be copyrighted to protect the artistic material. Basic geometric shapes, such as squares and circles, are not copyrightable, but artistic combinations of these shapes can be copyrighted. Typeface designs are also excluded from being copyrightable. Calligraphy would appear to be copyrightable if expressed in artwork, especially insofar as the characters are embellished, but not to be copyrightable if merely expressed in the form of a guide, such as an alphabet. Computer programs and the images created through the use of computers are both copyrightable.

Federal Copyright Duration

The copyright law enacted in 1978 ended the often confusing dual system of state and federal copyright protection. Designers now have federal copyright as soon as a design is created—without putting copyright notice on it or registering it with the Copyright Office. Copyrights created after January 1, 1978, as well as those already existing in work not published or registered, will last for the designer's life plus fifty years. If the designer is an employee, the copyright term will be seventy-five years from the first publication of the design and will, of course, belong to the employer. Legislation has been proposed to increase the duration of the copyright term.

Exclusive Rights

The graphic designer, as the copyright owner, has the exclusive rights to reproduce work; license work; prepare derivative works, such as a poster copied from a design; perform work; and display work (the owner of a copy of the work can also display it). Anyone who violates these rights is an infringer whom the designer can sue for damages and prevent from continuing the infringement. If the designer would have trouble proving actual damages, which include the designer's losses and the infringer's profits, the law provides for statutory damages that are awarded in the court's discretion in the amount of $500 to $20,000 for each infringement. The infringer can also be required to pay attorney's fees. However, to be eligible for consideration for statutory damages and attorney's fees, designs must be registered with the Copyright Office prior to the commencement of the infringement.

Fair Use

Fair use is a limited exception to the exclusive power of the designer, or client, if the designer has transferred rights to the client, to control the uses of designs. Fair use permits someone to use work without permission for a purpose that is basically not going to compete with or injure the market for the work, such as using a design in an article about the designer's career. The test for whether a use is fair or infringing turns on the following factors: (1) the purpose and character of the use, including whether or not it is for profit; (2) the nature and character of the copyrighted work; (3) the amount and substantiality of the portion used, not only in relation to the copyrighted work as a whole, but also, in some cases, in relation to the defendant's work (and this can be a qualitative as well as quantitative test); and (4) the effect the use will have on the market for, or value of the copyrighted work.

Transfers and Terminations

The copyright law explicitly states that copyrights are separate from the physical design, such as a mechanical or, more recently, a digital storage medium. Selling the physical design would not transfer the copyright, because any copyright or any exclusive right of use of a copyright must always be transferred in a written instrument signed by the designer. Only a nonexclusive right can be transferred verbally, such as when the designer sells a design to one client, such as a wallpaper company, but doesn't make the transfer exclusive so that it can also be sold to another client, such as a placemat company. Both exclusive transfers of copyrights or parts of copyrights and nonexclusive licenses of copyrights can be ter-

minated by the designer during a five-year period starting thirty-five years after the date of publication or forty years after the date of execution of the transfer, whichever period ends earlier. This right of termination is an important right, but it does not apply to works for hire or transfers made by will.

Copyright Notice

Copyright notice is now optional but not unimportant. The designer has a copyright as soon as a work is created and is not required to place copyright notice on the design at the time of publication. However, placing the copyright notice on the work, or requiring that it appear with the work when published, has certain advantages. The copyright notice is Copyright, Copr., or ©; the designer's name, an abbreviation for the name, or an alternate designation by which the designer is known to the public; and the year of publication. For example, notice could take the form of © Jane Designer 1998. If notice is omitted when a design is published, an infringer may convince the court to lower the amount of damages on the grounds that the infringement was innocent, that is, the infringer wasn't warned off by a copyright notice. In addition, copyright notice informs the public as to the designer's creative authorship of the work. The best course is simply to place the copyright notice on the design before it leaves the studio and make certain that copyright notice accompanies the design when published, even if, in some cases, the copyright notice on publication may be the client's rather than the designer's.

Work For Hire

Work for hire is a highly problematic provision of the copyright law. If a designer does work for hire for a client, or if a designer hires a supplier to do work for hire, the party doing work for hire loses all rights and can't even terminate the rights transferred after thirty-five years. A work for hire can come into existence in two ways: (1) an employee creating a copyright in the course of the employment; or (2) a freelancer creating a specially ordered or commissioned work if the work falls into one of several categories and both parties sign a written contract agreeing to consider the artwork as a work for hire.

This means, for example, that partners in design firms do not own the copyrights in what they create. Assuming the partners are employees, the firm owns those copyrights just as it owns the copyrights created by any other employee. If a partner wants rights to what he or she has created, a special contract will be necessary. Also, a salaried employee may

request a written contractual agreement that allows the employee to retain some copyright ownership.

For freelancers, the categories of specially ordered or commissioned works that can be work for hire include: a contribution to a collective work, such as a magazine, newspaper, encyclopedia, or anthology; a contribution used as part of a motion picture or other audio-visual work; and a supplementary work, which includes pictorial illustrations done to supplement a work by another author.

In my opinion, commissioned design rarely falls into a category that can be work for hire under the copyright law. Even if it did, I would advise designers against agreeing to it unless unusually generous compensation were being given (enough to cover all conceivable future uses in any medium whatsoever). Also, I believe that work for hire should almost never be used when designers are commissioning photographers or illustrators. Whether the designer is working for a client or is the client hiring a photographer or illustrator, work for hire demeans the creative process. It says, in effect, that the party who created the art is not the artist. It takes every conceivable right forever, when the value of these rights can hardly be ascertained and is almost never paid. It is a clumsy, antagonizing way to achieve usage rights. Corporate attorneys often rely on work for hire because they lack sophistication in parceling out the limited rights that their employers actually need. Or, in some cases, conglomerates may use work for hire with the intention of building inventories of stock images for resale.

Often the term work for hire is used loosely to mean a buyout or the transfer of all rights. It is important to understand that work for hire is defined in the copyright law, but neither buyout nor all rights have a universally agreed upon definition. For example, all rights might mean the transfer of all conceivable rights in every medium, or might simply mean the transfer of all rights in the first medium in which the design is used. Buyout might mean the transfer of all conceivable rights plus any physical objects incorporating the design, such as mechanicals or a digital storage medium, or might mean a lesser transfer of rights without ownership of any physical object. Because of these ambiguities, designers should spell out the rights transferred by type of use, media of use, duration of use, geography of use, and any other description that makes clear what the parties intend. Ownership of any physical objects contained in the work should also be clarified, and may have a bearing on whether sales tax has to be charged.

But, whether the contract refers to work for hire, a buyout, or all rights, the issue

facing the designer remains the same. Unless generous compensation is given to cover all conceivable future uses, the designer should seek to transfer only limited rights to the client. This will ease the designer's task in dealing with suppliers, since the designer won't have to negotiate for rights that may be considered too extensive. If the client demands extensive rights, obviously the designer will have to budget for acquiring extensive rights from any suppliers and should explain this cost to the client. Moreover, the designer might explain that such a cost is often unnecessary, since the client's desire for work for hire or all rights is often for the purpose of preventing the client's competitors from using the design or images in the design. The client can be protected against such competitive use by a simple clause in the contract stating, "The designer agrees not to license the design or any images contained therein to competitors of the client." This might be accompanied by the client's right of approval over some or any licensing of the design and incorporated images. The designer would then have to include similar restrictions in contracts with suppliers.

Designers must be careful to make certain that their contracts for rights with photographers and illustrators conform to the rights that the designers have contractually agreed to give their clients. Ideally, therefore, designers will resist clients that demand work for hire — both for themselves and for the allied creative professionals who will be asked to work on the design project. The designer will be wise to use a written limited rights contract so that both parties know exactly what deal is being agreed to.

Registration

Almost all designs can be registered, whether published or unpublished. But why would it be desirable to pay the $20 fee if copyright protection already exists simply by creating the design? There are several reasons: (1) almost all designs must be registered in order to sue, except if the design is not of U.S. origin; (2) registration is proof that the statements in the Certificate of Registration are true, such as the designer is the creator of the design; and (3) registration is necessary for the designer to be entitled to the statutory damages and attorney's fees discussed earlier with respect to infringement.

Registration allows the artist to make a record of the design and have that record held by a neutral party—the Copyright Office. Since registration is so significant if a lawsuit is necessary, the deposit materials that accompany the application are especially important. It is these deposit materials that will show what the designer, in fact, created. Groups of unpublished designs can be registered for a single $20 fee using an alternative form of de-

posit, such as slides or copies of the designs. This greatly reduces the expense of registration, since the designs will not have to be registered again when published.

The Copyright Forms

Most designs would be registered on Form VA (which stands for visual arts). If a designer wants to register a work with both text and design, Form VA should be used if the design predominates and Form TX if the text predominates. Since these classifications are only for administrative purposes, rights will not be lost if an error is made in choosing the correct classification.

Form VA is a simple two-page form with step-by-step directions explaining how to fill it out. A filing fee of $20 and copies of the work being registered should be sent with the application form to the Copyright Office, Library of Congress, Washington, DC 20559. There is also a Short Form VA which is even simpler than Form VA and can be used when the designer is the only author, the design is not work for hire, and the work is completely new. Registration is effective as of the date when an acceptable application, deposit, and fee have *all* arrived at the Copyright Office. Although the certificate of registration will be mailed later, this will not change the effective date. If there is an error in a completed registration or if information should be amplified, Form CA for supplementary registration should be used.

Group Registration

Unpublished works may be registered as a group under a single title for a $20 registration fee. This will dramatically reduce the expense of registration, and no copyright notice need be placed on unpublished work. The following conditions must be met to allow for group deposit: (1) the deposit materials must be assembled in an orderly form; (2) the collection must have a single title identifying the work as a whole, such as "Collected Designs of Jane Designer, 1998"; (3) the person claiming copyright in each work forming part of the collection must be the person claiming copyright in the entire collection; and (4) all the works in the collection must be by the same person or, if by different people, at least one of them must have contributed copyrightable material to each work in the collection. No limit is placed on the number of works that can be included in such a collection.

It is important that a work registered when unpublished need not be registered again when published. But, if new material is added to the work or it is changed into a new me-

dium—creating a substantially different work from that registered—it would be wise to register the work again to protect the changed version.

Deposit

One complete copy of an unpublished work or two copies of a published work must be sent to the Copyright Office with the registration form and fee. If a work is first published outside of the United States, only one complete copy of the work need be deposited. The Copyright Office regulations give details of the deposits required for different categories of art.

Sometimes an alternate deposit may be made in place of the actual work itself. Expense may be avoided by depositing something in place of copies of a work. For both published or unpublished works, generally only one set of alternate deposit materials needs to be sent in. Combining this with the group deposit provisions, the benefits of registration may be gained inexpensively. Alternate deposit is for pictorial or graphic works if: (1) the work is unpublished; (2) less than five copies of the work have been published; or (3) the work has been published and sold or offered for sale in a limited edition consisting of no more than three hundred numbered copies. If the work is too valuable to deposit, a special request may be made to the Copyright Office for permission to submit identifying material rather than copies of the actual work. Alternate deposit materials must be sent in for three-dimensional works and oversize works, which are those exceeding ninety-six inches in any dimension. If this mandatory requirement of alternate deposit would create a hardship due to expense or difficulty, a special request may be made to the Copyright Office to deposit actual copies of a work.

For works that are pictorial or graphic, three-dimensional or oversize, the materials used for alternate deposit can be photographic prints, transparencies, photostats, drawings or similar two-dimensional reproductions, or renderings of the work in a form that can be looked at without the aid of a machine. The materials used for alternate deposit should all be of the same size, with photographic transparencies at least 35 mm (mounted if 3-by-3 inches or less, and preferably mounted even if greater than 3-by-3 inches) and all other materials preferably 8-by-10 inches (but no less than 3-by-3 inches and no more than 9-by-12 inches). For pictorial and graphic work, the materials must reproduce the actual colors of the work.

The Value of Copyright

The value of copyright for the designer is undeniable. Knowing how to register work enhances this value by strengthening the designer's position in the event of a lawsuit. If a designer feels a work will be so successful as to be a target for infringement, that work should undoubtedly be registered. Since group registration for unpublished works is easy and inexpensive, office procedures might well be structured to include registration in appropriate cases. To be knowledgeable about copyright is not to take an antagonistic stance with respect to clients, since clients will also benefit from the designer's care in protecting designs.

When client and designer enter into a contractual arrangement, whether verbal or, preferably, written, allocation of the copyright is one issue to be resolved. With respect to the rest of the world, that is, potential infringers, the designer and client both want the same result—maximum protection for the copyright. There is no conflict or competition here. Certainly neither client nor designer benefits if the copyright is not protected in the best possible way.

Licensing

The value of copyright leads to the concept of licensing. If the designer understands that his or her work consists of many different rights, only some of which are needed by the client, then the designer will often want to retain rights. In some cases only the client will have any interest in using the design again, in which case the initial contract could provide for reuse fees. On the other hand, if there are unrelated uses for the design, then the designer may be able to license rights to additional users.

A license defines exactly what rights are being transferred to the client. For example, the license might be to use the design as a poster in the United States for a period of five years. Payment might be by a flat fee or, more preferably, by an advance against royalties. Royalties allow the designer to share in the success of the product. If an advance is paid, the designer has a guaranteed income which may grow if royalties are earned beyond the amount of the advance. If royalties are to be paid, the licensing agreement should provide for accountings and the right of the designer to inspect the books and records of the client. The designer would want samples of the product and would also want to be able to ensure that certain quality standards are achieved. The client would be expected to make best efforts to promote the product and might even specify certain promotional steps or a budget. The designer would not want the client to be able to assign the agreement without the designer's

consent. Of course, the designer would want to reserve the copyright and all rights not granted.

Both the grant of rights to the original clients and the grant of rights to a subsequent client for the same design are licenses. By licensing, the designer honors the creativity that goes into the design and retains a future connection to the design. That connection may result in residual income. In *Business and Legal Forms for Graphic Designers* (Allworth Press) the Project Confirmation Agreement and the Licensing Contract to Merchandise Designs each deal with many of the typical issues arising from licensing rights and are worth reviewing in this context.

Sources of Copyright Information

Legal Guide for the Visual Artist (Allworth Press) contains an extensive discussion of copyright. The Copyright Office makes available free information and application forms such as Form VA for a work in the visual arts. To obtain this information, the designer should request the Copyright Information Kit for the visual arts. The application forms and Copyright Information Kit are available from the Copyright Office, Library of Congress, Washington, DC 20559. Forms from the Copyright Office can also be requested by calling a telephone hotline: (202) 707-9100. The public information number for the Copyright Office is (202) 707-3000. Also, the Copyright Office has a site on the Internet at *lcweb.loc.gov/copyright*. Designers with the proper software can download the copyright forms from this site.

Infringement, Influence, and Plagiarism

by Tad Crawford and Steven Heller

Should the designer's standards of professional behavior be rooted in law, ethics, or both? That is the subject of the following dialog. Designers are often influenced by contemporary art and design and borrow elements for their own creativity. When does this borrowing become more than influence? When is it plagiarism and, if so, is plagiarism the equivalent of copyright infringement? Can the design profession police itself and set its own standards? Or are aesthetic standards too subjective, too vague, so that policing must be left to the heavier hand of the law?

Steve: There is a perilously fine line between infringement, influence, and plagiarism. How would we define these terms to make them manageable?

Tad: In general I think that designers are more likely to consider a work to have been plagiarized than I would as an attorney. This reflects a refinement of vision, but also relates to the disparity between what most designers consider plagiarism and the standard for copyright infringement.

Plagiarism is a moral term, while infringement is a legal term. As every law student learns (to his or her disappointment), there is often a gap between the moral and the legal. Also, the test for infringement under the copyright law may be very difficult for the designer to apply to his or her own work. That test is whether an ordinary observer who looks at an original work and an alleged copy will believe one to have been copied from the other. If the similarity is great enough, it will not be necessary to prove the alleged infringer had access to the original work to do the copying. Designers pride themselves on not being ordinary observers, and this may explain why the designers are likely to see plagiarism. From a lawyer's

point of view, what the designer considers plagiarism, a bad thing, might merely be influence, presumably a good thing. Do you think there is a higher standard to which designers must adhere, a standard derived, not from the vision of an ordinary observer, but from the vision of a designer versed in aesthetic issues?

Steve: Unlike the fine arts, which also has its share of sanctioned and unsanctioned thefts, graphic or advertising design is a commercial art, and like clothing or furniture design, it adheres to the knockoff principle. Styles, fashions, and even languages are built on the universality of certain forms. Then you have to factor in the intellectual property issue, which I understand is a dicey term: How can a creator protect his or her creation in the marketplace? This creation could be the basis for a livelihood or reputation, and if it is knocked off, or trivialized, then this has an adverse effect on the creator. But highfalutin talk aside, I think that styles can be copied, but ideas should somehow be preserved. As a lawyer, would you agree with these distinctions? And if so, how do you insure such rights?

Tad: No, I really can't agree. Neither style nor ideas are copyrightable. We have to keep in mind that copyright gives its owner a monopoly for the term of the copyright, subject to the fair use exception (see chapter 22). It would be counterproductive to creative endeavor to give anyone a monopoly on a style or an idea because it would prevent others from working in that style or with that idea. The classic legal distinction is based on the dichotomy between an idea and the expression of an idea. The idea is not copyrightable, but the expression of the idea is copyrightable. So, for example, the idea to create a book cover using a certain combination of typefaces and a negative image of someone's eyes (the idea for the cover of *Looking Closer 2*) is not copyrightable, but the actual cover as created by Michael Bierut is copyrightable. In terms of the idea-expression dichotomy, style would fall on the side of ideas. Of course, any specific work is copyrightable, even though the style in which the work is created is not copyrightable. Do you think that some ideas should be copyrightable, such as original ideas?

Steve: Originality is a difficult concept. Is David Carson's work original, or as an interpreter of the Zeitgeist, is his design a refinement of other experiments? Push Pin Studios incorporated Art Nouveau and Art Deco into their decidedly contemporary designs. Is there any lack of originality there because they invoked styles that existed in history? While

originality is difficult to define, it needs defining. And in the process I believe that standards of design behavior must be established. Ethically speaking, don't you think that a designer's unique ideas should be protected from abuse? Legally speaking, what elements of a design are undisputedly protected?

Tad: In part, this is the question of whether design is copyrightable. Often, design is created from many elements that are not copyrightable. Ideas are not copyrightable. Typefaces; colors; common geometric forms, such as circles, squares, or triangles; useful objects; and systems are not copyrightable. Yet a creative combination of uncopyrightable elements certainly is copyrightable. This means that original design certainly can be protected from abuse under the copyright law, although there may be some minimal designs that would be uncopyrightable. However, the copyright law may be an unwieldy way to approach issues of creative plagiarism. To litigate is expensive and a great waste of energy. Don't you think that the profession itself should define its own standards which, presumably, would be on a higher level than that of the ordinary observer?

Steve: Well, this goes back to the earlier question of ethics. The profession is not in a position to either establish or enforce such dicta. Moreover, as the sands of time shift, young art and creative directors take commissioning roles, and many of these people don't know who came up with what first. So often designers themselves are the ignorant culprits, and clients go innocently along for the ride. In the best of worlds there would be some arbitration group, but everyone would have to subscribe to their rulings. I don't see that happening.

Needless to say, we've been talking in generalities. What about clear cases of pilfering or, to be more generous, of influence? What about the case of the *Swing* magazine cover (November 1994) where the image is a head wrapped in words and wearing sunglasses, set against a blue background that is virtually identical to a cover of *PC Format* (May 1995). Presumably one copied the other, and the duplication is so brazen that it is embarrassing to look at it. How do you adjudicate something like that? But before answering, let me add a wrinkle. The presumably original *Swing* cover is itself a rip-off of a 1966 poster for *Caspar Magazine* by Frieder and Renata Grindler in the Museum of Modern Art poster collection and reproduced in their catalog *The Modern Poster*. In each case a little bit has been altered (it is not simply a pickup); so is this just the nature of commercial graphic art?

Tad: When we speak of blind justice, we might consider one aspect of the rules about copyright infringement. If two designers create an identical work, each without having seen the work of the other designer, there is no copyright infringement, regardless of who created it first. We also have to keep in mind the public domain, which is where all creative works go after their copyright expires or is lost. By public domain, we mean free to be copied by anyone, which would include most works by U.S. citizens published more than seventy-five years ago. If the cover of *PC Format* has been scanned and slightly altered, it will clearly be an infringement. If the idea for it has been stolen, it will depend on how closely an observer would say that the expression, as opposed to the idea, had been stolen; then it would be copyright infringement. At the same time, both works could be infringing the 1966 poster if it is, in fact, still protected by copyright, which would have to be established by exploring its particular copyright status. I should note that if a work is composed of infringing and noninfringing materials, the noninfringing materials are protected by copyright. But what are we to make of the fact that so many designers and illustrators are urged by their instructors in school to maintain reference files? Are such files intended to be for influence or for scanning and unauthorized reuse?

Steve: "Swipe file" is the common term for research or reference resources, which are mainstays for the average illustrator and designer. Strictly speaking though, a good illustrator or designer wouldn't actually steal the material therein or reuse it verbatim. Alterations are required, unless the designer is either so ignorant that he or she doesn't know any better or so corrupt that he or she doesn't care. I hope that when teachers encourage students to make these files, they are also warning them about the limits of such use. Even the New York Public Library picture collection—the greatest swipe source in New York—cautions users that copyrights may be in question. But in actuality, illustrators and designers are not taught about ethics in school. Most teachers ask students to make dummies or comps using existing printed material. I can only speculate whether or not this reinforces bad behavior, but students are usually the most influenced by the work they see in annuals and books, anyway. So here's a hypothetical situation: A young designer is told by his or her boss or client to appropriate a certain look. They are shown a particular design, say a poster by Pentagram or a type design by Neville Brody and told "this is how our job should look." There are various degrees of copying here. At what point would you say "stop, there is a legal problem here"?

Tad: Scanning has made appropriation so easy that educators should be rigorous in warning their students. The schools are obviously the best place to create and deepen awareness of professional standards, although professional groups like the AIGA and the Graphic Artists Guild also play important roles. Some instructors give their students misinformation about legalities. For example, one bit of wishful thinking is the frequently repeated, and incorrect, test for infringement: As long as you change 25 percent of an artwork you can copy it freely. This isn't true, since a part of a work can certainly be infringing if an ordinary observer would find it to have been copied. Taking your examples of a poster by Pentagram or a type design by Neville Brody, the legal standard would again be whether the ordinary observer believes the new work was copied from the existing work. However, I think that stealing style is hardly desirable, since it implies a lack of creative force, unless, of course, the theft is itself a commentary such as a parody. In this context, it's also worth mentioning that using images without permission in the course of creating in-house dummies also raises ethical questions, particularly if there is no intention of giving an assignment to the creator of the dummy. If knocking off a particular style goes beyond what we might call influence, as I think it does, I would say that the unauthorized use of art for in-house dummies is plagiarism and unethical. What do you think?

Steve: Whew! That's a toughie. Every creative act is built in some way on other creative acts. In the case of dummies, however, there is direct use of another's creation. But practically speaking, before expenses are incurred it is necessary to present the job in some concrete form. In the old days it was called comping. Commercial artists had to draw or trace everything. In the computer age designers comp from scanned pictures, and some of these are available from stock houses. But, I see your point. When one is using another's ideas to establish a particular context, they are, in fact, stealing the work. But in my hypothetical example I am asking what happens when an existing designer's work is the basis for a cultural or commercial style. Neville Brody invented a language, based on other graphic languages, that became the code for a new generation. Once that code is released in the air doesn't it become public domain? Another example is the Pentagram's poster by Paula Scher for the Public Theater; it is a synthesis of existing design languages—i.e., Victorian typography, and street placard imagery—filtered through the designer's vision into a distinct identity for the Public Theater. But, who is to say that she has cornered the market on the underlying language? Can't others use bold gothics and primary colors? Even if these

"influenced" designers don't know of the original historical source and take their inspiration directly from the Public Theater posters?

Tad: Your examples help draw a quixotic line in the aesthetic sands. Design certainly informs culture, which in its myriad diffusions casts the spell of influence. I don't think of that kind of influence as plagiarism, and it certainly isn't copyright infringement. However, if a designer instructs an assistant to create a work like another work, even though it may not be copyright infringement, it seems to me to raise the ethical question of whether it is plagiarism. This might also be true if the instruction is to create a work in the style of another artist without specifying a particular work. To return for a moment to the issue of comps, it is worth mentioning that the unauthorized scanning of an image for use in a comp is an infringement of copyright. If designers feel they can get away with this, "getting away" with something is quite a remove from doing what is right. Any designer would be outraged if his or her portfolio were used by another design firm to obtain a project. Shouldn't this same solicitude apply to unauthorized use of the work of other creative talent?

Steve: Isn't preventing scans of others' work for comp use just as unenforceable as tearing the "It is illegal to remove" sticker from a mattress? So here are two questions for you: One, can a prohibition on this kind of scanning be enforced? And two, which is an extension of this question as well as another question entirely; how can plagiarism be proven? Or put another way, what standard does the court use to decide whether or not something is actually either stolen or an airborne idea?

Tad: Prohibition is probably a good word to use, since prevention of something done so easily in private would be like the enforcement problems with people who wanted to drink alcohol during Prohibition. However, the fact that something is difficult to prove doesn't make it legal. Moreover, a disgruntled, or zealously ethical, employee might decide to blow the whistle on an employer making unauthorized use of art and photography. This isn't a consensual crime, since one party is absent and definitely not consenting. To move to your larger question: Copying is often inferred from the infringer's access to a work and the substantial similarity of the work alleged to be infringing. So the party suing may not have to show the infringer actually stole the work as long as the infringer had access (i.e., if the work has been published or distributed, the infringer probably had access), and the work was substan-

tially similar. The standard for judging substantial similarity is the ordinary observer test discussed earlier. The idea-expression dichotomy is used to determine if what is taken is copyrightable and therefore, capable of being infringed. Designers and other creators cannot protect ideas but only the expression of those ideas. Another point worth making is the substantial amounts involved in copyright infringements. The owner of an infringed work may get his or her damages plus the infringer's profits. If these infringements would be hard to prove, the aggrieved party may be able to ask the court for statutory damages, which are an amount between $500 and $20,000 for each work infringed. The $20,000 can be increased to $100,000 if the infringement is willful, that is, done with knowledge that the work is protected by copyright. The victor in a copyright suit may also be able to ask for the loser to pay attorney's fees and court costs, which can be substantial amounts. To be eligible for statutory damages and attorney's fees, the work must be registered prior to the commencement of the infringement. All of these dollar amounts suggest another reason why it is better for the profession to have high ethical standards that exceed the requirements of law. Whatever the benefit of knocking off people's work, I think there is a greater and practical benefit to having the highest standards and never needing to worry about exposure to expensive and time-consuming litigation.

Steve: Sometimes what appears to be infringement to the casual viewer is not really the case. I'm referring to the image used for the poster for the film, *Showgirls*, which shows a woman whose leg and torso is curvaceously framed by dark areas, which appear like an open coat or dress. It is sensual and surreal, but was it original? In fact, it was based on a photograph that was used as the cover for a book, *The Nude*, less than a year before the poster came out. What seemed like a clear case of plagiarism was sanctioned by the original photographer, who sold the image rights to his creation to an ad agency which then had the right to have another photographer alter the image. Okay, I realize that this is done all the time—novelists sell their books to the movies to adapt into screenplays, etc. But something's not right. I can't really put my finger on it. The photographer was presumably well paid—so its not theft, per se—but it certainly trivializes the originality of the work.

Tad: If I understand the facts, it would seem that there is no copyright issue. In fact, it is a good illustration of how the value of copyrights can be maximized through licensing multiple uses. If an identity symbol is successful, why should multiple applications

create an issue? For example, if a corporate identity program is expected to have multiple applications, why should it be surprising that a highly original image finds more than one use? That is the basis for stock photography houses and the concept of reuse fees following the licensing of limited rights. Yet, I think that you are on to something here, a subtle essence about what it means to create design and be a designer. If something disturbs your eye as an art director, but not mine as an attorney, it seems that we've returned to the place where we started. The very sophistication of the designer's vision calls for standards that exceed the mere requirements of the copyright law. Where these standards are forged is and will be in the heart—and eyes, and mind—of every designer.

CHAPTER 24

Fair Use and Permissions

by J. Dianne Brinson

Every time you use copyrighted material owned by a third party, you must determine whether it is necessary to obtain permission from the owner. For most uses, permission should be obtained, whether you are planning to use the copyrighted material in traditional media or on the Web.

Here are the basic rules for using copyrighted material owned by others:

- You need permission to use a third party's copyrighted work if your intended use of the work without permission would infringe any of the copyright owner's exclusive rights (see chapter 22).
- You don't need permission to use a copyrighted work if your use is "fair use."

The first section of this chapter, Fair Use, includes guidelines for deciding when it is reasonable to rely on fair use. The second section discusses the permissions process. The last section discusses some common myths about fair use and getting permission.

Fair Use

You don't need permission to use a copyrighted work if your use is fair use. The fair use of a copyrighted work is not an infringement of copyright. Copyright owners are, by law, deemed to consent to the fair use of their works by others. Examples of fair use are quoting passages from a book in a book review; summarizing an article, with brief quotations, for a news report; and copying a small part of a work to give to students to illustrate a lesson.

Unfortunately, it is often difficult to tell whether a particular use of a work is fair or unfair, as there is no definition of the term. Instead, determinations are made on a case by case basis by considering four factors:

- Purpose and character of use. The courts are most likely to find fair use where the use is for educational or other noncommercial purposes or where the use is "transformative." The use of a copyrighted work to create a new work is transformative if the new work adds some additional elements or has a different character or serves a different purpose. An example of a transformative use is a parody or satirization of an existing work.

    Nontransformative use, where the new work merely serves the same objectives as the original work, or supersedes it, is less likely to be fair use. In general, commercial use is not likely to be fair use.

- Nature of the copyrighted work. The courts are most likely to find fair use where the copied work is a factual work or a work that has already been distributed. They are least likely to find fair use where the copied work is creative or fictitious, or the work has never before been published.

- Amount and substantiality of portion used. The courts are most likely to find fair use where what is used is a tiny amount of the protected work. They are least likely to find fair use where much of the protected work is used. If what is used is small in amount but substantial in terms of importance—the heart of the copied work—a finding of fair use is unlikely.

- Effect on the potential market for or value of the protected work. The courts are most likely to find fair use where the new work is not a substitute for the copyrighted work. They are least likely to find fair use where the new work is a complete substitute for the copyrighted work.

Fair Use and the Internet

Some people think that there's an absolute fair use right to use someone else's copyrighted material on the Web because the culture of the Web is that it's okay to do this; "everyone is doing it." And, some people think that there's a fair use right to copy and use any material found on the Web.

The truth? There is no special fair use exemption for the Internet. The four-factor test discussed above applies to the Web as well as to traditional media.

Guidelines

Because getting permission to use copyrighted material can be complicated and costly, as explained later in this chapter, you may be tempted to skip the permissions process and just rely on fair use.

Before you yield to that temptation, please read these guidelines:

- If you are creating material that will be used for purely noncommercial purposes, for example, educational materials for the American Red Cross to use to train volunteers, it is possible that you can justify copying small amounts of material as fair use.

- If your work is designed for commercial use of any sort, for sale to consumers, for use in retail stores, or for use by a for-profit client, it will be hard to succeed on a fair use defense. It's better to get permission in this situation.

- If your project serves traditional fair use purposes, such as criticism, comment, news reporting, teaching, scholarship, and research, you have a better chance of falling within the bounds of fair use than you do if your work is sold to the public for entertainment purposes.

Getting Permission

Getting permission to use copyrighted material involves three steps:

- Determining who owns the copyright in the work you want to use
- Determining what rights you need
- Obtaining permission—known as a "license"—from the copyright owner

Locating the Owner

If the work you want to use contains a copyright notice (many works do, although use of copyright notice is now optional), the name on the notice is your starting point for locating the copyright owner. The name in the notice is the name of the copyright owner at the time the copy of the work containing that notice was published, although it is not necessarily the work's creator or the current copyright owner.

The copyright owner named in the notice may have assigned the copyright (transferred ownership) to someone else after your copy was published. You need to get permission from the current owner. For example, John, a freelance writer, assigned the copyright in his

book to Mega Books, Inc. If Sue wants to use excerpts from John's book, Sue must get permission from Mega Books.

You may find that the owner has already granted others permission to use the work you want to use. Unless you want an exclusive license, you don't need to worry about earlier nonexclusive licenses. An existing nonexclusive licensee has no grounds for complaint if you are granted permission to use the same work on a nonexclusive basis.

Exclusive licenses are a potential problem, though. A copyright owner cannot give you a license that conflicts with an existing exclusive license. For example, Web Publisher wants to use some excerpts from Reference Book Publisher's book in an online encyclopedia. If Reference Book Publisher has already granted another company, Massive, an exclusive license to use the reference book's text for an online encyclopedia, Reference cannot give Web Publisher the license it wants.

According to U.S. copyright law, an exclusive licensee can grant sublicenses unless the license agreement states otherwise. (An exclusive licensee is considered an owner of an interest in copyright.) In the previous example, Web Publisher should find out whether Massive has the right to sublicense. If it does, Web Publisher should ask Massive for a nonexclusive license to use excerpts of the reference book.

If the work you want to use incorporates several different copyrightable works, you may need more than one license. For example, Web Publisher wants to use text and an illustration from Bookco's book in an on-line magazine. Bookco does not own the copyright on the illustration, the freelance artist who created the illustration does (Bookco just has the artist's permission to use the illustration). To use the text and the illustration, Web Publisher needs permission from Bookco and the artist.

Determining What Rights You Need

The second step in the licensing process is determining what rights you need to license from the copyright owner. To shield you from an infringement suit, your license must authorize every type of use that you will be making of the licensed work. Consequently, you need to determine how you will be using the work and what rights you need before you seek your license. A license is no protection for uses not authorized in the license.

For example, Web Developer obtained a license to reproduce Photographer's photograph of the Golden Gate bridge in a Web site that Developer created for a client. Although the license did not authorize Developer to alter the photograph, Developer manipulated the

image to eliminate cars and pedestrians and create an uncluttered image of the bridge. If Photographer sued Developer for unauthorized exercise of the modification right, Developer's license would be no defense.

Using a licensed work in ways not authorized in the license may be material breach of the license agreement. If it is, the licensor can terminate the license. In the previous example, Developer's alteration of the photograph is probably a material breach of Developer's license agreement with Photographer. If Photographer terminates the license, Developer will no longer have even the right granted to Developer in the license.

If you want the right to use the licensed work in more than one project, the license must explicitly give you that right. For example, CD-ROM Developer obtained a license to use a five-second clip of Movieco's movie in Developer's interactive multimedia work, City Tour. Developer later used the same film clip in another multimedia work, Downtown. Developer's second use of the film clip is copyright infringement.

Obtaining a License

The third step in the licensing process is obtaining a license from the copyright owner. The terms of the license should cover the following seven points:

- Definition of the product or products in which the licensed work can be used (by title or by description or both). Pay careful attention to the definitions of the products covered by the license. If you want to be able to use the licensed work in future versions of your work or in sequels, include the future versions or sequels in the license's definition of the products. If your current project involves one medium, such as CD-ROM, but you might want to shift it to another medium in the future, such as an online interactive game, make certain the license does not limit your right to just the current version's medium. Given the rapid advances in technology, you should try to avoid limiting the product definition to a particular format or configuration.
- Whether the license is exclusive or nonexclusive
- Specific authorized uses, such as reproduction, modification, distribution, public performance, and public display
- License fee, whether royalties or a one-time fee
- Term (duration) of the license
- Territory limitations, if any. You probably want a worldwide license, but the li-

censor, the U.S. copyright owner with whom you are dealing, may not own the worldwide rights.

- Warranties of ownership and noninfringement. You should try to get the licensor to warrant three things: (1) that it is the sole and exclusive owner of all rights in the licensed material, (2) that it has the right to grant you the license, and (3) that the licensed material does not infringe any third-party intellectual property rights or other proprietary rights. If you are licensing a film or television show clip or a master recording of music, your license should also include a warranty that any applicable union reuse fees have been paid.

Exclusive copyright licenses must be signed and be in writing to be valid. It is a good idea to get exclusive copyright licenses notarized. Notarization is legal evidence of the signing of the license.

Oral nonexclusive licenses can be enforced if you can prove their existence. However, you should always get a written license so that you will have proof of the license and its terms.

Myths

There are a number of myths concerning fair use and the necessity of getting permission. Don't make the mistake of believing these myths.

Myth #1

"I don't need a license because I'm using only a small amount of the copyrighted work." It is true that *de minimis* copying, copying a small amount, is not copyright infringement. Unfortunately, it is rarely possible to tell where *de minimis* copying ends and copyright infringement begins. There are no "bright line" rules.

Copying a small amount of a copyrighted work is infringement if what is copied is a qualitatively substantial portion of the copied work. In one case, a magazine article that used three-hundred words from a 200-thousand-word autobiography written by President Gerald Ford was found to infringe the copyright on the autobiography. Even though the copied material was only a small part of the autobiography, the copied portions were among the most powerful passages in the autobiography. Copying any part of a copyrighted work is risky. If what you copy is truly a tiny and nonmemorable part of the work, you may get away with

it (the work's owner may not be able to tell that your work incorporates an excerpt from the owner's work). However, you run the risk of having to defend your use in expensive litigation. If what you are copying is tiny, but recognizable as coming from the protected work, it is better to get a license, unless fair use applies. You cannot escape liability for infringement by showing how much of the protected work you did not take.

Myth #2

"I don't need a license because what I am creating will only be used in-house by my client. It will never be shown or marketed to the public."

The U.S. copyright law does not permit copying for private use or in-house use other than under the fair use doctrine. How a work will be shown or used is relevant in determining whether you need permission to exercise the public performance right. However, even if you don't need a license for public performance, you need a license if you are planning to copy a third party's copyrighted work into a project.

Myth #3

"I don't need a license because I'm doing this project for a nonprofit group."

Copying for educational or public service use may be fair use, but it is not necessarily fair use. Type of use is one of the factors that determines whether a use is fair or unfair. Three other factors must be considered (see the section "Fair Use").

Myth #4

"The work I want to use doesn't have a copyright notice on it, so it's not copyrighted. I'm free to use it."

For works published on or after March 1, 1989, the use of copyright notice is optional. The fact that a work doesn't have a copyright notice doesn't mean that the work is not protected by copyright. Unless you have good reason to believe a work is in the public domain, assume that it is protected by copyright and get permission unless your use is fair use.

Myth #5

"Since I'm planning to give credit to all authors whose works I copy, I don't need to get licenses."

If you give credit to a work's author, you are not a plagiarist, as you are not pre-

tending that you authored the copied work. However, attribution is not a defense to copyright infringement.

Myth #6

"I don't need a license because I'm going to alter the work I copy."

You cannot escape liability for copyright infringement by altering or modifying the work you copy. You can use a copyrighted work's unprotected facts and ideas, as discussed in chapter 23, but if you copy and modify protected elements of a copyrighted work, you will be infringing the copyright owner's modification right as well as the copying right.

Myth #7

"Rather than just scanning in the copyrighted cartoon character I want to use on my Web site, I'll draw my own version of the cartoon character. That way, I won't need a license."

Drawing a facsimile of a copyrighted character, like scanning the character from print media, is a way of copying the character. Unless your use is fair use, you need permission to copy.

Myth #8

"We've used this song (photo, logo, illustration, text, etc.) in our productions in the past, so we don't need to get permission to use the work now."

Don't assume that past use was licensed use. Even if the past use was licensed, the license may not cover your use now because it may have authorized one-time use only or may have been limited in duration or there may have been other restrictions. Watch out, an old license that authorized you or your client to use material in specified print media will generally not give you the permission you need to use the material on a Web site.

Other People's Trademarks—
Using Them Without Problems

By Lee Wilson

Almost everyone knows that selling toothpaste or sneakers or brokerage services by using a trademark that belongs to someone else is a quick ticket to a federal suit for trademark infringement. The law allows marketers to protect themselves from interlopers who want a free ride on their commercial coattails; they do this by means of suits to preserve the integrity of their trademarks, which represent them to the public. The penumbra of protection granted an established trademark extends to identical marks and to marks which, although not identical, are similar enough to confuse consumers. Usually the comparison to determine trademark infringement is made between marks used to market similar products or services. However, the more famous or unusual the trademark, the wider the scope of protection trademark law grants it. No one can use Kleenex® or Coca-Cola® or Exxon® for *any* product without encountering serious opposition from platoons of trademark lawyers for those companies.

Because trademark owners are vigilant in protecting their trademarks, wariness in the matter of other people's trademarks is a very good idea. Such wariness can lead to an exaggerated fear of trademarks that belong to others and unnecessary maneuvering to avoid any mention or depiction of them. Surprisingly enough, there are some circumstances when using someone else's trademark is safe.

Broadly speaking, the law gives a trademark owner protection against any action that creates confusion about that trademark in the minds of consumers. This means that the dividing line between safe and unsafe uses of a trademark is where consumer confusion begins. Determining whether a given use of someone else's trademark will lead to a lawsuit is simply a matter of determining, under all circumstances, whether that use will confuse anyone.

There are two common varieties of use of someone else's trademark that are usu-

ally safe and one that is, by definition, almost never safe. An examination of each of these situations will demonstrate the considerations involved in using other people's trademarks.

Incidental Use of Trademarks

More than one advertising agency creative director has called in a lawyer to evaluate whether the presence of a Coke® can sitting on a table in a photograph is enough to disqualify the photo for use in an ad that isn't supposed to advertise Coke®. Before the lawyer can answer the question, he or she will have to see the photograph in question and read the ad copy, because the two important factors in an evaluation whether the Coca-Cola Company is likely to sue are the emphasis of the photograph and the context of the use of the Coke® logo.

Trademarks are a part of our world. They so pervade every environment of modern life that it is next to impossible to walk down a street or visit a public place or sit in a room without being surrounded by trademarks of every sort. This means that any realistic depiction of a street scene or restaurant setting or home or office situation will include representations of the trademarks found in that environment. Even though the trademarks that appear in such depictions are the valuable property of the companies that own them, in a way they also belong to the rest of us because they are a part of our lives. The First Amendment protects commercial speech, such as advertising, as well as other sorts of speech. This means that, as a matter of free speech, we have a right to mention the trademarks around us, either verbally or visually.

Which brings us back to the Coke® can in that photograph. Although free speech gives us the right to talk about or depict the world we live in, including trademarks, trademark law limits that right to some extent by discouraging certain sorts of uses of trademarks. The law would allow the Coca-Cola Company to sue the ad agency and the agency's client for trademark infringement if anything about the photo that included the Coke® can implied that there was some connection between Coca-Cola® and the product advertised in the ad for which the photo was used. The same would be true if consumers could infer from the ad that the Coca-Cola Company somehow sponsored the ad or the product it advertised. As a practical matter, it is not likely that either of these grounds for suit would exist unless the Coke® logo was legible and the can on which it appeared was a prominent element of the photograph; a background depiction of the can wouldn't create a problem, especially if the can wasn't an emphasis of the photograph.

Similarly, the context of the appearance in an ad of a borrowed trademark is important. If the Coke® can photograph depicted the scene around the pool at an upscale resort hotel in an ad for that hotel, implying, however obliquely, that Coca-Cola® is a favorite drink of carefree, wealthy people who look good in stylish bathing suits, the Coca-Cola Company probably would not object to the incidental appearance of its name and logo in the ad. If, however, the Coke® can appeared in an objectionable photograph or if that photograph were used in any unsavory context, the Coca-Cola Company would be inclined to take whatever action was necessary to halt any further use of the photo, especially if the Coke® can was prominent in the photograph. The Coca-Cola Company, along with everybody else in the world, knows that villains and heroes and every other variety of human being drink Coca-Cola® soft drinks. However, it is understandable that no one in Atlanta, except the lawyers who earn their keep by guarding the various valuable Coca-Cola® trademarks, would like to see an ad photo prominently depicting a Coke® can lying on a heap of rancid garbage or a broken Coke® bottle being wielded as a weapon in a bar fight. Similarly, an identifiable depiction of a Coca-Cola® product used in an ad for a topless bar or cigarettes or a personal hygiene product could earn the animosity of the Coca-Cola® Company. Any use of a trademark in an unsavory context can lead to a claim of product disparagement, which is like a defamation suit brought on behalf of a trademark.

Comparative Advertising

Strangely enough, there is one variety of calculated, obvious use of other people's trademarks that will seldom cause trouble if carried out carefully. This is the use of trademarks belonging to competitor companies in comparative advertising. Trademark law does not prohibit *non*-trademark or informational uses of the trademarks of others but, rather, punishes uses that confuse consumers. Comparative advertising informs consumers by explicitly comparing the merits of one product with those of another. The competitor's product, which always suffers from comparison with the advertiser's product, is mentioned specifically in the ad copy, and its package is usually pictured next to the advertiser's product in a head-on shot. Such ads require by their very nature that the products compared be carefully identified before the distinctions between them are drawn; only a clumsy ad would fail to make clear whether Joy® detergent or Dove® detergent cut grease faster in laboratory tests. The test for trademark infringement is whether the public will be confused by the use of the mark. Since the possibility of consumer confusion is eliminated in comparative

advertising, so is the likelihood of any charge of trademark infringement. However, only claims that are truthful and can be substantiated are safe. Exaggerated claims or claims that can't be documented can lead to false advertising suits or unfair competition claims. Every statement in a comparative advertising campaign should be carefully documented and every element of the campaign should be carefully designed.

Although properly designed comparative advertising does not usually lead to trademark infringement suits, there is one caveat. Whenever you use a trademark belonging to someone else in an ad, it is only prudent to state who owns the trademark in order to emphasize that the mark has no connection with the advertiser's product. This is easily accomplished by means of a "footnote" ownership statement appearing in the margin of a print ad or across the bottom of the frame in an audiovisual ad, that says something like, "Dove® is a registered trademark of the Lever Brothers Company." The competitor's trademark should be used in exactly the form it appears on the competitor's product; that is, if it is a federally-registered trademark and bears the ® symbol, that symbol should be used in the ownership statement. If the mark is not registered, no such symbol will appear, or the ™ symbol will be used in conjunction with the mark. In this event, the usage as it appears on the product should be duplicated and the ownership statement should read something like, "Grease-Be-Gone ™ is a trademark of the Sudsy Company." A statement that your client's competitor owns its mark should eliminate any claim that the comparative ad creates confusion regarding the ownership of the mark or the manufacturer of the product it names.

Trademark Parody

When a company decides to market a product under a name that is a parody of another mark, it is engaging in trademark parody. Trademark parody is almost always a bad idea, for two reasons. The first reason is that one of the kinds of confusion that trademark owners can legitimately complain about in court is "dilution," which is a claim that someone's use of an established mark is eroding the mark's strength, even though the complained of use is made in connection with a product that is unrelated to the product named by the established mark. If this fact alone isn't enough to convince you that trademark parody is almost invariably a dumb idea, consider this: only very famous trademarks are parodied—a parody of an obscure mark just wouldn't work. This means that the parodist is picking on a company rich enough to finance a trademark infringement lawsuit out of its petty cash.

The second factor in trademark parody that often contributes to the problems that

parodists face is that the parodied mark is often the butt of the parodist's joke, which may be an off-color joke. Nobody likes wise guys. The owners of the parodied mark may be so enraged by the parody of their mark that they rush to file a trademark infringement suit and ask for an injunction against the parodist. Courts are usually sympathetic to the interests of the owners of famous trademarks; as a result, trademark parodists are routinely enjoined from pursuing their bad jokes at the expense of the well-known marks they parody.

You can understand trademark parody better by considering a few trademark parody cases in which the parodists were ordered by the court to give up making jokes at the expense of the plaintiff trademark owners. The pairs of marks that were the subjects of these suits tell the story in themselves. If reading the list makes you wince, you're getting the right idea about trademark parody. Not surprisingly, all of these defendants lost in court.

Plaintiff Company Versus Defendant Trademark

- Coca-Cola Company: "Enjoy Cocaine" (used, on a poster, in a script and color identical to those used for the Coca-Cola® logo)
- Anheuser-Busch, Inc.: "Where There's Life . . . There's Bugs" (for a combination floor wax-insecticide, in a parody of the Anheuser-Busch slogan "Where There's Life . . . There's Bud")
- General Electric Company: "Genital Electric" (used, on men's underwear, in a script monogram similar to the General Electric® script logo)
- Johnny Carson: "Here's Johnny" (used, as the name of a line of portable toilets, in a parody of the phrase associated with the famous comedian; no trademark infringement was found, but the court found that Mr. Carson's right of publicity had been violated)

Not every trademark parody is ruled a trademark infringement. For example, the use in a florists' ad campaign of the slogan "This bud's for you" was held not to infringe the trademark rights of Anheuser-Busch, Inc. In its ruling, the court specifically mentioned the innocuous and pleasant nature of the florists' slogan. As a practical matter, all that this tells us is that sometimes parodists win in court. Since paying to defend a lawsuit is almost as much a misfortune as losing it, this is really no encouragement to would-be parodists. The best thing to do with famous trademarks is to steer clear of them, especially if your parody is smutty or would associate a famous mark with an unsavory product.

The Etiquette of Trademark Use

The only thing left to say about using other people's trademarks is that you should do so carefully. This boils down to a few rules:

- Trademarks are proper adjectives; remember to use them as such. It is a "Kleenex® tissue," not just a "kleenex," and you wear "Levi's® jeans," not just "levis."

- Trademarks should never be used as nouns or verbs; you do not "Xerox" a document, you make a photocopy of it, and it is a "photocopy," not simply a "xerox."

- Spell it right. Most importantly, capitalize trademarks; it is "Coke," not "coke," and "Cuisinart," not "cuisinart."

- Give a mark its due. If it is a registered mark, use the ® symbol in conjunction with the mark in at least the two or three most prominent uses of the mark in a text or an ad. If it is not registered, use informal trademark notice, i.e., the ™ superscript or subscript, if the owner of the mark does so on its products. (If the mark names a service, the trademark owner may use ˢᴹ to indicate this.)

Your rights won't be affected if you fail to follow these rules in using other people's trademarks, but theirs may be diminished. A trademark that is used incorrectly can become generic; that is, the mark loses its ability to refer to a particular product or service and comes to indicate a whole class of products. If this happens, the original owner of the mark loses the exclusive right to use it. This happened to "aspirin," and "escalator," and "thermos." In determining whether a mark has lost its significance as an indicator of one company's products or services, courts often consider whether a trademark owner has acted against infringers. You may have no legal duty to use the marks of others carefully, but they may have a good legal reason—the preservation of their rights—to challenge any misuse of those marks.

Because a trademark represents the reputation in the marketplace of the products or services of the company that owns it, it may be that company's most valuable asset. It is understandable that trademark owners pay close attention when their marks are used by people they never met in ways they don't necessarily approve. The way to avoid trouble when using other people's trademarks is to handle them like you would handle other people's money—carefully.

CHAPTER 26

Trademarks and Trade Dress

by Leonard DuBoff

Trademark law was once thought to be important and relevant only to a select group of persons or corporations whose legal interests were handled by specialists. Today it is recognized that trademarks are far more pervasive than most people realize. Similarly, the body of law known as trade dress has been developed to protect the "look and feel" of a distinctive product or service.

Trademarks

Trademarks, and the goodwill associated with them, are valuable assets to the businesses that own them, and any infringements are likely to be vigorously challenged. When, for example, Time Warner learned that an artists' organization in Sarajevo was publishing a magazine profiling survivors of the war in Bosnia-Herzegovina entitled *Life* with the *e* reversed in the spelling, it swung into action. Time Warner, owner of the *Life* trademark, was angered because the Sarajevan magazine appropriated the look and feel of *Life Magazine* and had a title that was confusingly similar to their magazine's protected title. The attorneys representing Time Warner insisted on having all of the infringing magazines destroyed, making it clear that trademark infringement is a serious offense.

Virtually every business, whether it deals in products or services, is involved with trademarks. Many established corporations, which aggressively compete in the marketplace for consumer dollars, consider their trademarks to be their business' single most valuable asset. From computers to rental cars, from magazines to crafts, it is the reputation associated with a trademark that may in the end become the decisive factor causing the consumer to choose one brand over another.

For some time, Queen Elizabeth II has permitted the House of Windsor name to be

used in connection with products ranging from furniture to rugs. The Church of Jesus Christ of Latter Day Saints has also permitted the use of its name as a trademark in connection with educational products and home decorating items. Even the Vatican Library has realized the value of its name as a trademark and the effect that its endorsement of products may have on consumers. Recently, it has been reported that the Vatican Library has commenced a licensing program permitting product manufacturers to include its official seal on authorized merchandise.

Oleg Cassini, the famous clothing designer responsible for creating Jacqueline Kennedy's look during her tenure as the First Lady and the first designer to use licensing, recently said, "Many times I've thought about it, what keeps me going, and I think it is a pride of trademark. That may seem like a commercial thing. But two of the greatest names in fashion today are Chanel and Dior, and they died years ago. I have young people in my company, and I like to think my trademark will survive me."

The same rationale affects smaller, growing businesses, such as your graphic design business and the clients it serves. As a result, disputes may arise regarding ownership of a mark in situations where a family business is placed in the middle of a marriage dissolution or an estate dispute.

Virtually every business will likely be involved with trademarks or infringement issues at some point. It is, therefore, important to have some rudimentary knowledge of this area of law in order to determine whether your graphic design business has a protectable intellectual property right or, conversely, whether you have, either intentionally or unwittingly, stumbled into a potential trademark dispute. Similarly, you should counsel your clients on the protectability of the trademarks you create for them, and be sure to avoid thrusting your client into a trademark dispute.

Trademark Infringement

Any name, symbol, logo, or combination of these items that is not generic, when used in connection with a product or service, may be protected as a trademark. Registration is by no means a prerequisite to creating a protected mark, and even unregistered marks are protectable and enforceable. Section 43(a) of the Lanham Act grants the proprietor/owner of a protectable mark the right to prevent others from using a mark that sounds like, looks like, or is confusingly similar to the protected mark.

"Likelihood of confusion" is a rather broad legal standard and may permit an in-

fringement claim, even if the challenged mark is not identical to the one protected. If a reasonable consumer would be confused and misled into believing that a product or service that bears the knockoff mark is manufactured, endorsed and authorized, or licensed by the owner of the protected trademark, then an injunction against further market confusion may be obtained. The trademark owner may recover defendant's profits, damages, and, in an appropriate case, the costs of the litigation. Thus, merely changing the spelling of a word or slightly modifying a logo will not avoid a charge of infringement. In addition, in certain circumstances, the trademark proprietor may also recover treble damages. The fact that the alleged infringer was ignorant of the protected mark is relevant only to determining whether the case is extraordinary, in which case attorneys' fees would then also be available.

Dilution

Pursuant to a new federal law, some marks can now be protected from others' use of similar marks, even where there is no likelihood of confusion. On January 16, 1996, President Clinton signed into law the Federal Trademark Dilution Act of 1995, which creates antidilution protection for "famous" marks. This act amends Section 43 of the Trademark Act by adding a provision entitling the owner of a famous mark to an injunction against another person's commercial use of a mark where such use begins after the mark has become famous and causes dilution of the distinctive quality of that mark. Willful intent to trade on the owner's reputation or to cause dilution of the mark may also entitle the owner of the mark to the same remedies as those set forth for trademark infringement, including damages, costs, and attorneys' fees.

Dilution is defined as "the lessening of the capacity of a famous mark to identify and distinguish goods or services, regardless of the presence or absence of: (1) competition between the owner of the famous mark and other parties, or (2) likelihood of confusion, mistake, or deception."

Although the term famous is not defined by the statute, a list of factors to be considered in determining whether or not a mark is famous is set forth in Section 43. These factors are:

1. the degree of inherent or acquired distinctiveness of the mark;
2. the duration and extent of the use of the mark in connection with the goods or services with which the mark is used;
3. the duration and extent of advertising and publicity of the mark;

4. the geographical extent of the trading area in which the mark is used;

5. the channels of trade for the goods or services with which the mark is used;

6. the degree of recognition of the mark in the trading areas and channels of trade used by the mark's owner and the person against whom the injunction is sought;

7. the nature and extent of use of the same or similar marks by third parties; and

8. whether the mark was registered under the Act of March 3, 1881, or February 20, 1905, or on the Principal Register.

Ownership of a valid registration under the Act of March 3, 1881, or February 20, 1905, or on the Principal Register is a complete bar to a state- or common-law antidilution action against an owner with respect to that mark. In addition, the following nonactionable uses of a mark are set forth in Section 43: fair use of a famous mark by another person in comparative commercial advertising or promotion to identify the competing goods or services of the owner of the famous mark; noncommercial use of a mark; and all forms of news reporting and news commentary.

Because the Federal Trademark Dilution Act is so new, there have been few cases interpreting it. One such case is *Dr. Seuss Enterprises, L.P.* v. *Penguin Book USA, Inc.,* in which the district court held that a parody of Dr. Seuss' *The Cat in the Hat* called *The Cat Not in the Hat! A Parody by Dr. Juice* did not violate the Federal Trademark Dilution Act, as parody is a noncommercial use protected by the First Amendment. There is also an unreported case involving Sunbeam Products, Inc.'s claim that a West Bend mixer dilutes the distinctiveness of its Mixmaster® Mixer.

While the 1995 Dilution Act does not provide as much protection for trademark owners as some state statutes, it is nevertheless a step toward unifying the remedies available to trademark owners.

Trademark Registration

A mark can be registered federally, in which case the process involves dealing with the Assistant Commissioner of Trademarks in Arlington, Virginia, and ultimately having the proposed mark published in the *Official Gazette of the U.S. Patent and Trademark Office.* This weekly publication is reviewed by trademark lawyers who look out for marks that may conflict with those of their clients. Anyone who feels that a mark that appears in the *Gazette* should not be registered may oppose registration, and a hearing will be conducted to

determine the rights of the respective parties. If no objection (or request for an extension of time within which to make an objection) is filed within thirty days after a proposed mark has appeared in the *Gazette*, then a Certificate of Registration will ultimately be issued. It is only then that the trademark proprietor may use the ® symbol in connection with a mark. Any other use of this trademark symbol is improper.

The symbols ™ and ˢᴹ may be used in connection with unregistered marks, as well as state registered marks. When a person desires to protect a mark she or he believes might be used in the future, an "intent to use" application may be filed even before the mark is actually used. If the mark is ultimately used in interstate commerce, then the intent to use registration may be converted into an actual registration by filing the appropriate documents with the Patent and Trademark Office.

United States Customs has been charged with the responsibility of policing American borders and aiding proprietors of registered U.S. intellectual property, including trademarks, by preventing the importation of material bearing infringing marks.

State Trademark Laws

A trademark may also be registered on the state level. Unfortunately, state registrations are geographically limited by the state's boundaries, although the legal remedies available against an infringer of a mark that enjoys state registration may be different from, and in some cases better than, those available under the federal statute.

For example, many states have their own antidilution protection. Essentially, this means that activities that might not be actionable under the federal statute may give rise to liability under state antidilution laws, which generally do not require that the infringed mark be famous.

Trademark Availability

It is essential to determine whether a name, symbol, logo, or combination of these is already protected and owned by another individual or business before using a particular mark. For this reason, graphic design businesses should commission a broad-based trademark search as a prerequisite to starting a new venture or identifying a product or service with a mark. Many law firms can actually conduct preliminary searches in-house. An experienced trademark lawyer can review the search results to determine whether the desired mark is potentially available and whether it would be prudent to commence using it.

Some things may not be protected as trademarks. If the proposed mark is generic, for example, the words describe the product or service (like "chair" to describe a chair or "car" to describe an automobile), then the mark cannot be protected. On the other hand, if the proposed mark is merely descriptive, then it may qualify for protection once the mark has achieved a "secondary meaning." Descriptive marks that conjure up images of the products or services that they represent are said to have achieved this secondary meaning and, therefore, are afforded protection. Thus, *TV Guide* is descriptive; yet, it has achieved secondary meaning and is protected. If the proposed mark is available, then there are a number of options that the business may select in order to protect it. As noted above, merely using a protectable mark in interstate commerce will give rise to protection under the federal trademark statute. It is, however, still a good idea to register protectable marks, since registration provides a trademark proprietor certain benefits in litigation as well as in public notoriety.

Trade Dress

A relatively new body of law has emerged known as trade dress. Initially, this doctrine was used exclusively for protecting unique and distinctive packaging when the packaging helped to identify the source of a product or service. More recently, trade dress law has been extended to the protection of products or services themselves. When, for example, the Hallmark Greeting Card Company appropriated the look and feel of the distinctive greeting card produced by the Colorado-based Blue Mountain Company, trade dress law came to the rescue. Since the Hallmark cards were not substantially similar to those produced by Blue Mountain, the Hallmark line did not infringe the copyright in Blue Mountain's distinctive cards. The court relied on the emerging doctrine of trade dress in holding that appropriating the look and feel of another's distinctive product or service is an infringement.

The U.S. Supreme Court endorsed this expansion of the trade dress doctrine by holding that the distinctive characteristics of a fast-food restaurant may be a protectable trade dress. In *Two Pesos* v. *Taco Cabana*, the court held that distinctive characteristics that are not functional and that are used to identify a product or service may be protectable, even though they do not enjoy copyright protection or are not traditional trademarks. All the plaintiff needs to prove is that the trade dress is not functional, that it is distinctive and notorious, and that the plaintiff is known by the characteristics claimed to be trade dress.

The trade dress doctrine has been used to protect the distinctive characteristics of an

artist's style, a craft show's format, a jewelry rack's unique characteristics, and many other products or services that may not enjoy other forms of intellectual property protection.

Graphic designers who create unique product designs, packaging, corporate personalities, or the like may be able to rely on the trade dress doctrine for purposes of protecting their creative work. There is no preregistration required for trade dress protection; rather, the law affords a remedy for the unauthorized misappropriation of the protected work.

Graphic designers should consult with a skilled intellectual property lawyer in order to determine whether the product or service in question is protectable under any of the intellectual property laws, such as patent, trade secret, copyright, trademark, or trade dress. A skilled attorney can advise you on the best method of securing the rights to your creations and what steps you should take in order to properly advise your clients.

The importance of the trademark and trade dress laws cannot be overemphasized. They pervade virtually every business, and nearly every business person will encounter them at some time. It is for this reason that all graphic artists should be familiar with these bodies of law and work with an experienced intellectual property attorney on a regular basis. Carelessness in dealing with these forms of intellectual property can result in serious consequences. Today there are both a vast array of reference materials available and an increasing number of attorneys who are adopting intellectual property law as a specialty.

With the advent of the World Wide Web, e-mail, faxes, and comparatively inexpensive long-distance telephone service, the world is shrinking. It is, thus, possible for you to consult with your attorney on a regular basis, even when you are half a world away. As a graphic artist, your stock in trade is your distinctive creations, which will only retain their value if you can protect them.

CHAPTER 27

Trademarks in Cyberspace

By Lee Wilson

Like all frontiers, cyberspace is largely populated by mavericks and rebels who like the cyberatmosphere of "if you can imagine it, you can do it." Unfortunately, the very dearth of rules that makes cyberspace so intriguing to everyone who has something to say or sell electronically is also causing problems. Americans often complain about overregulation by local, state, and federal governmental agencies and authorities. But many who are familiar with the problems that have arisen as everybody and his brother scramble for domain names would agree that, in some corners of cyberspace, *more* rules are needed.

One aspect of cybercommerce has produced disputes for which there is as yet no clear law; this is the ownership of domain names. A domain name is the heart of an e-mail address. In the e-mail address *johnjones@jonesventures.com, jonesventures.com* is the domain name. Domain names tell Internet users where to find companies and individuals in cyberspace. They function like ZIP codes for "snail mail"; they direct e-mail and other communications to the right cyberspace neighborhood to find the person or entity named in the first part of the e-mail address. They allow Internet users to visit World Wide Web pages.

The system of categorizing Internet user addresses according to type is familiar to most Net surfers. The five major nonmilitary domains are: *.com* for commercial entities; *.gov* for governmental bodies; *.edu* for educational institutions, *.org* for organizations; and *.net* for networks. Because innovative marketers are finding ways to sell everything from coffee to books online, the most crowded part of cyberspace is the commercial district, where all the .com addresses are located.

Internet addresses are actually a series of numbers. However, because people who want to locate an Internet merchant are much more likely to remember a verbal address than a series of numbers, domain names are alpha and/or numeric names that a computer

can convert to numeric addresses. There is presently no complete directory of domain names. Therefore, the best domain names look like the names of the companies that own them; this sort of domain name creates an expectation as to who is at the Internet address it names. If you are familiar with a company, and its domain name resembles the name of the company, you know what you will find at its address on the Internet. Such Internet addresses are easy to guess and to remember. For example, because ibm.com is one of the elements of the Internet address for IBM, anyone can guess that that address belongs to that company.

Obstacles on the Superhighway

So far, trademark disputes have been one of the biggest impediments facing Internet marketers. The gist of trademark law is that every marketer is entitled to his or her own reputation in the marketplace. Any interference with this—any act that causes consumers to confuse the products or services of one marketer with those of another—is trademark infringement. Although the legal status of domain names is not yet a settled area of the law, anyone who understands trademark law would agree that domain names are more than just virtual street addresses.

Problems with domain names usually arise when one company registers a domain name that is identical or similar to the name of another company. It is reasonable that a company whose name had been adopted as the domain name of another enterprise would feel that its rights in its trademark, the embodiment of its commercial reputation, had been infringed. Courts are likely to agree. One variety of trademark infringement is confusion of sponsorship or affiliation. If, on account of similarities between a domain name and the name of an unrelated company, consumers are likely to believe that there is some relationship between the owner of the domain name and the company, the company's trademark rights have been infringed.

Superhighway Robbery

Trademark disputes have in recent years resulted when competitors and pranksters have registered domain names that are logically related to the names of established companies. Many such domain name registrations were apparently made for the purpose of extorting fat buyouts from rich corporations. A journalist registered the domain name *mcdonalds.com* as a part of his research for an article for *Wired* magazine. Needless to say, McDonald's was chagrined to find that the most obvious domain name it could choose

had already been registered. Some overeager capitalist at Sprint Communications registered mci.com; not surprisingly, MCI Telecommunications objected. The Princeton Review, a leading test preparation company, registered kaplan.com, a domain name based on the name of its competitor, Stanley Kaplan Review, and planned to set up a Web site that compared the two companies' products, presumably showing the alleged inferiority of the Kaplan products. The domain name mtv.com was registered and used by a former MTV employee. The domain names *windows95.com* and *nyt.com* were registered by people who were not connected with Microsoft and the *New York Times*. Although several of these "land grabs" resulted in lawsuits, there are no reported court decisions to guide those who will face similar issues because all of these disputes were settled out of court. Most of the terms of the settlements in these disputes, including any amounts paid to the domain name hijackers, were not disclosed, but it is telling that all the companies that complained because someone else had registered versions of their names now own those domain names. Similar problems have arisen when companies have registered domain names that they had no intention of using. This has been done in the hope that some company that does want to use one of the registered domain names will buy it from the original registrant. This sort of kidnapping has been fairly common.

Eventually there will be a larger body of case law to guide lawyers on these issues because there will certainly be more disputes between trademark owners and cyberspace profiteers and pirates. One reason that more such disputes are likely is that many companies seem unaware of the race for domain names and have been dilatory in registering versions of their corporate names as domain names.

Superhighway Patrol

Formerly, the U.S. government's National Science Foundation assigned all Internet domain names, both military and nonmilitary. As the Net grew, this job became a big one. The National Science Foundation created the InterNIC (Internet Network Information Center) project to provide Internet management services. The National Science Foundation entered a contract with a Herndon, Virginia, telecommunications network integration company called Network Solutions, Inc. (NSI), and delegated to NSI the tasks of allocating and managing the registration of nonmilitary domain names.

In 1993 there were only eighty-seven hundred registered domain names; by mid-1996 NSI had registered more than four-hundred thousand. Currently, NSI handles about

fifteen thousand domain-name registrations each month. Most of these applications for new domain names come from private business—companies are greedy to stake their claims to cyberspace territory. For example, Procter and Gamble has registered more than two-hundred domain names, including dandruff.com, badbreath.com, and underarm.com. Kraft has registered one-hundred-fifty domain names.

In mid-1995 NSI announced a new policy on registration of domain names. This new policy attempted to end some of the abuses and disputes that had become familiar to would-be Internet marketers. Names were still assigned on a first-come, first-served basis, but, for the first time, an applicant had to represent to NSI that he or she had the legal right to use the name sought to be registered, had a bona fide intention to use the name, and had no unlawful purpose in seeking to register the name. If the owner of a registered trademark objected to another entity's registration of a domain name, the trademark owner could challenge the registration. NSI would then put a hold on the domain name, suspending its use until the dispute was resolved. The registration for the domain name was rescinded if the domain-name registrant could not show ownership of a trademark registration for the mark. If both the domain-name registrant and the objecting trademark owner could prove ownership of trademark registrations, the first company to register the trademark as a domain name was awarded the domain name. This situation sometimes occurred in disputes in which registrations in various jurisdictions were involved. The questions arose whether federal registrations should be given priority over state registrations, as is the settled protocol in U.S. trademark law, and what weight should be given to registrations in other countries.

NSI's new policy worked in most cases. However, it did not solve all of the problems that can arise between owners of trademarks and would-be registrants of similar domain names, especially in situations where the trademark and domain name are used by companies that are not directly competitive. Inconsistencies between U.S. trademark law and NSI's rules and policies led to several lawsuits involving trademark owners, would-be domain-name registrants, and NSI. NSI, which originally contemplated its role with regard to the Internet as being merely the registrar of domain names, found itself cast, by default, as referee between marketers competing for the same domain names. Since its rules and policies do not have the clout or effect of law and it is incapable of enforcing its decisions in the way court decisions can be enforced, NSI was anxious to avoid this role and the liability inherent in it.

In an effort to solve some of these problems, in August 1996 NSI announced im-

portant revisions, effective in September 1996 to its Domain Name Policy Statement. The revised NSI policy institutes three important changes in the way that domain names are registered:

1. A federal trademark registration obtained *after* a dispute arises between competitors for a domain name will not provide grounds for obtaining or avoiding an NSI suspension of the domain name in dispute. This means that a domain name owner will no longer be able to quickly apply for and obtain a foreign registration in an effort to counter a trademark owner's claims that the domain name infringes its rights in the trademark.

2. NSI will not suspend use of a domain name if either the would-be domain name registrant or the trademark owner files a lawsuit in the dispute over the domain name. (If such litigation is commenced, NSI will "deposit control of the domain name into the registry of the court," thereby passing the hot potato to the pertinent court, which will have judicial power to dispose of ownership of the domain name as it sees fit.)

3. NSI will abide by any court order (thereby dispensing with its prior policy of giving equal weight to decisions of the American Arbitration Association) so long as NSI is not itself named as a litigant and, if named, NSI "reserves the right to raise any and all defenses deemed appropriate." In addition, NSI continues to give preference to owners of trademarks registered federally in the United States, but will now suspend use of a disputed domain name only on the basis of the ownership of a Principal Register federal registration, which is like a first-class federal trademark registration as opposed to a second-class, and less powerful, Supplemental Register registration. NSI will continue to give equal weight to foreign federal trademark registrations as that given U.S. federal registrations.

Trademark owners will also gain substantial protection from the new federal Trademark Dilution Act, passed by Congress early in 1997. The Act codifies and formalizes several formerly somewhat vague principles of trademark law. It allows the owners of an existing famous trademark to sue to enjoin the use of the same mark by another company—even if there is no likelihood of confusion between the marks—on the ground that the defendant's use of the mark, even for noncompeting goods or services, "dilutes" the distinctive quality of the famous mark. This will eliminate, for the owners of truly famous marks, the obstacle pre-

sented by the use of their marks as domain names by the marketers of noncompeting goods and services. The first notable lawsuit brought under the new Act was brought by Hasbro, Inc., which owns the trademark CANDY LAND for a famous children's board game, against a company that had adopted the domain name *candyland.com* for a sexually-explicit Web site. Hasbro, Inc. was successful in having the domain name enjoined on the basis that its use would dilute the strength of the CANDY LAND mark. Other, similar, cases have followed.

NSI's newest policy is a big improvement, but it won't solve every problem that will arise involving trademarks and the Internet; nor will the Trademark Dilution Act, which is really useful only to the owners of demonstrably famous trademarks. Until the law of domain names has become a settled part of trademark law, the best course for any marketer is to immediately register any domain name under which you want to conduct business—or may want to conduct business—on the Internet. Stay away from any domain name that you know to be similar to the name or trademark of any other company, especially if that company is a competitor. And because the misuse and use without permission of trademarks in the content of Web pages seems likely to grow into another thriving area of trademark infringement, be careful how you use trademarks that you don't own. An example of content-based trademark infringement would be language in a Web page text that implies a connection between a famous product and the product of the Web site marketer. (See chapter 25 for principles applicable to the use of others' trademarks in Web sites.)

Signing Up and Signing On

Applications to register new domain names in the United States may be submitted electronically to InterNIC Registration Services. (Other entities are responsible for registering domain names in the more than 120 other world jurisdictions.) You can call InterNIC at (703) 742-4777 for information concerning registering a domain name or send an e-mail message to *admin@ds.internic.net*. You can also access this information at: *rs.internic.net/ contact.html*. If the name you choose is already in use, InterNIC will ask you to choose another. Otherwise, if InterNIC does not deem your name offensive, obscene, or otherwise objectionable, the system will process your application, send it back to you for verification, and tell you when you can begin to use it.

InterNIC's exclusive contract with the National Science Foundation expires in March 1998. Other organizations and groups are already proposing new methods of handling the issuance and registration of domain names, including initiating the use of more categories

of domain names, such as *.firm* for businesses; *.store* for merchants; *.web* for Web-related activities; *.arts* for cultural and entertainment sites; *.rec* for recreational and entertainment sites; *.info* for informational services; and *.nom* for individuals. However, there are many problems to be solved and competing interests to be considered before all of the questions involved in creating and managing a working worldwide system for domain names are answered. Stay tuned.

Ethics

CHAPTER 28

The AIGA Standards of Professional Practice

by Richard Grefé

The AIGA, as a professional association, has adopted standards of conduct for designers as a model for professional performance. They do not represent a restrictive code of behavior within the profession. Instead, they represent guidelines on interactions among designers and clients that reflect a high level of integrity and responsibility.

The graphic design profession is a community that shares a sense of its own talent, often the same educational experience, perhaps the same sense of its purpose, and certainly the same potential client pool. It could also be a strong community built as a cultural community is, from shared ethical habits and reciprocal moral obligations. These understood rules or norms give community members a reason to trust each other and for others in society to trust their expectations of dealing with a designer.

The AIGA standards have emerged from professional dialogue on current practices within the profession and the ethical guidelines of other professions. In joining AIGA, designers associate themselves with these standards; it is expected that they will conduct their business with respect toward the principles embodied in the professional standards.

The Need to Create Trust and the Role of Professional Standards

Trust is critical to a strong and productive designer-client relationship. If a client trusts a designer, he or she will provide the designer with the latitude to solve problems in ways that may exceed a client's original preconceptions. This latitude, in turn, allows more creative and more effective solutions, engaging the designer in ways which make the highest and best use of his or her expertise.

An effective designer-client relationship also requires that a client understand explicitly a design professional's sense of responsibility for privileged information. Trust over

confidentiality becomes critical to the evolution of a designer from a crafter of design solutions to a consultant on effective communications.

As much as every professional yearns for immediate trust from a potential client, trust cannot be asserted simply by producing a published professional code. Trust must be earned over time, either individually or collectively. To be effective, a profession's guidelines must be followed consistently and broadly, until there is a public appreciation that professionals, or the members of a professional association, adhere to certain expected standards of ethical practice, integrity, and professional performance.

These standards for professional practice can come to define a profession, distinct from those who seek similar work without the same level of knowledge or experience. They only work, however, if they are adopted by individual designers, one by one, and are adhered to in their entirety. The AIGA standards relate to performance between designers as well as between designers and clients. The use of standards to establish trust and expectations toward a profession can only occur if they also reflect a trust within a profession.

Standards can affect trust within a profession when they become broadly accepted and even promoted by many. Ultimately, they have achieved their role within the profession when individual designers realize that they should be followed even when they are not in the immediate self-interest of the concerned professional.

A code authenticated by a professional association offers validation to a client for the practices of a designer. This role can be critical when encountering a potential client who has worked with other professionals, for whom the norm is to sell time by the hour, with little concern over the ownership of creative content.

In some professions, standards are called "ethics." The word ethics, for most of us, implies moral values. Many of the issues which confront designers daily, however, are not moral in nature; they relate to norms for professional conduct.

The AIGA Statement of Policy on Professional Practices

The AIGA Statement of Policy on Professional Practices provides all graphic designers with a standard of professional conduct. It accompanies this chapter in its entirety.

The AIGA statement is consistent with model codes in many other countries as well. It is based on the Code of Ethics and Professional Conduct published by the International Council of Graphic Design Associations (ICOGRADA) and refined to reflect practices within the United States.

As with most professional codes, this policy covers the relationships between designers and their clients, their colleagues and the general public. For many professions, it is this code of conduct that separates a profession from a trade. This policy statement presumes the graphic designer serves as a trusted communications consultant for clients. It represents a set of norms for professional practice that define expectations for professional respect. Following the norms should allow each designer to work toward a product which meets client expectations, the designer's creative interests, and his or her financial imperatives.

Major Principles of the Policy

The policy contains a number of individual guidelines, each of which contributes to advancing certain major principles. An explanation of individual guidelines in the context of the broader principles may help to build a sense of the cohesion of the entire statement. It cannot serve its purposes if there is only selective adherence to individual guidelines.

The Designer's Responsibility to Clients

The most rapid means of achieving the respect of clients is to make clear the responsibilities the designer must assume in being retained by a client. The professional responsibility assumed by the designer defines the profession.

> 2.1. A designer shall acquaint himself or herself with a client's business and design standards and shall act in the client's best interests within the limits of professional responsibility.

Graphic design offers value to clients by solving complex visual communication problems. An effective solution requires an understanding of the client's business and design standards. Designers who provide design solutions without working closely with the client to refine the problem statement and understand the context in which the design will operate are unlikely to provide a service that draws on the full strength of graphic design discipline and expertise.

Failure to work in a manner which optimizes the value a client will receive hurts the client and the profession.

2.2. A designer shall not work simultaneously on assignments which create a conflict of interest without the agreement of the clients or employers concerned, except in specific cases where it is the convention of a particular trade for a designer to work at the same time for various competitors.

2.3. A designer shall treat all work in progress prior to the completion of a project and all knowledge of a client's intentions, production methods, and business organization as confidential and shall not divulge such information in any manner whatsoever without the consent of the client. It is the designer's responsibility to ensure that all staff members act accordingly.

The professional relationship between a designer and a client relies on trust. If that trust is at risk, the value of the professional relationship is damaged.

A designer will usually be most effective when she benefits from a thorough understanding of the business practices of a client, even as a part of larger firms' communications strategy team. It is difficult to be an informed participant in strategy without being privy to perspectives on a competitive marketplace that are proprietary to the client. A designer serving two clients in the same competitive marketplace would usually require the designer to advise one client in ways that would be damaging to another. Thus, the designer would be forced to make a decision on behalf of one client, diminishing value to the other client. This is clearly a conflict of interest.

In any case where there is a concern over a perceived conflict of interest, it is appropriate to discuss the issue with a client.

Compensation for Work and the Troublesome Issue of Speculative Work

Issues related to the value of a designer's work offer a forceful means of impressing upon clients that graphic design is a profession, not a craft.

Designers regularly receive requests for pro bono work and are sometimes naively asked for casual assistance on design problems, as if this were not a profession that has serious value associated with it. The intent of the standards is not to discourage informal and formative comments from designers to friends, clients, and the public which help others to appreciate and implement effective design. The purpose of the following specific guideline is

to communicate consistently and cumulatively that professional advice from a designer has substantial market value and should not be expected under terms that would be unacceptable in other professions, such as doctors or lawyers.

> 4.1. A designer shall not undertake any work for a client without adequate compensation, except with respect to work for charitable or nonprofit organizations.

Unless designers establish a consistent norm of asking for payment for their work, they will find it difficult to establish that the designer's judgment and experience have value.

> 4.2. A designer shall not undertake any speculative projects either alone or in competition with other designers for which compensation will only be received if a design is accepted or used. This applies not only to entire projects but also to preliminary schematic proposals.

Unacceptability of speculative work is not an ethical issue in the sense of a moral or natural right or wrong. Undertaking speculative work, particularly when expected to do so, represents an approach toward problem solving which few in the profession would sanction—it suggests effective design outcomes can be achieved from developing visual representations without the research and analysis stage, which is the most time consuming and must precede solutions.

The expectation that designers will undertake speculative work is a signal of disrespect for the value of a designer's work. Willingness to undertake it reflects lack of confidence in the value of one's own work. Every designer will be challenged on this practice and will make individual decisions on a case by case basis. Only if the profession as a whole acts consistently on the issue will a new norm be established. The norm will be established when each designer begins to follow it in his or her own practice, regardless of what others around him or her are doing.

This is one of the most difficult standards to accept for many designers because they react to its violation with the righteousness of a moral issue, yet feel forced to succumb to the practice as an economic issue. Ultimately, its consequence is neither. Its value is in defining the nature of the professional relationship which a designer is expected to have with

a client and a problem. Adopting the practice, even at some initial cost in lost prospects, will yield a stronger and more rewarding professional experience for all designers who adhere to the standards in the future.

There will always be some graphic designers who do not adhere to this standard. The profession cannot allow the ones who do not to define the nature of the profession. There needs to be a strong and consistent commitment to principles that will demonstrate the difference between those who are professionals and those who are not.

Speculative work has become a lightning rod in defining the nature of the work of this profession. This practice calls for designers to create images without having the time and resources to commit to solving the problem. This is not graphic design as it has evolved. It is a form of commercial illustration. The practice results in products and services which are misleading about what the profession of graphic design is.

Standing Up for the Profession

Designers must show respect for other designers in order to signal how seriously they take the norms against which they would like to be held. These standards, if applied, may disadvantage the individual designer who espouses them, yet all designers will benefit indirectly from the demonstration of a profession that strives for higher expectations. For instance, there is an effort to: encourage designers to promote selection processes which are based on open consideration of designers in ways which stress designers' effectiveness and the quality of his or her work; and assure that other designers are treated with respect if a client is seeking to change designers or use another designer's work.

Promoting an Accurate and Complete Impression of the Profession

In order to develop trust and respect for individual and collective responsibility, it is important to develop a profession-wide commitment to accurate representation about the capabilities of the profession; to demonstrate public respect for other designers; to assign credit and responsibility clearly and accurately; and to avoid misleading statements in promotional pieces. The adopted standards include specific expectations for publicity statements and authorship.

The Role of the AIGA in Promoting Professional Standards

Standards or norms within a profession are only meaningful if they are broadly respected within a profession; if there is public awareness of their existence as a distinguishing feature of professional performance; and if the profession is trained to fulfill the expectations which they create.

The AIGA is active in each of these areas. Over the past several years, it has been active in developing standards and promoting them within the profession. The AIGA is about to embark on a public awareness campaign within the business community that will promote professional graphic design and the existence of standards. All of AIGA's current activities at the national level are focused on informing the public and the business community that design is a problem-solving discipline in which graphic designers play a critical role and that good design has measurable value to them. Finally, the AIGA is currently working to develop accreditation standards for four-year graphic design programs and postgraduate programs that will provide further definition of the character of the profession.

To the extent that designers use the initials "AIGA" after their name or acknowledge membership in the AIGA, they are making a commitment to the professional standards. Some designers also place a small line at the bottom of each invoice that acknowledges that the firm's practice is governed by the standards for professional practice of the American Institute of Graphic Arts. The more frequent practices such as this become, the more effective the standards will become as accepted norms within the profession.

AIGA

Purpose

The purpose of the statement of policy on professional practices is to provide all American Institute of Graphics Arts members with a clear standard of professional conduct. The AIGA encourages the highest level of professional conduct in design. However, the policy is not binding. Rather, it reflects the view of the AIGA on the kind of conduct that is in the best interest of the profession, clients, and the public.

For the purposes of this document the word "designer" means an individual, practicing design as a freelance or salaried graphic designer, or group of designers acting in partnership or other form of association.

The designer's professional responsibility

1.1   A designer shall at all times act in a way which supports the aims of the AIGA and its members, and encourages the highest standards of design and professionalism.

1.2   A designer shall not undertake, within the context of his or her professional practice, any activity that will compromise his or her status as a professional consultant.

The designer's responsibility to clients

2.1   A designer shall acquaint himself or herself with a client's business and design standards and shall act in the client's best interest within the limits of professional responsibility.

2.2   A designer shall not work simultaneously on assignments which create a conflict of interest without agreement of the clients or employers concerned, except in specific cases where it is the convention of a particular trade for a designer to work at the same time for various competitors.

2.3   A designer shall treat all work in progress prior to the completion of a project and all knowledge of a client's intentions, production methods and business organization as confidential and shall not divulge such information in any manner whatsoever without the consent of the client. It is the designer's responsibility to ensure that all staff members act accordingly.

The designer's responsibility to other designers

3.1   Designers in pursuit of business opportunities should support fair and open competition based upon professional merit.

3.2   A designer shall not knowingly accept any professional assignment on which another designer has been or is working without notifying the other designer or until he or she is satisfied that any previous appointments have been properly terminated and that all materials relevant to the continuation of the project are the clear property of the client.

3.3   A designer must not attempt, directly or indirectly, to supplant another designer through unfair means; nor must he or she compete with another designer by means of unethical inducements.

3.4   A designer must be fair in criticism and shall not denigrate the work or reputation of a fellow designer.

3.5   A designer shall not accept instructions from a client which involve infringement of another person's property rights without permissions, or consciously act in any manner involving any such infringement.

3.6   A designer working in a country other than his or her own shall observe the relevant Code of Conduct of the national society concerned.

Revised 7/96   The American Institute   164 Fifth Avenue   Page 1
                    of Graphic Arts   New York, New York 10010
                                                 Telephone 212 807-1990
                    www.aiga.org   Facsimile 212 807-1799

Fees	4.1	A designer shall not undertake any work for a client without adequate compensation, except with respect to work for charitable or non-profit organizations.
	4.2	A designer shall not undertake any speculative projects either alone or in competition with other designers for which compensation will only be received if a design is accepted or used. This applies not only to entire projects but also to preliminary schematic proposals.
	4.3	A designer shall work only for a fee, a royalty, salary or other agreed upon form of compensation. A designer shall not retain any kickbacks, hidden discounts, commission, allowances or payment in kind from contractors or suppliers.
	4.4	A reasonable handling and administration charge may be added, with the knowledge and understanding of the client, as a percentage to all reimbursable items, billable to a client, that pass through the designer's account.
	4.5	A designer who is financially concerned with any suppliers which may benefit from any recommendations made by the designer in the course of a project shall secure the approval of the client or employer of this fact in advance.
	4.6	A designer who is asked to advise on the selection of designers or the consultants shall not base such advice in the receipt of payment from the designer or consultants recommended.
Publicity	5.1	Any self-promotion, advertising, or publicity must not contain deliberate misstatements of competence, experience or professional capabilities. It must be fair both to clients and other designers.
	5.2	A designer may allow a client to use his or her name for the promotion of work designed or services provided but only in a manner which is appropriate to the status of the profession.
Authorship	6.1	A designer shall not claim sole credit for a design on which other designers have collaborated.
	6.2	When not the sole author of a design, it is incumbent upon a designer to clearly identify his or her specific responsibilities or involvement with the design. Examples of such work may not be used for publicity, display or portfolio samples without clear identification of precise areas of authorship.

This document is based on the Code of Ethics and Professional Conduct published by the International Council of Graphic Design Associations (ICOGRADA). The AIGA Statement of Policy on Professional Practices is intended to conform with the ICOGRADA code, while at the same time clarifying its meaning and content in the context of U.S. practice.

CHAPTER 29

Ethics in an Electronic Age

by Don Brunsten

I can only say that, while my own opinions as to ethics do not satisfy me, everyone else's satisfy me less.   —Bertrand Russell

To the general public, the topics of design and ethics seem to go together like fifteenth-century Florentine principles of perspective and 401(k) plans: interesting subjects in their own right but not routinely connected. To the design community, however, professional ethics questions have acquired a new immediacy and relevance because of the rapid development of new digital tools, platforms, and distribution systems for design. On the Web, for example, emerging issues about hyperlinking and viewing source files or disclosures to clients regarding technologically cutting-edge design work are not adequately answered by existing legal standards. The absence of legal standards, however, does not make the search for ethical guidelines a philosophic luxury. On the contrary, designers should now feel compelled, as perhaps never before, to take a long, hard look at the new ethical issues generated by the electronic age. The search for ethical guidelines in design for the electronic age will be frustrating, at best, and susceptible only of rough answers. But if some notion of voluntary ethical conduct does not emerge and take root, the public interest, the courts, and the legislatures will eventually catch up to the design community. The result may be new layers of legal rules and property rights that are not especially design friendly.

While new examples of ethical issues could easily be drawn from a variety of design disciplines, Web design seems to present a particularly interesting case study. Accordingly, this article focuses on several ethical questions that have lately become relevant to Web design. These questions, however, are certain to find echoes in all branches of modern design.

Hyperlinks, Hot Lists, and Para-sites

In considering the application of trademark law to the Web, many would immediately think of the well-publicized disputes that have arisen over domain names, including fights over the rights in such names as Marilyn Monroe, James Dean, a famous New York jazz club, MTV, *Esquire* magazine, Planned Parenthood, and Microsoft Network. The current trend of legal thinking seems to be that existing trademark law is sufficient to protect the owners of valid, preexisting trademarks from having their Web space preempted by aggressive domain name claimants. A number of other, more subtle trademark issues for the Web are on the horizon, however, and may have no answer in current trademark law. The absence of legal answers suggests the need for ethical restraint by Web designers.

For example, it is now becoming clear that the underlying architecture of the Web presents an ethical conundrum for designers. As originally conceived, the Web's raison d'être was hypertext. The introduction of multimedia elements into the Web led to the somewhat expanded concept of hyperlinking. The highly distributed ability to cross-reference all kinds of information gives the Web, as we know it today, amazing power. As the Web becomes progressively more commercial, though, the interplay of trademark interests and the Web's hyperlinking architecture becomes more apparent and more problematic.

Web users are by now extremely familiar with "hot list," typically the incorporation in a Web page of a series of hyperlinks to other sites not controlled by the hot list publisher. Hot lists may reflect the personal tastes of the hot list publisher, or may be included simply to add value for the end user by pointing to outside sites that are especially relevant or worthy of observation.

Until recently, the incorporation of hyperlinks to outside sites or hot lists composed of hyperlinks has not generated substantial controversy. The prevailing theory—and the so-called spirit of the Web—seems to have been that any Web publisher maintaining an open site asks to be seen by the world at large; thus, other sites which point or cross-reference to a publisher's site can only be a boon to the targeted publisher. Furthermore, a hyperlink generally consists of a brief text description, perhaps one word, of the target site. The text description operating as a bookmark for the target site's URL is just a locator, so in one sense, a hyperlink is little more than publication of a phone number or street address. For these reasons, the inclusion in Web pages of hot lists or hyperlinks to outside sites has not been thought to require the permission of the owner of the target sites.

Guilt By Association, Part I

Companies are now asking, however, whether a hyperlink, either by itself or as a result of design and context, implies some connection with or endorsement of the target or dilutes the target's control of its own content and commercial value or, otherwise, tends to create confusion in the marketplace. A recently filed lawsuit on these matters brings into sharp relief the evolving concepts of fair play on the Web.

Microsoft recently began providing a Web service of entertainment and information guides for various cities. Microsoft calls this service Sidewalk. Ticketmaster, the nation's largest vendor of ticketing for live entertainment, entered into negotiations with Microsoft to create some form of online partnership or joint marketing program to funnel Sidewalk users to the Ticketmaster Web site for the purchase of Ticketmaster's inventory of events. The negotiations apparently broke down, but Microsoft wound up including in its Seattle Sidewalk site a hyperlink to Ticketmaster's site. Ticketmaster then filed suit for trademark infringement, contending that Microsoft engaged in "electronic piracy," diluted Ticketmaster's name and trademark, and illegally used Ticketmaster's name and trademark by providing links to its site. The lawsuit seeks a court order barring Microsoft from using the Ticketmaster name and its content on the Seattle Sidewalk site, as well as unspecified damages and fees. Ticketmaster has also implemented technology to block its site to visitors hyperlinking from Sidewalk.

Microsoft has contested Ticketmaster's legal contentions and, to some extent, breached Ticketmaster's fortress by creating "two degrees of separation": Microsoft switched from providing a direct hyperlink from Sidewalk to Ticketmaster to providing a hyperlink to the page of a search engine site, not under Microsoft's control, which in turn offers a hyperlink to Ticketmaster.

One of the remarkable things about this lawsuit is that it appears to run contrary to the hyperlinking tradition of the Web, if it is possible to have meaningful tradition after only a few years. Furthermore, it seems odd that Ticketmaster would reject a healthy increase in traffic through its site. Most site developers are only too happy to be the target of external links. Part of Ticketmaster's argument seems to be that the value of the Microsoft Sidewalk site—and its ability to sell advertising—is enhanced by reference to the name Ticketmaster and by incorporation of a hyperlink to Ticketmaster's site, and that is unfair for Microsoft to capture that value without compensation to Ticketmaster.

This case is merely an early salvo in what promises to be a long battle among various models of Web architecture and commerce. Unquestionably, hyperlinking creates a nexus and some blending between two sites. Legal standards may emerge from the Ticketmaster-Microsoft case, but it is more likely the matter will be settled before a court can enunciate any meaningful standard. Whenever the appellate courts finally get the opportunity to define the law in this area, the chances are we will not be given anything resembling a black-and-white rule.

Guilt By Association, Part II

A relatively new technique—the so-called para-site—brings the blending problem to the next level. A para-site is a Web site that wraps its own identifying frame around other third party sites that are linked from it. This technique keeps the user anchored to the para-site, even as the user is viewing third party materials.

At first glance, para-sites seem the answer to a Web designer's prayer. Designers know that hyperlinks to third party sites add value for the user, but users have an annoying habit of traveling to those outside sites and then failing to return, robbing the starting site of much of its influence. The para-site's use of the frame as an anchor allows hyperlinks to third party materials but tends to curtail user meandering. This consideration is particularly meaningful if the para-site is advertiser supported. But, how should the owners of the third party sites feel about this practice?

One recent action suggests that the owners of third party sites may be none too happy. The *Washington Post* and a number of other well-known news organizations that provide on-line products recently filed suit against an entity called *totalnews.com*. The *Washington Post* and its co-plaintiffs (collectively "the *Post*") alleged that *totalnews.com* designed a parasitic Web site to republish the news and editorial content of other Web sites in order to attract both advertisers and users. The *Post* specifically alleged that *totalnews.com* was designed to feature the content of the *Post*'s Web sites, inserted within a frame on the computer screen that included a *totalnews.com* logo and URL as well as advertising that *totalnews.com* had sold. The *Post* alleged that this framing caused the plaintiffs' Web sites to appear not in the form that the *Post* intended, but in an altered form designed by *totalnews.com* for its own economic advantage. Within the frame, the *Post*'s site did not fill the screen as it would had the user accessed the *Post*'s site directly (or by means of a hyperlink from a Web site that did not frame) and the *Post*'s URL did not appear at the top of the

screen as it normally would. The *Post* further alleged that totalnews.com provided little or none of its own content to the viewer.

Totalnews.com wound up quickly settling this lawsuit. In exchange for mutual releases of liability, *totalnews.com* agreed to cease the practice of framing content linked from the *Post*'s Web sites. The settlement agreement was particularly interesting because totalnews.com also agreed to license from the *Post* the right to publish simple, unadorned hyperlinks to the *Post*'s sites. Under the terms of the agreement, the plaintiffs reserved the right to revoke the license at any time upon fifteen days notice. One can understand *totalnews.com*'s decision not to fight well-heeled plaintiffs on the question of framing, the legal validity of which is unknown. More surprising, perhaps, is *totalnews.com*'s agreement to be bound by a revocable license covering simple hyperlinking, something most people believed it would have had a complete right to do in the absence of any license or permission. In this instance, the deep pockets of the *Post* and the threat of continued litigation appear to have been used to alter radically the extensive cross-referencing capability allowed and even encouraged in Web publishing as we have known it.

The *totalnews.com* case sets no legal precedent, and designers should not overreact to a settlement of expediency. The more general question, though, is at what point does the simultaneous viewing of the para-site anchor and third party content begin to imply an endorsement or connection between the two services? On the flip side, if a para-site adds valuable content of its own, it is not difficult to imagine clever design of frames or other elements to permit content from two or more unrelated sources to rub shoulders together in a more natural way than we have seen so far. Such design innovations could create a marvelous new medium or could create commercial chaos. The answer is likely to be in the eye of the beholder. Designers may rest assured, however, that the development of law to resolve this and similar questions will be both confusing and glacial compared to the advance of technology.

It should be noted that present Javascript techniques may permit Web designers to prevent capture of their pages within para-sites. However, this does nothing to protect the millions of Web pages that have already been designed without such defenses and for which the cost of reengineering would be prohibitive. Moreover, a technology snapshot at any moment in time is relatively meaningless. The arms race in Web technology obviously will continue, driven by competition between the incentive of Web publishers to control the audience's attention in a fluid environment and the incentive of third party publishers to maintain the integrity and branding of their own Web sites.

The Ethical Landscape

Until it is possible to see the actual effects of these techniques over time, the imposition of new legal rules, or the expansion of existing concepts, to preclude hyperlinks or para-sites without the permission of the target seems both harsh and unlikely, but far from impossible. In the meantime, the ethical challenge for designers, who may be dragged by clients to either side of battles on hyperlinking or para-sites, will be to remain focused on finding a workable balance. The first and perhaps most important step is simply to realize that the very interconnectedness of the Web requires ethical sensitivity. Specifically, the following notions of ethical restraint may prove valuable:

- Avoid hyperlinks to sites whose owners you reasonably expect may object to the link. This is neither the impossible assignment of anticipating all potential objections nor the unnecessary assignment of seeking permissions. This is merely the ethical maturity to ask yourself if the hyperlink is really necessary where you have reason to expect an objection would be forthcoming.

- Design of links and para-sites needs to be carefully executed to avoid any implication to the audience of connection with, endorsement or dilution of third party sites, or their advertising. Some Web sites have begun posting disclaimers that appear when hyperlinking to outside sites. This may protect the trademark interests of the third party and may also protect the interests of you and your client if the third party site turns out to have defective or unlawful services, products, or content.

- Obtain your client's approval for all hyperlinks to third parties and all para-sites or similar techniques which may implicate the rights of third parties.

- As a legal matter, more than as an ethical matter, have your written contracts with clients allocate to the client, as much as possible, the risks associated with hyperlinking, para-sites, or similar techniques which may implicate the rights of third parties.

Viewing Source

Current Web browsers, built around HTML, allow end users to see the source code of any document on the Web. The prevailing term for exploiting this capability is "viewing source." Access to underlying HTML code considerably simplifies the process of borrowing a "look and feel" from a third party Web page.

Some legal commentators have suggested that the look and feel of a Web page may be protected by copyright, while others believe that look and feel protection, if any, should be awarded only on a trademark basis, i.e., strictly to prevent public confusion as to the source of the services or products available through a Web site. Legal tests aside, many designers can testify to the bruised ego that goes along with seeing one's own laboriously crafted design concepts popping up at another site.

At the same time, the process of viewing source has clearly been instrumental in building the knowledge base of the design community. Viewing source may be no more an objectionable form of reverse engineering than print designers engage in when they study various publications for ideas to design the next project.

Two San Francisco–area Web publishers were involved recently in a dispute over a carefully crafted page design. The creator of the literary and art site *Fray* asserted that the HTML coding underlying a *Fray* page design, which took some thirty hours to create, was stolen by the Web magazine *Salon. Salon* asserted that it had used a similar concept much earlier but agreed that it had been inspired by *Fray* to modify its earlier work. The controversy was resolved by *Salon* posting a credit on its site for the influence of the *Fray* designers' HTML coding.

Not all disputes are likely to be settled so readily. Despite the difficulty of knowing how much intellectual property protection is going to be afforded to original HTML source code, the golden rule should be a minimum ethical test for design choices. Learn as much as possible about HTML from viewing source, but put yourself in the shoes of your fellow designer before deciding to replicate substantial portions of that designer's code.

Professional Know-How

The brave, new world seems to have given us a Web design "expert" on every corner. A brief tour of the Web leaves many designers grumbling that clients are being poorly served or even ripped off by some of these experts. Analysis of the ingredients that combine to make successful Web design is outside the scope of this article. Yet clearly one ingredient expected by clients is technological mastery of the medium.

The Web and the tools used to create content for the Web are undergoing technological change at a rate rarely seen in any field throughout history. In the ancient period of Web design, several months ago, required technical knowledge for designers included then-current HTML tags and perhaps the ability to create imagery with popular software tools,

such as Adobe Illustrator. Soon, CGI scripting, which could make a Web page the front end for a database, and other more advanced techniques began to appear. A discussion of Web design today would hardly be complete without mention of dynamic HTML, Javascript, Jscript, Active X Controls, CDF, "broad-catching," OpenType, SQL, "shocked" files, cascading style sheets, and a host of other newborn digital tools or standards. New acronyms will soon arrive to make these terms as quaint as "stagecoach" or "DOS." The rate of change seems unlikely to slow down any time soon, particularly as more bandwidth becomes available. In this environment, clients, even comparatively unsophisticated clients, have begun to expect a cutting-edge Web presence for their design dollars.

What should Web designers ethically be expected to disclose to their clients about their ability to hit a rapidly moving technological target? For example, should designers who hold themselves out as Web design experts already be knowledgeable about the newest iterations of dynamic HTML or Javascripting? Clearly some designers pride themselves on knowledge of bleeding edge methods. But, if designers are not completely *au courant*, do they have an ethical obligation to so inform the client in advance?

On one side of the equation, designers obviously face competitive pressures to appear knowledgeable about their craft, and there is certainly a long, if little mentioned, tradition of designers going to school on the client's project. Moreover, not every client expects or wants to pay for the most current technology for its Web site, and designers can legitimately sell the point that simpler or more established techniques may be better. Clients often approach designers based on the clients' knowledge of earlier projects by the designer and are comfortable with the designer's prior art. Some design firms provide extremely valuable design services or concepts with the understanding that those solutions will be implemented by others in the software or Internet domain.

But, at some point, Web designers are likely to run up against an ethical problem that confronts other professions whose knowledge base is complex and constantly changing. Web sites, for many businesses, are a primary window on the world, and a company's Web presence may account for an increasingly significant portion of its image, marketing, and sales. It therefore seems proper to assume, at least initially, that the client would want to know exactly what is possible today in its Web site. As between the client and the consulting professional, the professional is usually the party presumed to know the state of the art sufficiently to bring up what is possible.

Before neurosurgery, for example, patients expect the attending physicians to be intimately familiar with the latest surgical methods, even if those methods turn out to be unnecessary in the case at hand. Patients, like design clients, prefer to feel that the professional they have consulted is capable of implementing whatever technique, new or old, is best for the patient. Similarly, one would not wish tax advice, on the potential methods of disposing of real estate, from an accountant or lawyer who has only vaguely heard of tax-free exchanges and is not abreast of current IRS rulings on the subject.

This sort of ethical problem has not been on the front burner in the design profession, but Web growth has now raised the stakes for all clients, and "Internet time" has collapsed the traditional learning curve for Web designers into something resembling a vertical ascent. Designers thus have a growing ethical responsibility to maintain enough familiarity with rapidly evolving techniques to advise clients intelligently about those techniques and to be straightforward with them about the extent of his or her technical expertise. Fulfillment of this ethical responsibility means, in many instances, a considerable financial investment in new software or hardware and, of course, a major commitment to continued education and training.

Conclusion

Even in the vast reaches of cyberspace, it is easy to be seen as trespassing on the neighbor's property. As designers seek to maximize the value of their work for the client, constant thought needs to be given to design methods that may reduce the likelihood of conflict with third parties. In the short run, designers may not have a great deal of legal exposure from exercises in hyperlinking and para-sites, or from viewing source, but without a shared sense of ethical restraint, the friction in the Web will only increase. As friction increases, new intellectual property laws may make a sudden and possibly unpleasant appearance, much like a drunk who stumbles into the wrong party.

Web designers, and indeed designers from many disciplines, also need to accept that their ethical duties are becoming increasingly similar to those of doctors, lawyers, engineers, or accountants: clients expect to be advised about the latest and greatest developments in the field, even if the newest techniques are not, in the end, necessary for the client and even at the risk that the designer and client may determine that some other designer is right for the job. In medicine, law, engineering, or accounting, the potential liability for misleading a

client about professional know-how is severe. Don't be surprised, as clients experience the financial impact of rapid obsolescence in their design investments, to find the design profession held to similar, implied ethical standards.

Intellectual property laws sometimes seem to be based on a complicated set of policies, but upon close scrutiny, these laws more often reflect a legislature's or court's imprecise, gut reaction about what is right and wrong. Perhaps there are fewer illusions about the precision of ethical tests. Ernest Hemingway wrote, "I know only that what is moral is what you feel good after; what is immoral is what you feel bad after." The cleverest designers of the new electronic age will be those who simply take the time with each project to reflect upon the interests of clients and third parties, because they are the designers who will both remain one step ahead of new intellectual property laws and achieve some peace of mind.

Simplifying Design
(and Your Life)

by Eva Anderson

After nine years of deep immersion in eco-design, I am still trying to probe and stretch the limits of what that actually means. In early 1997, while in New York City as a judge for the American Institute of Graphic Arts (AIGA) "Greening of Design," I was able to dive further into this question. In addition to profound debate over what eco-design actually meant to each of the judges, we found several of the entries reflected the creators' naivete towards ecological choices in design. It seemed they believed that as long as their pieces were printed on recycled paper, they counted as eco-friendly, regardless of whether they were oversized, overprinted, or overdesigned.

But I, and the rest of the judges, wanted more than that. Although specifying re-cycled paper is a good first step, it was frustrating that there wasn't more overall progress reflected in the show. For many pieces, we wondered where the thoughtfulness behind the idea was. Did they consider the total impact—environmental as well as aesthetic? What about their responsibility—not only to their client but to humanity and the earth? Needless to say, the show was much smaller than we had originally anticipated.

The challenge of these issues and the conversations and interactions with my fellow judges left me stimulated and grateful and with more questions about the big picture. Eco-design was more than just tree-free or recycled paper, veggie inks, and alternative technologies. It was, I felt, somehow deeper.

My alter ego speaks:

Since acquiring my official title of "Green Designer" in 1988, I have been consci-entious and observant of my consumer patterns. Being observant has helped me consume less, but I suspect that I still consume at least twenty times more than a person in India, six times more than a Chinese person, and three times more than a person in Mexico.[1]

Having lived in a Third World country has reminded me of this, too. When it's not on the supermarket shelves, or it's astronomically expensive, you'd be amazed at how quickly your consumption patterns shrivel up (but they never really die—they're lying dormant, waiting to get you back in the U.S. of A.).

As conscientious as I try to be, I still have some of those old, bad habits acquired as a child of the fifties when we thought everything was abundant and disposable. Oooooh! A new toy to add to the collection that sits on top of my monitor or the ones that line the wall next to the toilet (well, hey, I get bored easily). And only a buck-fifty, I can afford that! Of course I can—it's just a drop in the bucket.

Which, I realize once I'm home and looking with shame at yet one more tchotchke cluttering up the place, is exactly what it is—a drop in the bucket. Trash. When I think about how easy it was for me to acquire it, and yet how difficult the payment will really be, I cringe. My short-term moment of happiness is dulled by the thought of long-term environmental degradation.

This leads me to thinking about the rest of my life. About how hard I have to work to buy the things I want. And it seems that the more I have to work to maintain this lifestyle, the less time I have to reflect on the purchases I'm making and the more convenience goods I have to buy to maintain my work life, because I don't have any time to do anything myself anymore.

It's a perplexing dilemma. One that my husband Gary and I talk about frequently. We have a strong desire to simplify our lives, but we're not sure where to begin. We're so entrenched in this routine that it's hard to break the cycle.

Which is why, when I went to New York City to judge AIGA's "Greening of Design," I stayed a couple of extra days to attend The Learning Alliance's "Voluntary Simplicity: Reducing Consumption, Building Community, Enjoying Life" workshop. Here at last, I felt, I might find some answers to the deeper meaning of eco-design.

Homecoming/Coming Home

Alas! None appeared specifically that I could apply directly to graphic design practices. Frustrated, I finally posed the question in a discussion group: "What message could I bring to *ECO* readers to help inspire them to share the vision of simplicity and living/designing lightly on the earth?"

"GAIA!," belted out the discussion leader. I turned to look at him in disbelief. "But I'm writing for *designers*. Many of them could care less about holistic principles. I need something more concrete, more basic!"

Gaia? That's it? How could I ever convey such a huge concept in this little article?

As I relaxed into the long train ride home, I reflected on my experience in New York City, and pondered the message that had been given to me.

Gaia. A big answer, yes. And yet, his response was brilliant. In its simplicity, Gaia is elegantly filled with meaning: Everything is connected to everything else. In design, what does this mean?

Let's go back to my example of oversized/overprinted pieces. If virgin paper is used, more trees are cut to make extra paper for the oversized piece; more petroleum is needed to power the trucks to transport the lumber to the mills; more energy, water, and chemicals are used to convert the lumber into pulp, then into paper; more petroleum is again needed to power the trucks to transport the paper; more soy beans are grown and more petroleum, minerals, and heavy metals are mined to make the inks for overprinted pieces; etc. And even if recycled or tree-free paper is used, extra energy, water, chemicals, and petroleum are still consumed. In each excessive design, there are corresponding environmental impacts.

Understanding this rationale on an intellectual level is fairly simple. However, for me, it still did not solve the dilemma of how to truly get designers to consistently integrate this way of thinking into their designs. There was still the chance that this example could be dismissed with "No one will know the difference with just this one small run" or some other rationalization.

Realizing that the solution is to help designers integrate the concept of Gaia into their everyday actions—not just in the studio, but at home and the world at large, in relationships with their partners, kids, community, pets, gardens, and *themselves*—I began to read.

What follows is an abbreviated description of historical and philosophical events and ideas that helped me understand how we got into this mess, some possible solutions, and how this all relates to graphic designers.

The Magic Paper Trick

The first book I happened upon was *Less is More*.[2] I ordered it from an ad I saw in *Common Boundary* magazine, thinking that I would learn about source reduction and living simply. Instead, it was "The Art of Voluntary Poverty." I was a bit put off at first, because I just wanted to simplify, not live in poverty.

Still, I read the book cover to cover and had some pretty incredible revelations (although I have yet to develop a desire to live in poverty!).

Money Is Not Good or Evil in Itself

Money is too abstract to carry any actual characteristics. Although we may have a piece of money in our hand, whether a bill, a check, or an ATM card, it is merely a representation of good intent. Today, it doesn't even represent a pile of gold the government keeps locked away. Nothing backs it except the well-placed motto "In God We Trust." Money represents our willingness to trust our government and is the tool that we have created to share what we produce. So how can it be good? Or bad?

On the other hand, money is our mirror. How we flow it into and out of our lives is a reflection of our own innate goodness or badness—or ignorance. How we use it reflects our views of how we want this world to be. Do we sell our design to promote a high-consumption, alienating culture? And turn around and buy products that are not essential to our lives? Do we sell messages and products that help inform and educate our communities, including a greater understanding of self and ecology? And buy only what we need from companies that are trying to help maintain a sustainable world?

Interestingly enough, I discovered that the word "wealth" originally meant "well-being".[3] Yet we have degraded and narrowed it to refer only to certain material goods measured by money, an object that really only has a certain value because those in power say so. And as commerce and banking continue their rampant development, money will correspond less and less to any tangible reality and become more and more abstract. (Is it any wonder that it is so hard to relate the value of the bill we hold in our hands to the hours in our lives that we have dedicated to acquiring the bill?)

I feel this way about a certain genre of design that has evolved with the latest round of computer technology. It is confusion behind masks and layers. It is speed and hype, and I feel alienated when I see it. The cacophony of image and text prevents me from attaining the silence I need to make sound judgments about the actual content.

"It's" Got You, Babe

Such is a great deal of magazine and television advertising and their accompanying design pieces. The promise of timeliness, "Buy Now!"; self-fulfillment, "You'll be left out if you don't because you're not hip/rich/beautiful enough!"; material gains as a source of stability, "Get richer quicker!"; and the quick fix, "We have the answer to your problems!" will never be fulfilled. There will always be some technology or thing that is newer, better, sleeker, and more efficient.

In this scenario, we are thrust into a void of intangible wants and needs. Yet because they will never be realized, we will always be kept at a distance from the "it" we are craving.

We have forgotten that, although it takes time to develop and nurture, "it" lies within us. The "it" we crave is the lost connection to our selves, to our communities and families, and the delicate balances of plants and animals and stars and planets and galaxies that give us our life. If we keep searching outside of ourselves for "it," we will continue on our path of ecological degradation and societal decay as we continue our patterns of consumption.

How Did We Get Here?

Until about the sixteenth century, nature was seen as animate. Animals and plants had souls, and spiritual and psychic entities permeated the world.

During the sixteenth and early seventeenth centuries, in both religion and science, the natural world was stripped of its *anima* (soul) and desacralized. This left nature unprotected from any religious or spiritual protection and up for grabs for exploitation.

In the book *Natural Grace,* Rupert Sheldrake explains that Sir Francis Bacon "Most clearly put forward a new agenda for human domination through science and technology. Through probing Nature's secret places, as he put it, man could find out her secrets so that he could more effectively bind her into servitude and have dominion and power over her— Mother Nature no longer had any intrinsic value of her own, but was simply there for man to use as he saw fit. Bacon helped prepare the way for the mechanistic revolution in science. The world was deanimated and effectively became regarded as an automatic machine with no soul, no spontaneous life, and no purposes of its own. Animals and plants were inanimate, thought of as machines and so was the human body."[4]

This mechanistic view still pervades today in Western scientific, medical, and agricultural philosophies and practices. It is promoted by the advertising and design industries with their bombardment of television, magazine, and printed propaganda.

Changes are gradually occurring, although mainly in the field of physics and alternative medicine. The cosmos is again seen as a living organism, and a good portion of society—even business—is responding to the transition. But we still have a long way to go to be fully involved in the next evolutionary phase.

Where Do We Go Next?

We are living in times of great decisions. All indicators point to environmental degradation and eventual failure within forty to sixty years. As Western society transitions from the Industrial Age, in which we are defined by extraction of natural resources for mass consumption, material possessions, and social position, we will need to relearn to simplify our lives if we are to survive and remediate the eco-degradation of our past patterns.

In modern physics, a sense is evolving that what the experimenter is looking for, and how one looks for it affects what is found. Moreover, what is observed is affected by the expectations of the experimenter. Therefore, it stands to reason that the way we view life and what we expect out of life will determine the outcomes of our lives.

Designing a Simple Life

Throughout my research, I discovered a thread that linked all readings: the practice of simplicity is the foundation for our success.

Duane Elgin, in his book *Voluntary Simplicity* elegantly relates, "In living more simply, we encounter life more directly. We need little when we are directly in touch with life. It is when we remove ourselves from direct and wholehearted participation in life that emptiness and boredom creep in. It is then that we begin our search for something or someone that will fill our gnawing dissatisfaction."[5]

As designers, when we run on automatic, zipping from deadline to deadline, being lulled into a computer daze, designing without regard to environmental or sociological impact, we give up a great portion of our capacity for voluntary, deliberate action.

If we slow down and become mindful, we remember ourselves. In the process of questioning/observing, we "re-member"—make whole again—versus "dis-member."[6] We live less and less in the almost incessant state of mental distractions our society promotes and become more thoughtful and aware of our feelings, thoughts, and behaviors. Once aware of ourselves, we can then become aware of the world around us.

Simplicity Is a State of Mind

Living and designing simply is not just about material frugality, recycled paper, or source reduction. It is a way of thinking about things. It is understanding and feeling that connection to everything else. It is Gaia. It begins inside each one of us, in our own unique way. Simplicity starts with small changes.

For me, I've decided to clear myself of credit card debt, so that I'm not living on "borrowed" time. This has meant spending far less and making conscious choices when spending. With limited finances, I am more aware of what's important to me and spend less time and money on things that are superfluous. Interestingly enough, I feel rather wealthy as I have realized how much I truly have: a healthy self that I continue to work on both inside and out, a loving husband and family, time to eat dinner together, and a warm place to lay myself at night.

In design, the seed of simplicity could be as minimal as spec'ing recycled paper — even if it's done because it's "the right thing to do." Potentially, a deeper understanding could develop. One may realize that trees are left undisturbed. The many levels of ecosystems in the trees that sustain insects, animals, plants, and birds are allowed to thrive. They, in turn, interact with other ecosystems that directly contribute to our own well-being. A profound sense of gratitude for the presence of these beings may evolve and touch our innermost core. At last, our void is filled! We have found "it"!

In isolation, these small acts seem inconsequential. But as the small changes accumulate over time and frequency, they have potential for lasting sociological and ecological transformation.

At the same time, we must be careful not to remain passive spectators. Much needs to be done, and many small acts by *all* citizens must be taken. We must push ourselves beyond that first good step and rise to the challenge within ourselves. We have to stay aware of the meaning behind our actions, keeping in mind the big picture, Gaia, and constantly questioning our motives and the impacts of our decisions. In other words, we must be conscious not only of the choices in front of us, but conscious of ourselves as we choose.

Simple design as the end goal. Applying the principle of simplicity to our communications design, we will tend to design more directly, clearly, and honestly. As we evolve into an increasingly more abstract, technologically-based society, we must remember to keep our spirit in balance. Equally, as design tools become more technological and abstract, we must

remember to stay centered and not get seduced into a design ethic that is alienating to ourselves and our audiences.

Just as John Ruskin said, "There is no wealth but life," there is no design *without* life.[7] As designers, we live to communicate. What we choose to say during this epic cultural shift is of utmost importance to the survival and wealth of our future. Individually, we each make our choices. Collectively, we all will shape the future of our species.

Endnotes

1. Mark Leiren Young, "Madison Avenue's Worst Nightmare," *Utne Reader,* Jan.–Feb. 97, 74.

2. Goldian VanderBroeck, *Less is More* (Rochester, VT: Inner Traditions, 1996).

3. *Ibid.*

4. Matthew Fox and Rupert Sheldrake, *Natural Grace* (New York: Doubleday, 1996).

5. Duane Elgin, *Voluntary Simplicity: Toward a Life that is Outwardly Simple, Inwardly Rich— Revised Edition* (New York: Quill/William Morrow, 1993).

6. *Ibid.*

7. Goldian VanderBroeck, *Less is More.*

Resources

Organizations for Graphic Designers

by Emily Ruth Cohen

Professional Organizations—International and National

The following is a list of national organizations; several have local or regional chapters. Please contact each organization for current chapter information and listings.

American Center for Design (ACD)

325 West Huron Street, Suite 711, Chicago, IL 60610

(800)-257-8657; *www.ac4d.org*

The ACD is a nonprofit national membership organization that serves the needs of designers of all disciplines. Its mission is to educate and inform design professionals about current research, ideas, and technology that affects design; to support excellence in design education; to educate the business community about the strategic value of design; and to build public awareness of design's role in shaping our culture and economy.

The American Institute of Graphic Arts (AIGA)

164 Fifth Avenue, New York, NY 10010

(212) 807-1990; *www.aiga.org*

The purpose of the AIGA is to advance excellence in graphic design as a discipline, profession, and cultural force. The AIGA provides leadership in the exchange of ideas and information, the encouragement of critical analysis and research, and the advancement of education and ethical practice.

Association of Professional Design Firms (APDF)

450 Irwin Street, San Francisco, CA 94107

(415) 626-9774

APDF is dedicated to elevating the standards of design and professional practice for design consulting firms.

Broadcast Designers Association (BDA)

145 West 45th Street, Suite 1100, New York, NY 10036

(212) 376-6222; *www.bdaweb.com*

BDA is a nonprofit professional association that advocates the value and usefulness of design in the television/audio and entertainment industries. BDA International strives to improve the efficiency of the design process and the quality of the design product in electronic media by fostering a continuous exchange of ideas, information, and experience.

Corporate Design Foundation

20 Park Plaza, Suite 321, Boston, MA 02116

(617) 340-7097; *www.cdf.org*

The Corporate Design Foundation is a nonprofit research and educational organization founded on the belief that individual and company interests can be best served through the effective use of product, communication, and environmental design.

The Design Management Institute (DMI)

29 Temple Place, 2nd Floor, Boston, MA 02111

(617) 338-6380; *www.dmi.org*

The DMI's vision is to inspire the best management of the design process in organizations worldwide. Its mission is to be the international authority and advocate on design management.

Graphic Artist Guild (GAG)

90 John Street, Suite 403, New York, NY 10038-3202

(212) 791-3400

(800) 878-2753; *www.gag.org*

The GAG promotes and protects the economic interests of member artists and is committed to improving conditions for all creators of graphic art and raising standards for the entire industry. The GAG is a union that embraces all creators of graphic art intended for presentation as originals or reproductions at all levels of skill and expertise.

Industrial Designers Society of America (IDSA)

1142 Walker Road, Great Falls, VA 22066

(703) 759-0100; *www.idsa.org*

IDSA is a professional organization dedicated to communicating the value of industrial design to society, business, and government. It provides leadership to and promotes dialogue between practice and education.

International Association of Business Communicators (IABC)

1 Hallidie Plaza, #600, San Francisco, CA 94102

(415) 782-4635; *www.iabc.com*

The IABC is the leading resource of effective communication. It provides products, services, activities, and networking opportunities to help people and organizations achieve excellence in public relations, employee communication, marketing communication, public affairs, and other forms of communication.

International Interactive Communication Society (IICS)

10160 SW Nimbus Avenue, Suite F2, Portland, OR 97223

(503) 620-3604; *www.iics.org*

Comprised of multimedia professionals, the IICS is a global organization dedicated to the advancement of interactive systems, techniques, and applications.

International Society of Graphic Designers (ISGD)

201 Main Street, Charlestown, MA 02129

(617) 241-7680

The ISGD's mission is to promote cooperation between American and other graphic designers and to foster increased communication within the international design community.

Organization of Black Designers (OBD)

300 M Street SW, Suite #N110, Washington, DC 20024

(202) 659-3918; *www.core77.com/OBD*

OBD is a nonprofit national professional association dedicated to promoting the visibility, education, empowerment, and interaction of its membership and the understanding and value that diverse design perspectives contribute to world culture and commerce. OBD

was founded to educate the design professions regarding the contributions of African-Americans and other people of color.

Package Design Council

481 Carlisle Drive, Herndon, VA 22070

(703) 318-7225; *www.packinfo-world.org*

The Council is a comprehensive international membership organization for the package design community.

Society for Environmental Graphic Designers (SEGD)

401 F Street, NW, Suite 333, Washington, DC 20001

(202) 638-5555

The SEGD is an international nonprofit organization founded to promote public awareness of and professional development in the field of environmental graphic design.

Society of Newspaper Design

129 Dryer Street, Providence, RI 02903-3904

(401) 276-2100; *www.snd.org*

SND is an international organization of designers, artists, editors, photographers, art directors, students, and faculty who design newspapers, magazines, and Web pages.

Society of Publication Designers (SPD)

60 East 42nd Street, Suite 721, New York, NY 10165

(212) 983-8585; *www.spd.org*

The SPD, an organization for magazine and newspaper design professionals, works to promote the art director's role as visual journalist and partner in the editorial process, and to recognize and reward quality and innovation in publication design.

Type Directors Club (TDC)

60 East 42nd Street, #721, New York, NY 10165

(212) 983-6042; *users.aol.com/typeclub*

An organization dedicated to the appreciation and understanding of letterforms and

calligraphy, the TDC has an international membership, sponsors an annual juried exhibition, and maintains a regular roster of events exploring and expanding the practice of typography.

Webmaster's Guild

P.O. Box 381231, Cambridge, MA 02238-1231

www.webmaster.org

The Webmaster's Guild brings together people involved in all aspects of developing and supporting World Wide Web sites and technology. Its goal is to provide a forum for sharing information within and across all of the Web disciplines. By doing so, it increases members' depth and breadth of knowledge.

Related Professional Organizations

ACM/SIGGRAPH

1515 Broadway, New York, NY 10036

(212) 869-07440; *www.siggraph.org*

SIGGRAPH is the ACM special-interest group on computer graphics. Its scope is to promote among its members the acquisition and exchange of information and opinion on the theory, design, implementation, and application of computer-generated graphics and interactive techniques to facilitate communication and understanding. SIGGRAPH serves the entirety of the computer graphics community, including artists, technicians, researchers, and the academic and business communities.

The Advertising Council

261 Madison Avenue, 11th Floor, New York, NY 10016

(212) 922-1500; *www.adcouncil.org*

The Advertising Council is a private, nonprofit organization of volunteers who conduct advertising campaigns for the public good. The Council is the largest source of public service advertising in this country and is credited with creating the category of public service advertising.

Advertising Photographers of America (APA)

National Headquarters

7201 Melrose Avenue, Los Angeles, CA 90046

(213) 935-2056; *www.apanational.com*

APA is a national nonprofit trade association. Its key goals are to promote the highest standards of business practice within the industry, and to promote an awareness and understanding of the role of advertising and commercial photographers within the creative community.

The American Advertising Federation (AAF)

1101 Vermont Avenue NW, Suite 500, Washington, DC 20005

(202) 898-0089; *www.aaf.org.*

The AAF is the unifying voice for advertising. It is the only professional advertising association that binds the mutual interests of corporate advertisers, agencies, media companies, suppliers, and academia. The AAF's Web site has a comprehensive list of affiliated local federations, including local art directors' clubs.

American Association of Advertising Agencies (AAAA)

405 Lexington Avenue, 18th Floor, New York, NY 10174

(212) 682-2500; *www.commercepark.com/AAAA*

AAAA is the national trade association of the advertising agency business. It is a management-oriented organization, offering its members the broadest feasible depth of information regarding the operation of advertising agencies, encompassing management, media, print and broadcast production, secondary research on advertising and marketing, international advertising, and more.

American Institute of Architects (AIA)

1735 New York Avenue NW, Washington, DC 20006-5292

(202) 626-7300; *www.aia.org*

The AIA is a nonprofit educational organization dedicated to cultivating the public's understanding of architecture and the human experience.

American Society of Interior Designers (ASID)

608 Massachusetts Avenue NE, Washington, DC 20002

(202) 546-3480; *www.asid.org*

ASID is a professional organization for interior designers. Professional members must pass rigorous acceptance standards; they must have a combination of accredited design education and/or full-time work experience and pass a two-day accreditation examination.

American Society of Landscape Architects (ASLA)

4401 Connecticut Avenue NW, 5th Floor, Washington, DC 20009

(202) 686-2752; *www.asla.org*

ASLA is a national professional society that represents the landscape architecture profession in the United States.

American Society of Media Photographers, Inc. (ASMP)

14 Washington Road, Suite 502, Princeton Junction, NJ 08550-1033

(609) 799-8300; *www.asmp.org*

ASMP is a trade organization that promotes photographers' rights, educates photographers in better business practices, and produces business publications for photographers.

Color Association of the United States (CAUS)

409 West 44th Street, New York, NY 10036

(212) 582-6884; *(Web site may be launched in July)*

CAUS is an international organization representing leaders in every branch of fashion, textiles, design industries, and general trade in which color is a factor. The Association serves as the authority and arbiter of commercial colors in the United States and in this role exerts great influence on American production and businesses worldwide.

Color Marketing Group (CMG)

5904 Richmond Highway, Suite 408, Alexandria, VA 22303

(703) 329-8500; *www.colormarketing.org*

CMG is a not-for-profit, international association of 1,500 color designers involved in the use of color as it applies to the profitable marketing of goods and services. CMG members are highly qualified color designers who interpret, create, forecast, and select colors for manufactured products.

Graphic Communications Association (GCA)

100 Daingerfield Avenue, Alexandria, VA 22314

(703) 519-8160; *www.gca.org*

GCA is a volunteer nonprofit membership association formed to apply computer technology to printing, publishing, and related industries. No other organization brings such a diverse pool of competitors, customers, and suppliers together to better the information technologies and print communications industry.

International Digital Imaging Association (IDIA)

84 Park Avenue, Flemington, NJ 08822

(908) 782-4635; *www.idia.org*

IDIA serves the digital imaging industry by pursuing the development of standards for the storage, management, output, and distribution of digital data.

International Interior Design Association (IIDA)

341 Merchandise Mart, Chicago, IL 60654-1104

(312) 467-1950; *www.iida.com*

IIDA is a professional nonprofit association with members holding the highest qualifications in the profession and representing all specialties of interior design.

National Association of Schools of Art and Design (NASAD)

11250 Roger Bacon Drive, Suite 21, Reston, VA 20190

(703) 437-0700

The major responsibilities of the Association are the accreditation of postsecondary educational programs in art and design, and the establishment of curricular standards and guidelines.

National Directory of Artists' Internships

c/o National Network of Artist Placement (NNAP)

935 West Avenue 37, Los Angeles, CA 90065

(213) 222-4035

NNAP provides job placement career counseling of fine and performing artists. NNAP's mission is to shorten the distance between artist emergence and paid professional.

The One Club for Art and Copy

32 East 21st Street , New York, NY 10010

(212) 979-1900; *www.oneclub.com*

      The One Club for Art and Copy is a nonprofit organization founded in 1975. The Club serves the creative community in advertising and has a membership of approximately nine-hundred members, including copywriters and art directors.

Picture Agency Council of America (PACA)

P.O. Box 308, Northfield, MN 55057

1-800-457-PACA; *www.pacaoffice.org*

      Trade association of stock picture agencies in North America.

Printing Industries of America (PIA)

100 Daingerfield Rd., Alexandria, VA 22314-2888

(703) 519-8100; *www.printing.org*

      PIA is the world's largest graphic arts trade association and is in the business of promoting programs, services, and an environment that helps its members operate profitably.

Society of Illustrators (SI)

128 East 63rd Street, New York, NY 10021

(212) 838-2560

      The SI aims at fulfilling and continuously extending its function in the community to promote and stimulate interest in the art of illustration, past, present, and future, and to give impetus for high ideals in the art by every means of communication.

Society of Photographers and Artists Representatives (SPAR)

60 East 42nd Street, Suite 1166, New York, NY 10165

(212) 779-7464

      SPAR is a nonprofit association of professional representatives of illustrators, photographers, and related talents.

University and College Designers Association (UCDA)

209 Commerce Street, Alexandria, VA 22314

(703) 548-1770

UCDA promotes excellence in visual communications for educational institutions.

Volunteer Lawyers for the Arts (VLA)

1 East 53rd Street, 6th Floor, New York, NY 10022

(212) 319-2910

VLA provides free arts-related legal assistance to artists and nonprofit art organizations in all creative disciplines who otherwise could not afford it.

Conference Only Organizations

International Design Conference at Aspen (IDCA)

P.O. Box 664, Aspen, CO 81612

(970) 925-2257; *www.idca.org*

TED Conference

P.O. Box 186, Newport, RI 02840

(401) 848-2299; *www.ted.com*

Professional Organizations—Local

Advertising Club of New York

235 Park Avenue South, 6th Floor, New York, NY 10003

(212) 533-8080

Art Directors Clubs (ADC)

The ADC has no central organization or formal network. Each ADC typically consists of leading creatives in advertising, graphic design, interactive media, broadcast design, typography, packaging, environmental design, photography, illustration, and related disciplines. The American Advertising Federation's Web site (*http://www.aaf.org*) has an extensive list of affiliated local federations, including local Art Directors Clubs. The following is only a partial listing:

Art Directors and Artists Club (ADAC)

2791 24th Street, Sacramento, CA 95818

(916) 731-8802; *www.adac.org*

ADC of Denver

P.O. Box 1324, Broomfield, CO 80038

(303) 466-7888

ADC of New Jersey

75 Kearny Ave., Kearny, NJ 07032

(201) 997-1212; *www.adcnj.com*

ADC of New York

250 Park Avenue South, New York, NY 10003-1402

(212) 674-0500; *www.adcny.org*

ADC of Houston

P.O. Box 271137, Houston, TX 77277

(713) 961-3434; *www.mediaplace.com/adch*

ADC of Metropolitan Washington

1620 Greenbrier Court , Reston, VA 20190

(703) 742-8055; *www.adcmw.org*

ADC of Philadelphia

994 Old Eagle School Road, Suite 1019, Wayne, PA 19087

(610) 971-4850; *www.adcphila.org*

Cleveland Advertising Association

2000 East 9th Street, Cleveland, OH 44115

(216) 241-4807; *www.cleveadmedia.com*

The Connecticut ADC

P.O. Box 639, Avon, CT 06001

(860) 651-0886

Dallas Society of Visual Communicators (DSVC)

3530 Highmesa Drive, Dallas, TX 75234

(972) 241-2017; *www.dsvc.org*

Western ADC

P.O. Box 996, Palo Alto, CA 94302

(415) 321-4196; *www.designlink.com/WADC*

Artists in Print

665 Third Avenue, San Francisco, CA 94017

(415) 243-8244; *www.design.link.com/aip*

Artists in Print is nonprofit resource and support center for the Bay Area graphic arts community.

Selected Bibliography

by Emily Ruth Cohen

The following books cover topics related to the business and legal aspects of graphic design. Theoretical, historical, inspirational, how-to, and technical books are not included within this bibliography.

Business and Legal Forms for Graphic Designers, by Tad Crawford and Eva Doman Bruck. Allworth Press.

The Business of Graphic Design: A Sensible Approach to Marketing and Managing a Graphic Design Firm, by Ed Gold. Watson-Guptill Publications.

The Business of Multimedia, by Nina Schuyler. Allworth Press.

The Business Side of Creativity, by Cameron S. Foote. W. W. Norton & Company.

Careers by Design: A Headhunter's Secrets for Success and Survival in Graphic Design, by Roz Goldfarb. Allworth Press.

Clients and Designers, by Ellen Shapiro. Watson-Guptill Publications.

The Complete Guide to Eco-Friendly Design, by Poppy Evans. North Light Books.

The Designer's Common Sense Business Book, by Barbara Ganim. North Light Books.

Electronic Design and Publishing: Business Practices, by Liane Sebastian. Allworth Press.

Electronic Highway Robbery, by Mary E. Carter. Peachpit Press.

The Graphic Artist's Guide to Marketing and Self-Promotion, by Sally Prince Davis. North Light Books.

Graphic Artist's Guild Handbook of Pricing and Ethical Guidelines. North Light Books.

Graphic Design: A Career Guide and Education Directory, compiled by the AIGA. Watson-Guptill Publications.

Graphic Design Career Guide, by James Craig. Watson-Guptill Publications.

The Graphic Design Portfolio: How to Make a Good One, by Paula Scher. Watson-Guptill
　　Publications.

The Graphic Designer's Source Book, by Poppy Evans. North Light Books.

How to Make Your Design Business Profitable, by Joyce M. Stewart. North Light Books.

Legal Guide for the Visual Artist, by Tad Crawford. Allworth Press.

Licensing Art & Design, by Caryn R. Leland. Allworth Press.

Marketing and Promoting Your Work, by Maria Piscopo. North Light Books.

The New Business of Design, by The International Design Conference in Aspen. Allworth Press.

1997 Artist's & Graphic Designer's Market, edited by Mary Cox. North Light Books.

Pricing, Estimating & Budgeting, by Theo Stephan Williams. North Light Books.

The Professional Designer's Guide to Marketing Your Work, by Mary Yeung. North Light
　　Books.

Selling Graphic Design, by Don Sparkman. Allworth Press.

Setting the Right Price for Your Design and Illustration, by Barbara Ganim. North Light
　　Books.

Web and New Media Pricing Guide, by JP Frenza and Michelle Szabo. Hayden Books.

Magazines

@Issue: The Journal of Business and Design, Corporate Design Foundation, 20 Park Plaza,
　　#321, Boston, MA 92116; (617) 350-7097; *www.cdf.org*

AIGA Journal of Graphic Design, The American Institute of Graphic Arts (AIGA), 164 Fifth
　　Avenue, New York, NY 10010; (212) 807-1990; *www.aiga.org*

Communication Arts, 410 Sherman Avenue, P.O. Box 10300, Palo Alto, CA 94303; (415)
　　326-6040; *www.commarts.com*

Corporate Annual Reports Newsletter, Ragan Communications, 212 West Superior Street,
　　Suite 200, Chicago, IL 60610; (312) 335-0037; *www.ragan.org*

Creative Business, 275 Newbury Street, Boston, MA 02116; (617) 424-1368; *www.
　　creativebusiness.com*

Critique, The Magazine of Graphic Design Thinking, P.O. Box 51572, Palo Alto, CA 94303-
　　9407; (888) 274-2748

Design Issues, c/o The MIT Press, 55 Hayward Street, Cambridge, MA 02142; (617) 253-
　　2889

Design Tools Monthly, 400 Kiowa Place, Boulder, CO 80303; (303) 543-8400; *www.csd.net/~dtm*

Design World, 2323 Randolph Avenue, Avenel, NJ 07001; (800) 688-6247; *www.designgraphics.com.au*

Emigre, 4475 D Street, Sacramento, CA 95819; (916) 451-4344; *www.emigre.com*

Eye, EMAP, 151 Rosebery Avenue, London ECIR 4QX, England; (800) 633-4931

Graphic Design USA, Kay Publishing Corporation, 1556 Third Avenue, Suite 405, New York, NY 10128; (212) 534-5500

Graphis, 141 Lexington Avenue, New York, NY 10016; (212) 532-9387

How Magazine, F&W Publications, 1507 Dana Avenue, Cincinnati, OH 45207; (513) 531-2690; *www.howdesign.com*

I.D., 440 Park Avenue South, Floor 14, New York, NY 10016; (212) 447-1400; *www.idonline.com*

Innovation, Industrial Designers Society of America, 1142 Walker Road, Great Falls, VA 22066; (703) 759-0100; *www.idsa.org*

Metropolis, 177 East 87th Street, New York, NY 10128; (800) 344-3046

Print , 104 Fifth Avenue, New York, NY 10011; (800) 222-2654; *www.printmag.com*

Publish, 501 Second Street, San Francisco, CA 94107; (800) 656-7495; *www.publish.com*

Step-by-Step Graphics, Step-by-Step Electronic Design, 6000 North Forest Park Drive, Peoria, IL 61614; (800) 255-8800; *www.dgusa.com/vip*

U&lc, The International Journal of Graphic Design and Digital Media, The International Typeface Corporation, 228 East 45th Street, 12th floor, New York, NY 10017-2991; (212) 949-8072; *www.esselte.com/itc*

Wired, 520 Third Street, 4th Floor, San Francisco, CA 94107; (415) 276-5000; *www.hotwired.com/wired*

About the Contributors

EVA ANDERSON is principal of Eva Anderson Design and managing editor/designer of *ECO*, a newsletter dedicated to environmental issues faced by graphic designers, their clients, and suppliers. She has served on the board of directors of the New England Businesses for Social Responsibility and has received an EPA Environmental Merit Award and a grant from the National Endowment of the Arts.

AUBREY BALKIND is the founding partner and CEO of Frankfurt Balkind Partners, a 25-year-old strategic communications agency with over 150 people in offices in New York, Los Angeles, and San Francisco.

J. DIANNE BRINSON is a copyright attorney and co-author of *The Multimedia Law and Business Handbook*. The *Handbook* is available from Ladera Press, (800) 523-3721; (415) 854-0642.

EVA DOMAN BRUCK is operations manager of the Digital Production Studio of Time Warner Interactive in New York City. She teaches at the School of Visual Arts, and is co-author of *Business and Legal Forms for Graphic Designers*.

DONALD J. BRUNSTEN is a principal of the Law Offices of Donald J. Brunsten, based in Los Angeles. Mr. Brunsten specializes in intellectual property, business transactions, and business litigation, and represents a number of design firms. Mr. Brunsten is also the director of the Design Coalition, a group of leading design firms developing common solutions for hot legal issues in the practice of design.

EMILY RUTH COHEN is a graphic design business consultant who specializes in writing estimates, proposals, contracts, and studio profiles for graphic design firms. An active AIGA member, she has lectured extensively at AIGA events, Parsons School of Design, and the School of Visual Arts. Her articles have appeared in *How* magazine, *ID* magazine, and the *AIGA Journal of Graphic Design.*

TAD CRAWFORD, president and publisher for Allworth Press in New York City, is the author or co-author of eleven books on business and the creative professions. A columnist for *Communication Arts* magazine, he was the recipient of the first Walter Hortens Memorial Award awarded by the Graphic Artists Guild for service to artists and also received a grant from the National Endowment for the Arts for his writing on behalf of artists.

LEONARD DUBOFF is a business lawyer specializing in intellectual property and corporate law. As a member of the Special Task Force appointed by the Oregon State Bar and the Corporations Division, he was involved in drafting the Oregon Business Corporation Code, as well as the Oregon Nonprofit Corporation Code. He is the author of numerous books including *The Desk Book of Art Law, Art Law in a Nutshell, The Book Publisher's Legal Guide,* and a *Law (In Plain English)*® series which includes books for small businesses, writers, photographers, craftspeople, high-tech entrepreneurs, and gallery owners.

COLIN FORBES has been the partner responsible for identity design programs and other design projects for clients including Lucas Industries, British Petroleum, and Kodak in the United Kingdom; American-Standard and Neiman Marcus in the United States; and Nissan, Hankyu, and Kubota in Japan. He has written several articles and has lectured in the United States, Europe, and Japan on corporate identity and corporate communications.

ED GOLD is a Full Professor in the University of Baltimore's Graduate Program of Publications Design, Division of Language, Literature and Communications Design. He is a frequent lecturer to professional design and communication groups and has written numerous articles on design and the design professions for such national and international design publications as *Business, Step-By-Step Graphics* magazine, the *AIGA Journal of Graphic Design, CASE Currents,* and *Communication Arts* magazine. Gold is the author of *The Business of Graphic Design.*

JESSICA GOLDFARB is a recruitment consultant, specializing in new media at Roz Goldfarb Associates. She is an employment lawyer and was a policy analyst for Vice President Gore and the U.S. Department of Labor during the first Clinton Administration.

ROZ GOLDFARB is President of Roz Goldfarb Associates, a management consulting and recruitment firm, specializing in creative marketing and executive personnel for design, new media, and advertising. Ms. Goldfarb's activities include establishing mergers, acquisitions, and new business ventures for creative businesses. She is also the author of *Careers by Design*.

RICHARD GREFÉ is the executive director of the American Institute of Graphic Arts.

DK HOLLAND is a partner in the Pushpin Group, design issues editor of *Communication Arts* magazine, and business editor of the *AIGA Journal of Graphic Design*.

STEVEN HELLER is senior art director at the *New York Times* and editor of the *AIGA Journal of Graphic Design*. He is the author of more than 60 books on graphic design, design history, and design criticism and is a co-editor of *Looking Closer* and *Looking Closer 2*.

CARYN LELAND, author of *Licensing Art and Design*, is an attorney in Soho in New York City who represents fine and commercial artists in the field of intellectual property law, including copyright and trademark law, art law, and computer law.

ED MORRIS is the partner in charge of the Tax Department at Rosenberg, Neuwirth, & Kuchner, CPAs. He is a member of the AICPA and NYSSCPA.

SHEL PERKINS is a graphic designer who is active on the business side of professional practice. He is director of operations for MetaDesign San Francisco and was previously VP of operations at Clement Mok designs. President of the San Francisco chapter of the American Institute of Graphic Arts, he is on the board of directors of the Association of Professional Design Firms.

PETER L. PHILLIPS is an internationally recognized expert in developing corporate and brand identity strategies and programs. He is the former Director of Corporate Identity &

Design for Digital Equipment Corporation. He currently serves as a member and is the secretary of the board of directors of the Design Management Institute.

MARIA PISCOPO is a creative services consultant who has worked as an art/photo rep since 1978. She teaches for Dynamic Graphics Educational Foundation and has produced four videos on the subject of marketing and business. Her articles appear in magazines such as *How, Step-By-Step, ID,* and *Communication Arts.* She is the author of *The Photographer's Guide to Marketing and Self-Promotion.*

MONONA ROSSOL is a chemist, artist, and industrial hygienist. She is the founder and president of ACTS (Arts, Crafts and Theater Safety), a not-for-profit corporation based in New York City and dedicated to providing health and safety services to the arts. She is also the author of *Stage Fright: Health and Safety in the Theater* and *The Artist's Complete Health and Safety Guide.*

ELLEN SHAPIRO, a graphic designer and writer, is president of Shapiro Design Associates Inc. in New York. She is author of the book *Clients and Designers* and more than 50 articles for magazines including *Communication Arts, Print, How, Critique,* and the *AIGA Journal of Graphic Design.*

V. A. SHIVA is recognized as a world authority on interactive marketing and has lectured on the subject throughout the United States, Europe, and Asia. A graduate of MIT's Media Lab, he maintains Millennium Production's Art Technology site on the World Wide Web and consults with small and large companies on the use of the Internet for publicity and marketing. He is the author of *The Internet Publicity Guide* and *Arts and the Internet.*

DON SPARKMAN is president of Sparkman + Associates, Corporate Communications in Washington, D.C., and author of *The Design and Printing Buyer's Survival Guide* as well as *Selling Graphic Design.* He is a past President of the Washington Metropolitan Art Directors Club and currently President of the Washington chapter of the International Design by Electronics Association (IDEA). He has also published in *Step-By-Step Graphics* magazine.

RAY TAYLOR is an insurance broker working with artists, graphic designers, and photographers. He is a principal of Taylor & Taylor.

SCOTT TAYLOR is a member of the New York State Bar and an insurance broker of 15 years. He works with photographers, commercial producers, equipment rental companies, and others in the film industry. He is a principal of Taylor & Taylor.

ROGER WHITEHOUSE is a member of the Architectural Association, an Associate of the Royal Institute of British Architects, and is licensed as an architect in the United Kingdom. A past director and vice president of the American Institute of Graphic Arts, he is the author of several books and legal documents for graphic design professionals, including *The Standard Form of Agreement Between Designer and Client* (AIGA).

LEE WILSON is an attorney with a special expertise in the areas of copyrights and trademarks. She is the author of *The Copyright Guide* and *The Trademark Guide*.

About AIGA

The American Institute of Graphic Arts is the oldest and largest national organization committed to the promotion of excellence in graphic design. The AIGA consists of a network of forty-one chapters and forty student groups nationwide with over ten thousand member graphic designers and related professionals. Founded in 1914, the AIGA national office is located in New York City.

The AIGA coordinates initiatives that focus national and grassroots effort on eight areas of crucial importance to graphic design:

- Business. Promote dialog and strong ties between graphic designers and the business community, including corporations, educational institutions, business leaders, and those governing commerce.
- Design history. Become a primary information resource for the history of graphic design and establish a national permanent archive of AIGA work.
- Education. Sponsor actions and programs that encourage educational institutions to improve and update the quality of design education in America.
- Environmental responsibility. Foster understanding of the environmental consequences of graphic design and promote education and actions that protect the planet from further ecological damage.
- Internationalism. Advance the exchange of ideas and information to increase awareness within the profession of diverse international perspectives about design, culture, and economics.
- New technology. Promote understanding of how new technologies are affecting the profession and increase the participation of designers in the development of new forms of communication and media.

- Professional practice. Promote professional practice among graphic designers and provide a forum for discussing values and practices that can positively influence the profession.
- Public service. Encourage the involvement of the graphic design profession in public service.

Credits

1. "Worst of Times, Best of Times" by Ellen Shapiro. ©1997 Ellen Shapiro. Originally published in the "Design Issues" column of the *Communication Arts Design Annual,* 1997. Reprinted with permission of the author.

2. "Negotiating: Lessons from a Caveman" by Ed Gold. ©1998 Ed Gold.

3. "The Process of Setting Fees" by Eva Doman Bruck. ©1997 Eva Doman Bruck. Originally published as "Studio Management: A Wake-Up Call" in *Step-by-Step Graphics,* January/February 1997. Reprinted with permission of the author.

4. "The AIGA Standard Form of Agreement" by Roger Whitehouse. The Standard Form of Agreement for Graphic Design Services has been prepared by the AIGA Professional Practice Committee. ©1988 The American Institute of Graphic Arts. Reprinted with permission of the American Institute of Graphic Arts.

5. "AIGA Standard Terms and Conditions for Designer/Client Relationships" by Emily Ruth Cohen. ©1996 The American Institute for Graphic Arts. Reprinted with permission of the American Institute of Graphic Arts.

6. "Negotiating the Key Issues for Web Site Design" by Caryn Leland. ©1997 Caryn Leland. Originally published in *Communication Arts,* May/June 1997. Reprinted with permission of author.

7. "Payment Strategies" by Emily Ruth Cohen. ©1997 Emily Ruth Cohen. Originally published in *How,* June 1997. Reprinted with permission of the author.

8. "The Design Firm and Its Employees" by Roz and Jessica Goldfarb. ©1998 Roz and Jessica Goldfarb.

9. "The Design Firm and Its Suppliers" by Don Sparkman. ©1998 Don Sparkman.

10. "Legal Structures for the Design Firm" by Leonard DuBoff. ©1996 Leonard DuBoff.

Originally published in *Communication Arts,* January/February 1996. Reprinted with permission of the author.

11. "Principles of Design Firm Management" by Shel Perkins. ©1998 Shel Perkins.

12. "Transition" by Colin Forbes. ©1992 Colin Forbes. Originally published in *Communication Arts Design Annual,* 1992. Reprinted with permission of author.

13. "Principles of Managing the Corporate Design Department" by Peter L. Phillips. ©1998 Peter L. Phillips.

14. "Large Project Management" by Eva Doman Bruck. ©1994 Eva Doman Bruck. Originally published in *Step-by-Step Graphics,* September/October 1994. Reprinted with permission of author.

15. "Audits and the Design Firm" by Aubrey Balkind. ©1997 Aubrey Balkind. Originally published in *Communication Arts Advertising Annual,* 1997. Reprinted with permission of the author.

16. "Valuing the Graphic Design Firm" by Ed Morris. ©1998 Ed Morris.

17. "Insurance Basics for the Designer" by Ray and Scott Taylor. ©1998 Ray and Scott Taylor.

18. "Managing Health and Safety in the Design Studio" by Monona Rossol. ©1998 Monona Rossol.

19. "Discovering America (or Someplace Close Enough)" by DK Holland. ©1997 DK Holland. Originally published in *Communication Arts,* July 1997. Reprinted with permission of the author.

20. "Marketing the Design Firm" by Maria Piscopo, from *Marketing and Promoting Your Work* (North Light Books, 1997). ©1997 Maria Piscopo. Reprinted with permission of the author.

21. "Internet Marketing Strategies" by V. A. Shiva, from *The Internet Publicity Guide* (Allworth Press, 1997). ©1997 V. A. Shiva. Reprinted with permission of the author.

22. "Copyright and Licensing" by Tad Crawford. ©1998 Tad Crawford.

23. "Infringement, Influence, and Plagiarism" by Tad Crawford and Steven Heller. ©1998 Tad Crawford and Steven Heller.

24. "Fair Use and Permissions" by J. Dianne Brinson, from *The Multimedia Law and Business Handbook* (Ladera Press, 1997). ©1997 J. Dianne Brinson. Reprinted with permission of the author.

25. "Other People's Trademarks—Using Them Without Problems" by Lee Wilson. ©1995

Lee Wilson. Originally published in *Communication Arts,* March/April 1995. Reprinted with permission of the author.

26. "Trademarks and Trade Dress" by Leonard DuBoff. ©1996, 1998 Leonard DuBoff. Originally published in *Communication Arts Advertising Annual,* 1996. Reprinted with permission of the author.

27. "Trademarks in Cyberspace" by Lee Wilson. ©1996 Lee Wilson. Originally published in *Communication Arts,* 1996. Reprinted with permission of the author.

28. "The AIGA Standards of Professional Practices" by Richard Grefé. ©1998 Richard Grefé.

29. "Ethics in an Electronic Age" by Don Brunsten. ©1998 Don Brunsten. Originally published in *Communication Arts,* January/February 1998 and March/April 1998.

30. "Simplifying Design (and Your Life)" by Eva Anderson. ©1997 Eva Anderson. Originally published in the *ECO* newsletter of *Communication Arts,* May/June 1997.

Index

I

IBM, 6, 236

identity, 4, 5, 9, 10, 11, 137, 209, 212, 231, 236, 240
  brand, 110, 122, 175, 211, 227, 259
  corporate, 26, 122

illustration, 35, 36, 52, 90, 132, 198, 208, 216, 288
  organizations for professionals in, 251, 276, 283, 284, 286

implementation services, 32, 35, 74

income, 98, 99, 145–146. *See also* profit; tax, income
  and cash flow, 66, 74, 108, 112–114, 116, 171–172
    discretionary, 145
    small business, 66, 69
  and inflation, 112
  and "wealth," 268, 269, 270, 271
  future, 144–145
  royalty, 26, 98, 111, 217
  salary, 33, 77, 113
    and bonuses, 78, 79, 80
    and hourly rates, 21–24, 25, 33, 75, 98

indemnification, 61

independent contractor, 75, 140, 163

India, 265

Individual Retirement Account (IRA), 152

industrial park, 178

information management, 177–178

Info*Seek*, 185

installations, 32, 56, 57, 131

institutions, goods and services for, 172

insurance, 147–152, 300. *See also* retirement
  carrier, 152
  disability, 150, 152
  liability, 21, 36, 55, 61, 92, 95, 97–99, 102, 148–151
  life, 145
  medical, 74, 75, 79, 98, 145, 149, 152
  personal, 152
  unemployment, 140
  workers' compensation, 149, 150, 163

Internal Revenue Service (IRS), 75, 96, 163

International Council of Graphic Design Associations (ICOGRADA), 246

Internet, 59, 63, 214, 294, 300
  domain names, 235–241, 256
    registration of, 237–241
  marketing on the, 183–189
  service provider, 186

intranet, 22

J

Japan, 4

Javascript, 259, 262

Joint Ethics Committee (JEC), 37

Jscript, 262

K

Kanawa, Kiri Te, 6

Karan, Donna, 173, 175

Kennedy, Jacqueline, 228

Keogh Plan, 152

Kirpich, Judy, 9–10

L

Landress-Bowkett, Ellen, 175

Lanham Act, 228

Lauren, Ralph, 173, 175

law, 4, 21, 30, 54–55, 88, 138, 140, 159, 291
  and business organization, 95–100, 116
  and legally binding evidence, 65
  and litigation, 61, 69, 70, 98, 199, 202, 205, 225
    defamation, 223, 225
    false advertising, 224
    libel, 148
  anti-discrimination, 77
  applied to cyberspace, 59
  arts, 284, 288, 292
  "at will," 74
  copyright, 36, 195–196, 198, 205, 207, 216, 218, 219, 232. *See also* copyright
  firm, 5
  labor, 71, 75, 81–82, 149
  multimedia, 291
  product labeling, 154, 165
  proprietary rights, 60–62
  Right-to-Know, 164
  state, 57, 139, 140, 149, 150, 158, 231
  tax, 137, 138, 139, 140, 263. *See also* tax
  trade dress, 227, 232–233, 301
  trademark, 222, 227, 228–232, 233, 236, 238–240, 256–259. *See also* trademark
  workplace safety, 158, 159, 163, 164–165

Leeds, Castle, 116

Legal Guide for the Visual Artist, 203

Less is More, 268, 272

Lewin, Cheryl, 134

Lewin/Holland, 134

Books from Allworth Press

Design Culture: An Anthology of Writing from the AIGA Journal of Graphic Design, edited by Steven Heller and Marie Finamore (softcover, 6 3/4 x 10, 256 pages, $19.95)

Emotional Branding: The New Paradigm for Connecting Brands to People, by Marc Gobé (hardcover, 6 3/4 x 9 7/8, 256 pages, $24.95)

The Graphic Designer's Guide to Pricing, Estimating, and Budgeting, by Theo Stephan Williams (softcover, 6 3/4 x 9 7/8, 208 pages, $19.95)

Careers by Design: A Business Guide for Graphic Designers, Third Edition, by Roz Goldfarb (softcover, 6 x 9, 256 pages, $19.95)

Digital Design Business Practices, by Liane Sebastian (softcover, 6 3/4 x 10, 384 pages, $29.95)

Business and Legal Forms for Graphic Designers, Third Edition, by Tad Crawford (softcover, includes CD-ROM, 8 1/2 x 11, 160 pages, $29.95)

The Graphic Designer's Guide to Clients: How to Make Clients Happy and Do Great Work, by Ellen Shapiro (softcover, 6 x 9, 256 pages, $19.95)

Inside the Business of Graphic Design: 60 Leaders Share Their Secrets of Success, by Catharine Fishel (softcover, 6 x 9, 288 pages, $19.95)

Looking Closer 4: Critical Writings on Graphic Design, edited by Michael Bierut, William Drenntel, and Steven Heller (softcover, 6 3/4 x 10, 288 pages, $18.95)

Selling Graphic Design, by Don Sparkman (softcover, 6 x 9, 224 pages, $18.95)

Licensing Art and Design, Revised Edition, by Caryn R. Leland (softcover, 6 x 9, 128 pages, $16.95)

Legal Guide for the Visual Artist, by Tad Crawford (softcover, 8 1/2 x 11, 256 pages, $19.95)

Please write to request our free catalog. To order by credit card, call 1-800-491-2808 or send a check or money order to Allworth Press, 10 East 23rd Street, Suite 510, New York, NY 10010. Include $5 for shipping and handling for the first book ordered and $1 for each additional book. Ten dollars plus $1 for each additional book if ordering from Canada. New York State residents must add sales tax.

To view our complete Web catalog, or to order books online, go to *www.allworth.com*.